TRADE UNION EDUCATION

This is one of the first two publications
of a new publishing venture between
the General Federation of Trade Unions
(GFTU) and New Internationalist
called Workable Books. Dr Mike Seal of
Birmingham University and Dr Jo Grady
of Leicester University join me to represent
the GFTU on this new imprint and we
work closely with our colleagues from
New Internationalist: Chris Brazier,
Dan Raymond-Barker and Kelsi
Farrington, to offer a new publishing
platform for trade unionists throughout
the world.

Doug Nicholls
*General Secretary of the General Federation
of Trade Unions*

TRADE UNION EDUCATION

TRANSFORMING THE WORLD

Edited by Mike Seal
with introductions by Doug Nicholls

WORKABLE

Trade Union Education
Transforming the world

First published in 2017 by Workable Books, an imprint of New Internationalist and the General Federation of Trade Unions (GFTU)

New Internationalist
The Old Music Hall
106-108 Cowley Road
Oxford
OX4 1JE
UK
newint.org

GFTU
84 Wood Lane
Quorn
Leicestershire
LE12 8DB
UK
gftu.org.uk

Edited by Mike Seal with introductions by Doug Nicholls

Designed by New Internationalist
Cover design by Andrew Kokotka

Printed by TJ International Ltd, Cornwall, UK, who hold environmental accreditation ISO 14001

British Library Cataloguing-in-Publication Data
A catalogue record for this book is available from the British Library.

Library of Congress Cataloging-in-Publication Data
A catalog record for this book is available from Library of Congress.

ISBN 978-1-78026-425-7
ISBN ebook 978-1-78026-426-4

Contents

Introduction

Doug Nicholls

There was a significant lightbulb moment for myself and most other delegates in a recent GFTU union-building conference. We had asked popular educators from the youth and community-work sector to lead a session on what education really is, and they helped us to recognize that every single active trade unionist is an educator. You can't be an organizer without being an educator. How can you deal with management, let alone the employers, without educating them as to the errors of their ways?

The brother sitting next to me in my group had been a shop steward, then convenor, all his life in a furniture factory. His entire post-16 educational experience had been provided by the GFTU education programme, but he had never thought of himself as an educator. But then, during this session, he, like others, recognized that everything he had ever done had included strong elements of educating others: negotiating, talking to members, listening, organizing, digesting and analysing information and talking about it: campaigning, building the union, formulating policies and implementing democratic decisions. He, like us all, is an educator.

Education is a constant dialogue with others, with workmates. We learn all the time throughout life. Unions are learning organizations. The best go out of their way to include all members and exude a democratic confidence. The worst are alienating and hierarchical; they stifle debate, or have so much debate that they never make decisions.

- The art of negotiation, persuasion and increasing knowledge that we use to secure our members' rights are all acts of educational practice.
- Education is embedded in the very core of trade union work. Becoming a better educator means becoming a better trade unionist.
- If, as a representative, you explain matters to a distressed member seeking representation – perhaps the legal implications, the limits of what is possible in their case, the breaches of procedure of which management are guilty, the need to do this or that to avoid future problems – then you are educating them.
- When you tell the employers what you think of their pay offer or their terrible reorganization proposal you are actually educating them, reflecting views gathered from your members and projecting them in the most effective way possible.

- In presenting your reasons for opposing a government decision to a Member of Parliament you are using the best words you can find to counter injustice. This is a deeply educational role.
- Education is about action and change. There is no point learning on your own.

Much trade union education in Britain for the past nearly 40 years of the neoliberal period has been based on the technical training required by activists in the previous social democratic period when unions were strong and collective-bargaining coverage high and when there was a consensus amongst parliamentary political parties that they should respond to the people to make beneficial social reforms. The dynamics of this previous period have disappeared. There is no sense therefore in carrying on with the old ways that so blatantly failed.

The educational nature of trade unionism has had the stuffing pulled out of it by years of low-level, outcomes-driven, purely functional training. Trainers think they have information in their heads which should be implanted in their students' heads unquestioningly and if they apply this knowledge in the workplace things will improve. This is not education. It's more like a zero-hours contract.

Education is about inspiring a critical consciousness and ability to think confidently and flexibly to solve problems and organize collectively with others. Trade union educationalists in Britain have largely operated outside of the worldwide traditions of popular education and radical learning theory. Their approach sometimes has been a softened form of chalk and talk – a mechanical function of conveying information and interesting anecdotes about their lives years ago on the shop floor. If your factory is about to close and you can't afford decent housing, there's not much point understanding Clause Six of the Health and Safety at Work Act.

Education must always tackle the real issues and the question of social and class power. It must enable and empower learners to change the structural and big obstacles to progress for themselves and others like them. The ruling class puts us to shame in this respect. They start training their successors to rule the world in prep schools at six. In their private elitist education system, from public school to Oxbridge, they learn the art of arrogance. Self-confidence and an ability to talk about any subject without knowing anything about it, to sound smart when your words are empty, or in fact defending social injustice and exploitation, lie at the heart of the elite's education system.

Their core subjects for their politicians, media pundits and functionaries are politics, philosophy and economics. These are exactly the subjects that trade unions have stripped out of their programmes for decades. They must be restored. Political and economic illiteracy lie at the heart of our difficulties in rebuilding our movement.

Our rulers' other strong subject is history. They've ruled the world and they know how to keep doing so because they constantly learn from past successes and mistakes; they encourage us to think they were born to rule and life will always be this way. Working-class history was once central to trade union education. It lifted our spirits and made us realize that we changed the world and rulers were forced to respond. We appreciated that we are the powerhouse of progress and the source of all wealth and value and culture. Now we are in danger of being forgotten and erased from the country's past, and the disappearance of the role of our ancestors in social change helps to disempower us today and leads us to forget our potential human agency.

Working-class history is missing from most trade union education programmes. There's a lot of truth in the statement that you don't know where you are going unless you know where you have come from. The history of the trade unions and the working class is the most impressive and inspiring there is – after all, it created all the rights and democratic practices and structures that have civilized the country. Without a knowledge of it we go nowhere. We don't like capitalism, we protest against this and that, yet we have no confidence in a socialist alternative, so a volatile and unpredictable populism surfaces from the fragments of discontent.

The GFTU commissioned Banner Theatre to create a performance piece in words, images, songs and interviews to convey a sense of trade union history. I like to have it performed as the first item at new members' and young workers' schools, whatever their stated subject. It can have a bigger effect in an hour than a whole week of technical training about wriggling round anti-worker employment legislation.

You can teach an important subject, for example working-class history, but teach it so badly that trade unionists are put off it for life and fail to be empowered by a sense of belonging to a class and a movement that has shaped all history. Instead of making our history relevant and present today, bad teaching can make history seem dead.

Economics is a comparable case. Until the 16th century the Catholic priesthood taught the word of god in Latin, a language that only a few of the population could understand. There was a long struggle for which many sacrificed their lives to translate the Bible into English so that the 'merest ploughboy could understand the word of god'. These days professional so-called economists deliberately seek to portray economics as a subject that only computers can understand and portray the economy as something beyond human intervention and control.

From our point of view, economics is having a good breakfast, it is the relationships between people, it is the product of our labour; and the laws of how the economy works are surprisingly simple. Economics and politics are inseparable. This whole subject must be demystified. The whole austerity agenda was based on simple, colossal lies, for example, and was an ideologically driven, politically motivated phenomenon.

Politics fares even worse in some teaching styles. We are encouraged to believe that only professional politicians do politics. Yet politics is what happens to us every day, how we struggle to survive, how we have aspirations and beliefs. It is not something confined to the Westminster bubble. To suggest that only political parties and politicians do politics is to distance workers from the life they create themselves and to disempower them again in the educational arena.

So how we convey our knowledge and concerns is vital. Our learning techniques and theory must match our content and purpose. Going into the education course as a tutor with pre-ordained learning outcomes to tick off is almost immediately a sign that something is wrong with your approach. If a tutor assumes that they have more to teach their group of participants than to learn from them they have in my view got something badly wrong. Everyone has more to learn than to teach, not least teachers. Yes, people come to trade unions wishing to learn, but learning to ask the right questions is often the most powerful tool of all.

I feel immensely privileged to have been part of two amazing British educational worlds: youth and community work; and trade union education. I have been part of them all my life. Youth and community workers who are trained in popular-education techniques are some of the most transformative and inspiring educationalists there are. Trade union educators cover topics at the heart of the intense and difficult struggles for social and workplace justice. There should be much more mutual exchange between these two spheres.

Popular educators find ways of seizing the moment for learning and informally engaging a group in learning from each other and building self-confidence and self-esteem. They find a way of embedding critical thinking and questioning into people's minds for life. This gift is essential to any active, alert, organized, democratic trade unionist as well as to any community activist or confident young person navigating the seas of misfortune that all too frequently bedevil their lives.

Popular-education traditions can end up with an obsession with the warm processes of group learning devoid of content and transformative social purpose. The trade union education tradition can end up obsessed with chunks of information devoid of learning theory. A new balance must be struck. We need a new theory and practice, a new set of organizing principles for trade union education. This book seeks to assist us in that new direction.

We need the best popular-education techniques applied to the most important subjects of trade union education. It is all about power – who has it and why others don't, and how those of us who don't can get more. Being an organized trade unionist is an essential start, and developing popular-education techniques in the unions is a basic requirement, empowering participants beyond all previous recognition.

As a beautiful song by Peggy Seeger on a GFTU CD of workers' songs says:

What is more important within a trade union, the ability to negotiate, to represent members at work, to campaign, to organize, or to educate?

Unless the union is able to unequivocally answer that it is to educate, members it will flounder. It will neither organize, nor campaign, nor win for members in the workplace.

You cannot negotiate without knowing your facts, the possibilities, how to argue, how to twist and turn with positions and events.

You cannot campaign without knowing what you are campaigning for and against and how to persuade others of your case. How can you campaign against neoliberalism without members understanding basic economic theory?

You cannot organize without analysing workplaces, workplace cultures, members' psychologies, the employers' obstacles.

In all of these three central areas of union work members have to be educated and to educate others. The educative process is fundamental to the key elements of union development. It is therefore without doubt the most important force for change and progress in a union.

- Education is not something that takes place in a classroom, equipping reps with knowledge and information.
- Learning and sharing knowledge is required in every element of union activity. Education is ever present in everything we do and learning should be constantly drawn from what we do.
- The basic question 'what have we learned from that?' should be asked during and after every union meeting and event.
- Every member of the union is a teacher and a learner. This awareness and reality should be promoted and encouraged.
- Negotiators and casework representatives need specific skills and knowledge, but can only function effectively on the basis of a strongly organized membership with whom they are in regular communication.

- Campaign leaders can only motivate and inspire and win if they are supported by a conscious and aware membership prepared to stand up and be counted.
- Organizers can only organize if their motivational ideas are grounded and have resonance and if those they organize take responsibility for the union and own its events and policies.
- Key all the time to union progress is an organized, conscious, educated membership.
- This is why developing a learning culture throughout is vital and why prioritizing the carburettor-like function of education is essential.
- Ultimately, solidarity is cemented by a recognition of our common interests and learning constantly from each other provides the strongest binding force.
- It follows that you cannot create an activists' culture without a learning culture. The creation of a learning culture is more important.

At heart the neoliberal agenda and culture have sought to remove democratic control from elected organizations of people, from regulatory bodies and parliament, and to replace them with the hidden hand of the market led by the banks working beyond national controls. This has led to a reduction of the idea that human agency changes and controls the world. Education and lifelong learning delivered through the popular-education method are critical to restoring the idea of human agency as the source of all democratic change.

This book aims to push that agenda along.

Doug Nicholls

Notes from the editor

Mike Seal

On terminology

There are several terms used throughout the world and in different organizational contexts to describe a form of democratic learning which seeks to engage participants in collective action and critical analysis of an exploitative social system. We prefer the term 'popular education', which is the term also used in Latin America. In the British tradition it has been generally known as youth and community work but this has not included much of adult education, where a more progressive approach to adult learning was called radical adult education. For a period in the 1970s and 1980s the term community education was used to describe local-education-authority commitments to transforming schools into sites of lifelong learning. Some academics have described the very broad spectrum of non-formal education approaches as 'informal education'. In the university the term 'critical pedagogy' or 'critical education' is used to describe processes of learning which seek to undermine conventional authority and confined, de-politicized ways of teaching and learning. The term popular education is the most popular and inclusive term and best expresses our understanding of a new way of sharing education with a social purpose.

On structure

It is usual within an introduction to a book to have a section which describes each section and each chapter within that section. Instead of doing this we decided to have a slightly expanded introduction to each section from Doug Nicholls, General Secretary of the GFTU. This is both an attempt to examine common themes within the chapter and to reflect on their wider context. Section One examines key concepts within trade union and popular education, as well as their historical development, concentrating on the UK. Section Two then examines particular contexts and challenges, from the need to connect to self-help and wider social movements, to the need to re-invigorate the sometimes narrow concerns of trade union education, to repoliticize and engage with the wider community. Section Three gives a series of case studies of attempts to change and re-invigorate trade union education from particular contexts such as schools and universities to new approaches such as the GFTU youth festivals, as well as how to think differently within traditional educational settings and contexts. The final section examines two case studies from elsewhere in the world and at different points in time.

You will also notice that there is a wide variety of writing styles between chapters. Partly this is a reflection of the different authors, but also of the different audiences for this text. It is primarily aimed at trade union educators, but we also wanted to reach out to academics, policymakers and politicians, as well as ordinary union members. Our selection of authors also reflects that, and includes contributions from seasoned trade union writers and thinkers, academics that are fellow travellers, and trade union activists and representatives. We recognize that there is not just one voice or approach in the movement and this needs to be honoured. One of the principles of popular education is to be inclusive and find common ground, but also to recognize and work though tensions and contradictions, seeing them as a fulcrum around which to develop new ideas. Popular education is not about finding a middle way or a compromise; it is about finding new ways of thinking rooted in dissent. We hope this book will act as both a provocation and a call to action.

Section One

Key concepts and historical developments

Introduction to Section One

Doug Nicholls

You do not know where you are going unless you know where you have come from. There is a lot of wisdom in this idea and it is important that we begin our consideration of trade union education by looking at its history and how it has defined itself.

John Fisher's opening chapter considers how trade union education has been defined, and the contested definitions and purposes which have emerged over the years. Taken in its generality, trade union education has been an amazing part of mass working-class education but, as with all other elements of this, the way it has been delivered and what has been delivered have expressed various ideological prejudices. By reflecting back on these influences and definitions of the role of trade union education, John enables us to begin our reconsideration of the subject with a firm grounding in what has gone before us.

What is clear from this history is that 'active learning' or the form of popular education that we are advocating in this book has been a strand within, rather than a dominant organizing force in trade union education until now. By asserting the development of popular education approaches in trade union education we seek also to develop away from the idea that trade union education is composed neatly of four key defining elements, although those identified by John are real and helpful. We seek to include all of those elements in a new dynamic approach to learning for social change and a shift of power away from the one per cent.

Mike Seal takes up this development in his chapter, outlining the key concepts in the popular-education tradition, and adds a sense of sharpness and socially critical purpose in every element of the new education method. The rich theory and practice of this tradition, much of which was developed in Britain, but is also a truly internationalist tradition, can be found on the excellent informal education website infed.org.uk, which should be considered a fundamental reference resource for this whole discussion about transforming education.

Mike's chapter is also a fundamental resource for the development of trade union education and the enrichment of it with theories from other related sectors. Two experiences come to mind when I consider this chapter. I had the privilege of visiting the Paulo Freire Institute in Brazil and the education department of the CUT Union. Freire is known throughout the world as a pioneering theoretician in popular education. But he was also very well grounded. He was one of the founders of the Workers' Party of Brazil and he was the key inspiration for the whole of the trade union education programme of CUT.

Another related experience was once to watch a brilliant youth worker at work. She was a very active trade unionist and a very skilled youth worker. I watched her work with a very lively group of 16- to 18-year-olds. What struck me was that she said very little. The group was analysing the newspapers and how they all commented on young people, and were relating this to their own predicament as a largely unemployed group with few prospects. The youth worker's words were like prompts, strokes of encouragement, tricky little questions, jokes, perceptions from different angles. The few words revealed an acute awareness of how the press operates and the impact of different ideas and how they help or hinder the emancipation of young people. The group session was full of oxygen: all participants had their say as they gradually illuminated each other about the different perspectives of the overall hostile attitudes of the media. You could feel a huge learning experience developing. For the first time these participants recognized how the press and its words convey subliminal and overt messages not in the interests of young people.

It is unusual in my experience for trade union trainers to say very little. There is a culture of dominating a group from the front – often standing over them. This reflects the traditional 'banking' theory of education which Mike's chapter exposes.

We have now considered a definition of trade union education and a definition of critical education. We return in the next chapter to consider the history and context of UK trade union education. John Fisher succinctly takes us through the main ideological and organizational trends that have shaped our origins. In a new world order in which the gains of this social democratic past have been pulled apart and in which collective-bargaining coverage has been reduced from its peak position of 80-per-cent coverage in 1980 to just 20 per cent today, things surely have to change. The basic role of unions in pay bargaining has been neutered by years of pay restraint in the public sector and by the most brutal reduction in the share of wages as a percentage of Gross Domestic Product in history. The few have been ascendant over the many, but the full dangers and horrors of this are just being fully recognized and a new spirit of asserting the values of the many is breaking out.

This spirit will be charged and revitalized as the sleeping giant wakes by a more purposeful approach to education, we argue. This means reclaiming earlier commitments to progressive education that have existed within the peasant and working-class movements in British history. These have remained present, often in subterranean form, throughout our history and have broken out into popular forms at various moments of danger in our history.

In Britain there is a long and proud tradition of working-class education. Workers fought to establish the state education system, including free comprehensive education and accessible primary and secondary schools in all parts of the country. But in addition to this there are various strands of thinking about teaching and learning methods and forms of learning that are linked closely to the socialist struggle for change. People have developed learning to liberate themselves from exploitation and oppression and class division.

Prior to the industrial period the struggle to ensure that the Bible was translated into English and to get church services conducted in English was part of a progressive reforming movement which sought to inspire everyone with the egalitarian interpretations of the scriptures. 'When Adam delved/And Eve span/Who was then the gentleman?' was the revolutionary question that the radical peasantry asked.

The spread of literacy and printing meant that, by the time of the 1649 English Revolution, radical democratic movements and leftwing religious groupings, and most of all the Levellers and the Diggers, were able to engage in the struggle of ideas and promote their democratic cause in an eloquent English plain style that found expression in the mass circulation of leaflets and pamphlets. Reading and study and the examination of the value of ideas became established in the early socialist movement.

This continued throughout the pre-industrial period and, as EP Thompson, the great working-class historian, and others have shown, the progressive learning and thirst for knowledge inspired the Sunday School movement, which radicalized many generations, including of course the early trade unionists. Leftwing religious groups were versed in the humanist traditions of a counter culture that opposed the Church and King and the established order.

It was not surprising that education became essential to the early trade union and socialist movements. Thomas Paine's *The Rights of Man* sold in hundreds of thousands of copies within a short time of publication, testifying to a highly literate working class. The Tolpuddle Martyrs wrote eloquently of their struggle, reaching a wide readership. Songs, and later, in the Chartist period for example, pamphlets would communicate the news of class-based struggles from village to village and town to town.

With the creation of mass industry, education for survival and liberation became the order of the day. Philanthropists established a tradition of providing education for the urban poor. Social reformers joined in, seeing the need to link training of the mind with questions of morality and behaviour and social direction. The industrial unions began to establish their libraries and training courses. Mass leftwing book clubs were established. Socialist study groups developed. Even the first scouting organization in Britain was a socialist one, established by Robert Blatchford. It sought to spread socialist ideals in the police, army and society generally.

Into the twentieth century there were well-developed socialist and trade union learning programmes. There were also artistic forms of mass education, socialist theatre and choirs, a revived tradition of political song, disciplined study in political parties, a vast new literature of scientific socialism, a network of socialist bookshops, and demanding trade union study programmes on the nature of capital and the extraction of surplus value.

There was also a strong tradition that drew on the works of many educationalists throughout the world of developing teaching and learning techniques that would engage learners and teachers in new, more dynamic ways of learning. These often sought to break down the various forms of bourgeois ideology and manners developed within a hierarchical education system. The curriculum and teaching methods of an education system established to create the reserve army of labour and reproduce docile labour began to be criticized.

Learning was extended beyond the classroom over the decades by socialist, working-class effort: trade union education, radical adult education, community work, youth work, play work; these all developed from the nineteenth-century socialist impulse to liberate minds and broaden the appeal of collective learning. Socialists continually established additional forms of learning for workers excluded from the full benefits of a state and university education. Trade unions encouraged a love of learning. Many of the self-educated and trade union-educated workers who emerged were without doubt some of the most knowledgeable and learned people in the country and could outpace many who had spent their lives in academia. The age of the self-taught person with an insatiable appetite for learning sometimes seems long gone.

This rich history, summarized briefly here, is still in part evident in many areas of life. But, like everything else of value to workers, it has been attacked by a resurgent capitalism. The state has moved more and more into trade union education, for example. This has transformed the curriculum from one of understanding the workings of capitalism and organizing against it to learning the technical ways of coping with decline. Community work which was once linked to collective action against injustice, linking trade unionists in the workplace to community groups in the neighbourhood, is funded now only if it has more modest aims, and trade unions generally lack interest in the local community. The professional autonomy of teachers and lecturers has been threatened with the mechanistic and fragmented nature of 'competencies' and the fragmentation of learning into modules and marketable units of 'knowledge'. The whole education system now faces the workings of the market. University departments sell bits of information to paying clients.

Education has always been the battleground where competing ideas about class interests and the future direction of society have been fought. These struggles can be about curricula matters, forms of teaching and learning, methods of delivery, funding mechanisms or levels. Such struggles are now intense, with capitalism seeking to put education in its totality onto the market. New towns are planned on the basis that all of their schools will be run by private companies. The student grant to higher education – which enshrined the working-class recognition that education, including knowledge at its highest levels, was a right, not a privilege – has gone.

In this context the rich seam of radical education that has been developed in Britain should be mined again, renewed and changed, recognizing that education is the key to social transformation and human equality.

Those trade unionists who founded the GFTU had high aspirations for unions and their wider role:

'We want to see the necessary economic knowledge imparted in our labour organizations so that labour in the future shall not be made the shuttlecock of political parties. Our trade unions shall be centres of enlightenment and not merely the meeting place for paying contributions and receiving donations… our ideal is a co-operative commonwealth.'
Tom Mann and Ben Tillett, *The New Trade Unionism*, 1890

Such sentiments drew into the trade union movement the best thoughts of the past about education as a powerful emancipatory force. This was dominant in the first part of the twentieth century, but then, as John's article shows, started to divert away from the trade union movement. It detoured into youth and community work, adult education and, for a time, into community education – a philosophy and practice that sought to transform schooling and encourage concepts of lifelong learning for all. Alan Smith and Mike Seal look in their important chapter at the understated but extremely beneficial impact of these services in the UK. So important did these services become to working-class communities that the coalition government of 2010-15 targeted them for eradication. The Youth Service became the first public service in most parts of England to face 100-percent cuts and it no longer exists in most areas. It was destroyed because it empowered and politicized young people. Community work suffered the same fate.

Youth and community organizations were in many ways like trade unions outside of the workplace and they achieved community cohesion and action at street level, fostering enlightened views in collective endeavour and active citizenship. They also imbued people with a critical faculty that enabled them to challenge social injustice in a powerful and informed way. It is why there is much to learn in trade union education from the learning techniques deployed in this area of work. This cross-fertilization of domains is something that the GFTU is taking up in its new 'training the trainers' courses, which started in 2017. As active trade unionists and youth and community-work trainers, Alan and Mike have been able to cross the rivers and make a unique contribution to trade union thinking in this area.

1
What do we mean by 'trade union education'?

John Fisher

The outburst of energy and activity associated with the trade union education programmes raises a number of important questions about the past and future role of trade unions, and of the process of education, particularly the education of adults. The great majority of the participants in trade union education were manual workers with little or no formal education, who would have been unlikely to come into an educational process if it had not been for their membership of their union.

Apart from the short-lived ABCA programme during the Second World War,[1] trade union education, if we include the work of the Workers' Educational Association (WEA) and Labour Colleges, was the most important mass adult-education programme carried out for specifically working-class people during the last century and into this century. For those reasons alone, the programmes are interesting in the light of the debates around adult education, day release, human resources management and employee development and, latterly, lifelong learning. Most of all, though, it is a story of *activism*; of the motivation of thousands of students and hundreds of tutors, who studied or taught, often for little or no financial gain, and believed that education played a central role in developing themselves, the unions and the labour movement as a whole. What moved the students was commitment to an ideal and the need to gain as much knowledge and as many skills as possible in order to move nearer to their goal; and the tutors and organizers were more often than not motivated by a belief in the value of learning, found in all good educators, coupled with a wider commitment to the labour movement.

In some quarters, it is suggested that trade union education is a mechanism for social integration under capitalism, and essentially strengthens trade union bureaucrats at the expense of rank-and-file members, and some of the more extreme criticisms of the Trades Union Congress (TUC) programme as being the tool of the government's attempt to regularize industrial relations steer close to this.[2] In the Thatcher period, for example, questions were raised as to the value of the TUC's previous collaboration with the

Callaghan government, and the effect of this in sanitizing TUC education and preparing the ground for the Tories.

Overall, such a view would only be tenable if one took the view that because trade unions exist *within* capitalism, they acted as maintainers of the system, and not even Marx and Lenin took such a one-dimensional view, though they recognized that trade unions were essentially contradictory. They do of course help to regularize industrial relations and sometimes 'police' agreements, but they also organize the working class and are the main vehicle for opposition and working-class political education.

The story in the main is one of a formal education programme funded partly by the individual unions, and partly through contributions from outside agencies and organizations, mainly the state, employers and educational providers such as the WEA and Labour Colleges. It cannot be emphasized enough, however, that the informal system of trade union education – conversations in the workplace between the experienced worker and the novice, hard lessons learned through the failure or success of a particular episode of industrial action or similar event, involvement in the local trades council or political party organization, attendance at conferences, visits overseas, significant books read, and so on – played just as important a part in the development of the individual trade unionist and of the unions and the movement as the formal system did. The point has been well made by Michael Welton in his discussion of Canadian workers' education:

We are all aware of the difficulties in delineating the boundaries of workers' education. For my purposes, the boundaries of workers' education ought to be drawn so that we can study both the 'schools of labour' and 'labour's schools'. Simply defined, the schools of labour are the socially organized workplaces, embedded in networks of economic, social and political control. Important technical, social, political and ideological experiential learning is occurring in the workplace...Labour's schools are those spaces workers themselves, their leaders, or sympathetic pedagogues open up for reflection on the meaning of their work and culture. Labour's schools take many forms: (a) 'educational moments' woven into particular social practices such as the assembly meeting or political party activity; (b) specific educational forms created by the workers themselves (journals, newspapers, forums, and so on); and (c) educational forms provided for workers by agencies and institutions outside the workers' own organization (WEA, University extension programmes). (Welton, 1993 p.220)

Thus, formal trade union education is primarily 'labour's schools', but the key distinction made by Welton is there throughout, and many of the changing priorities of the formal education system are directly linked to the experiences and struggles of union members in their workplaces and of union organization in the wider political and industrial context.

Trade union education as a whole, although familiar to many in practice, needs definition, especially for those who have not encountered it before, or who are unclear as to its purpose. Such attempts are rare, and as J. Holford points out, 'no theory of trade union education has emerged. It is truly remarkable that no book-length study has been published...apart from official and semi-official reports' (1994, p.250). One of these reports was written in 1959 for the WEA by Hugh Clegg and Rex Adams. It presents a reasonably comprehensive survey of trade union education in the late 1950s, but is more concerned with practical advice for the improvement of trade union education programmes than with attempting definitions. However, its main conclusion was that 'the central purpose of trade union education must be to provide education suited to the needs and the abilities of active or potentially active trade unionists' (ibid., p.6). No-one would dispute this, but it cannot be held to be a comprehensive definition. In September 1950, an article in the *TGWU Record* by William Morgan, then Assistant Labour Information Officer in the US Economic Co-operation Administration, attempted to characterize it as follows:

> Trade union education today has three main strands. Firstly, there is education for specifically trade union purposes – a study of union histories and procedures, and other topics most necessary to hold union posts. Then there is general education of a liberal kind – usually in the social studies. As a bad third there comes semi-technical training in problems of particular industries in joint consultation, and training for management. (TGWU Record, September 1950, p.6)

In a period when modern trade union education was still in its infancy, this was a good attempt at a definition, covering as it does the core of internal role education with a link to wider lifelong learning on the one hand and workplace industrial relations on the other. It should be noted that this definition plays down education as skills training, whether in the initial basic skills usually taught in schools, or vocational skills of whatever kind. On the other hand, the skills of advocacy and representation, and the wider range of inter-personal and transferable skills, are very much implicit in the definition. A similar definition was given by Jim Fyrth in 1980: 'Trade unions are vehicles for learning. Unions are in the business of defining and analysing problems and seeking solutions' (p.162). He went on to define trade union educational objectives as 'Internal Education', aimed mainly at supplying activists;

'Industrial Education', based on dealing with workplace problems; and 'Social and Political Education', looking at economics, politics and so on (ibid., p.6). These broad definitions were echoed some years later by Philip Hopkins, who defined what he called 'Workers' Education' as 'that sector of adult education which caters for adults in their capacity as workers and especially as members of workers' organizations' (Hopkins, 1985, p.167). He went on to identify five major components:

- Basic general skills
- 'Role skills' for trade union activity
- Economic, social and political background studies
- Technical and vocational training
- Cultural, scientific and general education.

While such definitions set the scene in which trade union education operates, they do not answer questions regarding elements of purpose and activity in trade union education, which might outweigh other elements, nor do they allow for different emphases in the actual process of education, which are important in determining the policy within the education providers. So, for example, a typical Labour College class may have included material from some of Hopkins' categories but completely excluded content from others, while a Training Within Industry scheme would have had a completely different emphasis. Such differences have been central to the debates around the definition of trade union education down the years, and indeed played an important part in defining the actual character of such education, as provided by the various organizations involved.

Government inquiries into adult education stressed different aspects of trade union education in their definitions. The *Interim Report of the Committee on Adult Education* or '1919 Report', established as part of the post-war process of reconstruction, emphasized the benefits to the individual and to the wider society. In a passage most likely drafted by R.H. Tawney and Basil Yeaxlee, the report noted that:

> Workers demand opportunities for education in the hope that the power which it brings will enable them to understand and help in the solution of the common problems of human society. In many cases, therefore, their efforts to obtain education are specifically directed towards rendering themselves better fitted for the responsibilities of membership of political, social and industrial organizations. (HMSO, 1918, p.3)

Fifty-five years later, the 1973 'Russell Report', *Adult Education: A Plan for Development,* emphasized role education, especially training and development for individuals in their roles as shop stewards and other trade union positions. This was in response to pressure from TUC leaders, who were looking for legal and financial support for trade union education on the basis of its contribution to more harmonious industrial relations: 'In a period when industrial relations are becoming increasingly complex, it is of vital importance that the large numbers involved on both sides of industry should be given the opportunity to study the problems and acquire the necessary techniques' (HMSO, 1973, p.6).

That trade union education contains a range of elements, from the philosophical through to the practical skills of industrial relations, has not really been in doubt, but the most important disputes have been about the different emphases within this range, and, implicitly or explicitly, the political purpose and consequences of trade union education.

Among those engaged in teaching and organizing within trade union education, there has been an intensive debate about the purpose and direction of such education. The earliest debate was between the WEA, who were championing the Workers' Educational Trade Union Committee (WETUC), and the National Council of Labour Colleges (NCLC), contrasting individual betterment and cultural awareness with the strengthening of collectivism through 'independent working-class education'. It was argued by the Labour College movement that the working class should control its own education, free from the capitalist state, and that the WEA, its rival, by accepting state funding, was compromised and was a 'sheep in wolf's clothing', weakening the movement through the dissemination of bourgeois ideology and the seduction of potential working-class leaders into the academic world. The WEA, on the other hand, saw the Labour College movement as propagandist rather than educational.

An equally intensive debate came later, in the 1980s, especially in the pages of *The Industrial Tutor,* journal of the Society of Industrial Tutors, and *Trade Union Studies Journal,* produced by the WEA (Caldwell, 1981; Gowan, 1983; Gravell, 1984; Edwards, 1983; Miller, 1983; McIlroy and Spencer, 1985; McIlroy, 1980, 1996; Nesbit and Henderson, 1983). This controversy touched on a number of issues of the time – corporatism and state funding at a time when the overtly hostile Thatcher government had arrived; paid release and joint training with employers – but mostly concerned itself with the ostensibly technical issue of active learning methods. At some stages it resembled a theological debate about seemingly obscure matters; the initiated, however, recognized the issues as codes for fundamental questions of doctrine. The main protagonists were John McIlroy of Manchester University on the one hand supported by others such as Bruce Spencer of Leeds University, and

Doug Gowan of the TUC and Tom Nesbit, Education Officer for Region 8 of the Transport and General Workers' Union (TGWU) on the other supported by Doug Miller of Newcastle Polytechnic and others such as Simon Henderson. The real issue was the alleged removal of political content from trade union education by the TUC. In its 1968 policy statement, *Training Shop Stewards*, the TUC had defined such training in a way which distinguished training from education:

> Training means systematic instruction, study and practice that will help to equip union members to be competent as representatives of their union in the workplace. Obviously this excludes consideration of their educational needs, as citizens or even potential general secretaries, or cabinet ministers. The boundaries to the training task, are, therefore, set by the richly varied duties and responsibilities of the workplace representatives themselves. (TUC, 1968, p.9)

The issue went back to the establishment of the TUC scheme in 1964, when J.P.M. Millar, General Secretary of the NCLC, bitterly accused the TUC of removing political content through the elimination of a number of politically related courses that had been offered by the NCLC, and through its narrow focus on collective bargaining skills. Millar commented that 'the less the members know about Socialism, the more the TUC like it' (quoted in McIlroy, 1980, p. 212). The election of the Thatcher government, with millions of trade unionists' votes, and the splits within the TUC over 'respectable' trades unionism and accommodation with this government brought the issue to a head. Key policy documents of the 1960s and 1970s had stressed the role of trade union education in 'inculcating the notion of constitutionalism and the need to respect agreements' in the minds of shop stewards (McIlroy, 1980, p.212) and the Royal Commission itself, under Lord Donovan, had specifically attached this function to trade union education:

> The need for shop steward training is immense...Additional resources are undoubtedly required. They should be used...with a view to using training of stewards as part of a planned move to more orderly industrial relations based on comprehensive and formal factory or company agreements. This is where shop steward training will be able to make its biggest contribution. (HMSO, 1967, pp.190-191)

At this time, the TUC was strengthening its links with further-education colleges, and insisting that courses follow a 10-day release format and essentially only concern themselves with basic shop stewards and safety reps training. Also, active learning methods were encouraged, with the tutor as 'facilitator', rather than lecturer or leader in the traditional adult education style. It was claimed that these methods were more democratic as they were more participative, and many references were made to the value of active learning, in contrast to the 'rote learning' that took place in schools. McIlroy and others argued that focus on student-centred learning methods obscured the 'wider questions of content, curriculum, what is to be learned and the nature of the power system within organized education which determines these questions' (McIlroy, 1979, p.47). He quoted the Marxist educationalist Douglas Holly:

> We must, of course, distinguish between…genuinely progressive methodology and *progressivism*. Progressivism can be defined as the mysticism of method, the belief that the only thing that matters in learning is the technique, or at best the social relationship between learner and teacher in the narrow. Progressivists delight in enquiry as an end in itself and rejoice when the classroom atmosphere is happy no matter what bunkum is being taught. (Holly, 1976, p.6)

The argument was that the focus on method went along with an extremely restrictive definition of what trade unionists wanted or needed, one essentially related to workplace industrial relations:

> TUC education appears to accept that there *is* a trade union knowledge 'out there', but a knowledge based on an extremely limited view of shop stewards. Yet what many trade unionists want today is social, political, economic knowledge – rooted in the workplace, yes, but qualitatively transcending it as well…And now we are reaching the real problems. What *is* the 'end' of trade union education for the educators and the students? Is it the provision of the preconditions for social change, as many of us believe, or is it, as the Code of Practice prescribes, 'improved industrial relations'? Until we address ourselves to these questions, then whether a tutor talks for three minutes or three hours in the classroom s/he may be talking to little effect. (McIlroy, 1979, p.53)

The implication, of course, was that the TUC was ensnared by its acceptance of state funding (a throwback to the NCLC/WETUC controversy) and did not want to jeopardize the continuation of that funding, even from the Thatcher government: 'Until 1979 the state operated with the carrot of rights. After 1979 the carrot was maintenance, the stick the threat of withdrawal of support' (McIlroy, 1996, pp.4 and 15). Later, as the controversy deepened, McIlroy was more strident:

Skills are important but in the harsh world of the 1980s the basic 'battle of ideas' is even more vital. Core TUC courses do not deal with the ownership of industry and managerial control of the workplace, the historical development of trade unions and their present predicament, the economic context or the political dilemmas. TUC education is in its own sealed world; its overwhelming focus on plant bargaining is like using bows and arrows to combat nuclear technology…In essence, the TUC Education Department have taken certain aspects of pedagogy and inflated them into dogma…we accept the need for the most imaginative learning methods. But we need those methods *as part of* a learning strategy. *That learning strategy requires a curriculum*…Education in terms of self-liberation is replaced by education in terms of utility for the enterprise and for the economy. (McIlroy, 1986, p.281)

Looking back on the debate 10 years later, McIlroy summed up his view:

The ideology that informed trade union education and industrial relations training was based upon Labourism's split between industrial and political. It emphasized a 'unitary', hierarchical, 'common-sense' conception of trade unionism with unproblematic goals, blurring differences of objective or interest between leadership and members and asserting politics as outside the realm of 'workplace industrial relations'…The presentation of workplace skills training as neutral failed to acknowledge that exclusion of a critical examination of politics and power in unions, industry and society, taking the wider context as given, was liable to legitimize existing authority relations and the politics of the *status quo*. Or that industrial relations training carried a view of trade unionism as centred on workplace collective bargaining at the expense of a view of trade unionism as a social movement with a political mission. And a conception of lay activists as a subaltern stratum was at the expense of conceiving lay activists as a critical, empowered, cadre. The economistic ideology of skills training reduced real divisions of purpose and policy to a simplistic, conservative technicism. (McIlroy, 1996, p.283)

There was also criticism of the TUC approach from those who were supportive of active learning methods in principle, but who felt that the TUC was not using them as part of an overall progressive approach. One such was Dan Vulliamy of Hull University, who identified a paradox in the TUC approach:

British trade union education, particularly as defined by the TUC Education Department, focuses on what British trade unionism is best at and overwhelmingly ignores its weaknesses. The result of the paradox is that the front line against continued workplace reorganization, plant closures and redundancies, imposition of new working methods and tighter discipline, hostile government legislation and other policies is manned by shop stewards who are now the best note-takers in the world, can calculate statutory redundancy entitlements in seconds and are all too aware that most forms of effective resistance have just been outlawed, but have no idea what to do when management take unilateral action or bypass the union with direct appeals to members, are largely unaware of alternative political and economic strategies which can be implemented at local and wider levels, and have often accepted the ideological barrage of Government and media about the inequities of the closed shop, the illegitimacy of effective industrial action and the responsibility for the mess of Communists, women, blacks and part-timers...in certain respects the contribution of trade union education in recent years has been worse than inappropriate, by fetishizing collective bargaining as the sole method and joint regulation as the sole purpose of trades unionism, and by encouraging a reliance on legal methods and written agreements in preference to more traditional trade union methods. (Vulliamy, 1985, p.54)

Vulliamy argued that participative and small-group learning methods were an important step forward in trade union education, but that their main function had been to highlight the inadequacy of the workplace organizations that existed at the time.

The response to these charges came on two levels. On the one hand, leading members of the TUC Education Department justified the TUC's approach on the grounds of its being an appropriate policy for the time, and claimed that the emphasis on participative methods was of value in itself. They also claimed that McIlroy and his supporters over-emphasized the focus on skills, and that TUC education was more broadly based. Thus Alan Grant, the Head of Education at the TUC:

The three legs of the educational school are 'attitudes', 'skills' and 'knowledge', and even the most basic course should operate on all three fronts...However, the acquisition of skills and the questioning of what passes for 'common sense' cannot take place in a vacuum. The context must be formally based upon employee/employer relationships at work. This context is established through the students' experience as the starting point, but must go on to extend knowledge to areas and issues beyond the students' experience. The view that the sum total of students' experience provides sufficient knowledge and information for a course and should itself set the limits of the syllabus, is...not the TUC view, but a parody of it. The most important person in this process is the tutor and I have very little patience with tutors who feel that their effectiveness increases with their invisibility. (Grant, 1985, p.12)

These comments kept the argument within the area of method, and did not acknowledge the demand for education dealing with economic and political issues put forward by McIlroy. Nor could such an official ever make a response that McIlroy would find satisfactory, given his starting point of education for social transformation. However, Grant did acknowledge that the TUC Course Development Unit had gone too far in the period before he took over, and in practical terms less extreme positions were taken up in the 1990s.

A more theoretically substantial response came from practitioners who argued that the use of active learning methods was itself a political and developmental process, taking their theoretical cue from Paulo Freire (1972a) and their practical one from their own experience as trade union tutors. It is an open question whether the TUC Course Development Unit ever perceived the process of active learning in this way, but radical tutors such as Tom Nesbit, Simon Henderson and Doug Miller certainly did. They argued that a 'dialectic pedagogy' based around active learning engaged workers in building a collective consciousness, which was itself a necessary learning process in trade union development. They criticized McIlroy and others for viewing the Labour College movement through rose-coloured glasses, arguing that their preferred methods were based on a passive process and only reached an already motivated elite. They argued that mass trade union education based on day release was far more significant in the development of activism in trade unions:

In our experience, one of the ways union members and representatives become active is by learning how to learn. We believe that by concentrating on the content (the 'what-is-to-be-learnt') to the exclusion of 'how the content is to be learnt' (methods), assumes a false division between the two. Knowledge is 'created' by the process of learning – defining and clarifying a problem, questioning, observing, generalizing, verifying and applying – not by memorizing someone else's questions…We believe that people are most interested in the issues which affect them and that the best time to learn anything is when it is most immediately useful to us. By encouraging people to become actively involved in those issues, the cause of unionism is advanced. (Nesbit and Henderson, 1983, p.5)

At this stage, these writers even argued that courses for trade unionists specifically concerned with training in active learning methods had significant political value. Tom Nesbit refined this view into a more comprehensive definition which tried to link political objectives and learning methods together:

> Although no education programme can resolve deep-seated economic changes, it can, however, help identify the causes of such changes, encourage an understanding of options, and challenge the apathy that overwhelms many in the face of crisis. Labour education can also encourage workers to rediscover the wider perspectives essential to development of real alternatives and policies, while simultaneously equipping workers with the skills and organization to implement them. (Nesbit and Henderson, 1983)

There have been other debates relevant to a definition of trade union education. In his book *The Third Contract*, set in a mainly Australian context, Michael Newman tried to deal with the separation between trade union education and other forms of adult education, and to examine the relationship between the educator and the requirements of union policy (Nesbit, T., 1991, p.6). He argued that there are three 'contracts' involved in trade union education. The first is between the union and the trainer: 'the union will set the objectives for its training programme and these are likely to be organizational ones to do with equipping members and officials with the necessary skills and knowledge to make the union function more effectively' (Newman, 1993, p.16). The second contract is between the trainer and the participants, which will need to be in accord with the union's policies and objectives. However, he argues that there is a third contract

> between the participants in the course and the union they belong to, and [it] is summed up in the saying: 'the members *are* the union'...The trainer is not party to this contract, but can influence it...we need to ensure that the members know that the union is theirs, that the officials are their servants, and that the structure they are a part of has been constructed to serve their interests as workers and members. And we need to ensure that they have the necessary skills and the motivation to act on this knowledge...The third contract is essential to the continued success of a union. If the interaction between a union as a sum of its members and a union as an organization is vigorously and continuously democratic, then the union will be able to resist domestication by employers, governments and its own peak bodies and, when necessary, will be able to engage in radical action. Defining, redefining, establishing and continually re-establishing this third contract must be the overriding purpose of all our training. (Newman, 1993, p.269)

This might be thought to be dangerous stuff, portraying the education programme as a Trojan horse for disruptive elements, and in some circumstances it could be so. However, it does focus attention on the exhilaration which all trade union educators have experienced when trade union members begin to understand their own organization and develop the confidence to take part in it and, in the longer run, extend their control over it. Education, then, can be an internal force for democracy and development within trade unions.

Much of the above discussion has centred on the motives of the organization and of the educators, but what of the students themselves and their motives? Although there may be a small amount of 'press-ganging' by officers, trade union education is almost entirely a voluntary activity on the part of the students, who are self-motivated, but little work has been done to identify what their motives are, and indeed, how the process of trade union education is viewed by the students, beyond asking them if they enjoyed the course or whether it was of benefit or not. The TUC and the unions have always operated 'course assessment' by students and tutors alike, and over the years the government-supported Workplace Industrial Relations Surveys have asked both managers and trade unionists to evaluate courses undertaken (Daniel and Millward, 1990). Overall, and not surprisingly, most trade unionists and managers felt that trade union education had been a useful exercise, with high percentages recording that in their role they, or industrial relations generally, benefited from involvement in it. More analytical was the attempt by Tom Schuller and Don Robertson to develop a framework of evaluation using 86 union representatives from two unions as a sample (Schuller and Robertson, 1984). They developed a number of measures of change, ranging from 'a waste of time' to 'a life-changing experience'. Most of the results were above average. They were able to identify one central result:

> The outstanding impression we have had from our research is that there is certainly one way in which shop steward training has an immensely powerful influence: that is in the growth of general confidence in carrying out the steward's duties. Seventy-two per cent of the stewards said that the course made them more confident and willing to make decisions. (ibid., p.10)

The problem with these approaches, however, was that they did not really measure the key requirement which unions themselves make of their education programmes; namely that they lead to an increase in *activity* amongst members, and especially representatives.

An attempt to measure this was made in 1992 by Doug Miller and John Stirling of Newcastle Polytechnic, on the basis of following up students involved in the TGWU Region 8 'Distance Learning' course (Miller and Stirling, 1992). They found that the course had resulted in a significant increase in activity. One student became a convenor, two more became branch secretaries and overhauled branch procedures; others stood for and were elected to various union conferences and committees, and increased their Labour Party involvement; others increased their participation in TUC and international trade union bodies. They also reported attitude changes over subjects like sexism and racism: 'The increased confidence that the course engendered has meant that members now make proposals at work and in the union that they would never have believed a year ago' (ibid., p.23).

Miller and Stirling made no grandiose claims for their study, pointing out that it is notoriously difficult to measure the impact, and especially the effect, of education:

> We are unable to say how much change would have occurred anyway, without the courses. In the opposite direction we also have the question of how much change can occur...Finally, we should bear in mind that almost any opportunity that allowed representatives to meet each other and exchange experiences would be likely to have a beneficial effect on trade union activity. In that respect, courses provide an important environment but they must go beyond that. (ibid., p.24)

Nevertheless, putting together their own experience as tutors on this particular course and their observation of the students, and the evidence of union activity where there is *no* education programme, it is reasonable to judge that such courses do give a boost to activity, at least for a time.

Michael Barratt-Brown attempted a historical approach to the relationship between trade unionists and their education programmes:

> What I would like to explore is the actual content of educational courses for workers as they have developed over the years. Given the interaction between tutor and class in adult education, this must give us some clues to the educational demands of workers and thus to the way that they and their tutors have perceived their needs. (Barratt-Brown, 1968, p.7)

In the first period, he noted that the syllabuses of the Central Labour College, Ruskin College, in the 1920s and the WETUC were very similar, covering a wide range of academic social sciences. Syllabuses in 1950s extra-mural classes were more problem-orientated, covering issues such as 'The Causes of Unemployment' and 'The Future of the Colonies'. By the 1970s almost the whole range of syllabuses of both short and long courses were workplace- and practically oriented, and by the 1980s there was a much greater emphasis on 'the group': women, black workers, miners' wives, single parents and so on. He deduced that in the 1920s and 1930s the emphasis was on self-advancement and making up for non-existent or inadequate initial education. During the war and in the post-war period, the need was to understand power and to end the misery of the 1930s, whilst in the 1960s and 1970s the demand was for knowledge and skills relevant to bargaining with employers. By the 1980s, the demand was from particular groups, often using local authority powers and funds to build bastions against Thatcherism and to promote their own particular advancement; what has now become known as 'identity politics'.

Overall, Barratt-Brown's point is that trade union education is a moveable feast, which constantly changes as part of the interaction not only between students and tutors, but also between the union organization and students and the economic, political and social context. For these reasons it is unwise to attempt a 'once-and-for-all' definition. This is again recognizing the presence of contradiction and the key dialectical processes, which make an unchanging definition of trade union education untenable.

It does, however, relate to what might make up the first part of any attempted definition, taking into account these debates and issues, namely, that trade union education should not be separate from the rest of union activity, and that it should as far as possible share the objectives of the union, and not be something which stands aside from these. These objectives may change over time, as Barratt-Brown has shown, and trade union education should also change. This part of the definition raises the question as to what the objectives of trade unions, or a particular trade union, are, but at least the organization must feel that whatever its debates on policy and overall direction, then its education programme is part of these and can be called on to assist in the realization and furtherance of policy.

A second element in trade union education is compensation for missed or unavailable initial educational opportunities. Even though priorities may change, the phenomenon of confidence-building and the unlocking of people's potential is just as much, or more so, an essential feature of trade union education as it is of adult education as a whole. If there is one way to characterize the trade union activist (or official), particularly in manual or general unions, it is someone whose ability outstrips his or her formal educational achievement. Often, regardless of trade union education, that is why people come forward as union representatives in the first place: because their routine work dulls the brain whilst union activity stimulates or tests it. Trade union education has been able to respond to this particular element of demand, whether through an NCLC discussion of fascism in the 1930s, a role-play matching a union negotiator's wits against an employer in the 1950s, or a confidence-building exercise on a women's course in the 2000s. It is also this element which has fitted so well into the accreditation of courses since the 1990s: often this has only made formal what already existed, as research into such schemes has found (Capizzi, 1999).

A third element is the widening of perspectives on the trade union movement. This was the essential issue in the 1980s dispute on methods set out in this chapter. It is often said, especially by socialists, that without education, trade union consciousness will remain parochial, at the level of 'factory gate' or 'office door'. With no explicit political content, and with the scope of inquiry limited by active and discovery learning methods, it would in theory be possible to engage in trade union education and come out with no wider perspective than when one went in. We have considered the debate and will not repeat it, but what evidence there is suggests that whatever methods are used, the effect of education is to broaden horizons beyond a person's immediate experience. This should, of course, be no surprise and should be applicable to all genuine education. Perhaps the essence of the problem in trade union education is the motives of the union and the tutors, rather than the methods. Do they *want* their students to learn about the history of the movement and its national and international objectives? Do they see themselves as part of a *movement* at all?

A fourth element would be the unlocking of the union organization itself, and the role of trade union education in maintaining or promoting the democratic health of the union as an organization. This is the 'third contract' element considered in this chapter. All unions claim to be democratic, and most have a formally democratic constitution. Breathing life into this, however, has not often shown itself to be the first priority of union leadership. One of the functions of trade union education is to build the necessary knowledge and confidence amongst the membership to encourage them to take part in committees and other activities of the organization, and to make democracy a reality, rather than a mere form.

I would propose that putting together these four elements comes somewhere near a descriptive – but not a prescriptive – definition of trade union education, and it also shows what a powerful force can be produced by this mix. Breathing life into unions through education programmes has affected the lives of millions of working people and their families over the years, and has also had a major impact on the state and the body politic. Of course, it is the labour movement itself, rather than its constituent parts (the TUC and less so the individual unions), which really impacted on society in the twentieth century, but the whole is only made up of its parts, and trade union education programmes made an important contribution. They present a fascinating story of activism and adult education at its best.

1 ABCA: the Army Bureau of Current Affairs was introduced as a programme of using educational methods to instil war aims, but was taken over by progressive tutors and students alike and, in the first half of the war at least, was turned into a debating society looking at social policies for the post-war world and criticizing what had gone on before the war. It was said to have played a role in the Labour victory of 1945. See S.P. Mackenzie, *Politics and Military Morale*, Clarendon Press, 1992; P. Addison, *The Road to 1945*: London, Quartet, 1975.

2 Perhaps the nearest is John McIlroy, 'Adult Education and the Role of Client: The TUC Education Scheme 1929-1980', in *Studies in the Education of Adults*, No 2, 1985.

2
Key concepts
in popular education

Mike Seal

Introduction

> Trade union training got locked into considerations of a very narrow range
> of technical and vocational areas, tutors became purveyors of information
> and facts, classes looked more like school rooms than workers' discussion
> circles, qualification replaced empowerment, learners were told what to
> learn instead of encouraged to learn from their experience, rigid curricula
> stifled debate. (Nicholls, 2017)

As we can see from the above quotation, there is a perception that education
within trade unions has become de-politicized, over-technical, and has
lost touch with wider social and economic issues. Discussions with trade
union educationalists at the GFTU conferences in 2015 and 2016 concurred.
Trade union education is often delivered in a very traditional way, based on
schooling, that is strangely at odds with our more dynamic radical history.

In some ways it is not surprising. Trade unionists, including educationalists, are often products of their own experience. Many will have gone through
at least 12 years of indoctrination into what education is, and could be, and
while this may have been a negative experience, it is nonetheless what they
expect when they go into a classroom, as teacher or learner. As a counter to
this the first thing I give to students on courses I teach is a document called
'How we teach', which tries to pull apart and reconstruct expectations of
education. I will refer to it several times in this document as it tried to put the
idea of popular education in lay terms. The opening lines of the document are:

> You might have thought university would consist of a teacher, who 'knows'
> the 'subject', at the front of a classroom giving a 'lecture' i.e. giving you
> information which you are to write down. At some point you will be required
> to regurgitate this information back in the form of an essay or exam to show
> that you understood. You then promptly forget this information to make
> room for the next bit of knowledge you are meant to 'learn'. For us this is

not education, this is temporary rote learning of uncontested information. In this day and age, you can quickly access what we could give you in terms of information via the internet in seconds – so what is the point of that? For us education is something else, it is helping you become critical thinkers to discover, or uncover, knowledge and assess its worth.

This implies that we also need to challenge associated structures of education, such as exams, assignments and trade union 'workbooks'. While they may still have a place, they should perhaps not be as central as they currently are. Fundamental for educators is to give students, trade union activists, and people in general, the tools to undo, rethink and challenge their received wisdoms about what constitutes knowledge and education. This view goes against a tradition of teacher-dominated education where the learner and teacher operate, what Freire (1972b) calls a 'banking' view of education whereby the student receives a fixed curriculum that they accept unquestioningly. I think the undoing and reforming of educational expectations needs to be an active process. Ira Shor, a popular educationalist, says we are trying to cultivate in learners:

> Habits of thought, reading, writing, and speaking which go beneath surface meaning, first impressions, dominant myths, official pronouncements, traditional clichés, received wisdom, and mere opinions, to understand the deep meaning, root causes, social context, ideology, and personal consequences of any action, event, object, process, organization, experience, text, subject matter, policy, mass media, or discourse. (Shor, 1992, p.129)

This is the starting point for the tradition of popular education, sometimes called critical pedagogy. Some trade unionists see that need for change. Below are quotes from trade unionists cited in the 'future of trade union' documents the General Federation of Trade Unions produced in 2015 that re-iterate this, but also point towards another way.

> The movement has dangerously moved away from proper education in trade unions to educate the minds and knowledge base of members into a very narrow range of vocational and technical areas. This will not do for the future and the GFTU will need to transform its provisions of education quickly to meet the needs of the challenge. (GFTU, 2015, p.3)
>
> Trade unions have a vital role to play in overcoming the neoliberal ideology that caused the financial crash, justifies 'austerity' and underpins the enduring power of the banks today. (GFTU, 2015, p.4)

This chapter will explore the key concepts of popular education, and assess whether the approach has potential resonance with trade union educationalists looking for 'another way' and wishing to make trade union education vital and relevant again. It will look at popular education's background, its different view on the nature of knowledge and learning, and examine some key principles of its educational approach and some of its characteristics and techniques.

Background on popular education

Critical pedagogy has existed as an approach to education for over 40 years. It is one of the main influences on youth and community work (Seal and Frost, 2014, Seal and Harris, 2016). However, as Doug notes in his introduction, pedagogy is not the word we have chosen to use in this book. This is mainly because we do not think it has resonance with a trade union audience, but also because there are some inherent tensions within the concept that make it problematic. However, advocates of the concept of pedagogy have a number of pertinent things to say about education, including how restrictive a term it has become. We should take heed of them. The word pedagogy also has currency with many of our European colleagues. However, we will use the term popular education.

The idea behind popular education was first described by Paulo Freire (1972b) and has since developed, described as popular education or critical pedagogy, largely in the United States, by authors such as Henry Giroux, Ira Shor, Michael Apple, Joe L. Kincheloe, Shirley R. Steinberg and Peter Maclaren. It is a broad school that combines critical theory, a neo-marxist approach, and educational theory. It grew out of a concern amongst certain educationalists with how education was being used as a method to re-inscribe power relations in society.

It seeks to illuminate the oppressed about their situation in which the state and the education system create a 'common sense' that re-inscribes dominant elites' social positions as 'natural and inevitable'. It seeks to interrogate received wisdoms and 'go beneath surface meaning, first impressions, dominant myths, official pronouncements, traditional clichés, received wisdom, and mere opinions' (Shor, 1992 p.125). As well as Marxism, popular education draws on other influences including humanism, existentialism and post-colonialism (Seal, 2014, Davies, 2012). Giroux (2012) describes it as a 'educational movement, guided by passion and principle, to help students develop consciousness of freedom, recognize authoritarian tendencies, and connect knowledge to power and the ability to take constructive action' (Giroux, 2012, p.1). This statement contains many of the fundamental ideas behind critical pedagogy.

Knowledge and education: what are they and who creates them?

What is education?

Before we try to identify how to improve and revitalize the educational approaches of unions, it seems important to outline and undo our pre-conceptions about what education is and what it is not – and also what knowledge is and is not. These relate directly to one of the principal aims of popular education outlined above, to challenge accepted ideas about the nature of knowledge and education – another being to de-neutralize education and acknowledge its inherently political nature.

Popular education seeks to challenge traditional concepts of both knowledge and education. A common association with knowledge, and particularly theory, is that it is something created or discovered by 'objective', 'neutral' 'experts', often under scientific conditions. Ideally it is universal in application, although this knowledge might subsequently be challenged by other experts with other ideas that fit the facts better. Knowledge and theory are therefore abstracted from most people's everyday lived experience.

Education is then traditionally seen as the process whereby this 'knowledge' is transferred, often via a teacher who 'knows' it, to students who do not. The process of students absorbing this knowledge is called 'learning'. When a student applies this 'learning' to their experiences, it should make sense of them. However, if it does not apply they have either not understood the knowledge properly, or applied it properly, or their experiences are 'not representative'. As said, popular education challenges these views on knowledge and education at many levels – on what constitutes knowledge, its neutrality and objectiveness, where and when it is applicable, how and who creates it and how we educate and enable others to learn about and engage with it.

What is knowledge?

Popular education has a particular view about what constitutes knowledge, particularly knowledge about people. Aristotle makes a claim for three types of knowledge. The first is 'Episteme', which is scientific knowledge that largely does not change (although this idea is itself heavily contested). Second is 'Techne', which is the technical knowledge and skills a person needs to put this science to use. When looking at issues of, say, health and safety at work we will often be drawing on both these kinds of knowledge – facts about what constitutes a hazard could be 'epistemic knowledge' while the laws about health and safety could be seen as a 'technical knowledge of how these hazards are managed in the workplace'.

His third type of knowledge is 'Phronesis', which is very different in character. It is hard to translate and is therefore often translated simply as 'practical wisdom'. However, this translation underestimates Phronesis's importance and seems close to 'Techne'. While 'Techne' is how we apply science to the world, 'Phronesis' says we need to ask *why* we are applying this knowledge – what our aim for doing this is and what moral values we are operating to when we do. So fundamental questions about why we define and look at hazards in the ways we do, why the laws have developed in the ways they have, how we understand our underlying motivations and intentions, and of management in a negotiation around health and safety, and the tactics on how to do this, are 'Phronesis'. We may have lists of negotiating tips, based on valid experiences, but the real skill is learning to apply these ideas in particular real situations, often in the moment, where a lot of other factors come into play which might make those tips redundant, and we have to draw on other ideas or create knowledge there and then.

The person is making a judgement about what is *right* to *do* in *particular* situations and we should not try to find universal truths that apply to people as the variables are so great and in flux. Why and how we apply knowledge has to be applied differently in different situations and the person applying it actively involved in creating this knowledge. Aristotle saw this as particularly important when talking about people and society rather than objects. I am reminded of being at a conference where a representative of the Confederation of British Industry (CBI) was in attendance. Some presenters were proudly telling her about how they had applied industrial models to their workplace in evaluating a piece of work with young people. The CBI representative asked why they were doing this – those models were meant for machine parts, not people.

There are political dimensions to this freezing of the debate. Marx recognized that to try to separate people from such decisions is deeply alienating for the individual, and is also about denying working people knowledge and a part in its creation. Everyone has a view on society and what is valuable; therefore this knowledge is not neutral and we should all be a part of creating it. Those privileged in society have been less honest and see the power of presenting the status quo as somehow inevitable and natural and immutable. Much of what is presented by ruling elites and educational systems as Episteme, i.e. as facts that are objective, neutral and natural, are in actuality 'Phronesis', knowledge that is a result of, and underpinned by, a particular moral view, a choice, and as such, could be different. Much in society, including the idea of education itself, is not neutral, but stems from a particular ideology. Indeed, attempts to say education should be neutral, again reinforces a view of society that favours existing power structures and hinders change.

Who gets to create knowledge: Praxis

A part of not being neutral, and having values and morals behind the application of knowledge, is that knowledge, for popular educationalists, needs to relate to the lived experiences of people and, where necessary, seek to change it for the better. One word for this is praxis and popular education has consistently described itself as a praxis (Batsleer, 2012; Smith, 1994; Ord, 2000). Praxis is often interpreted as the synthesis of theory and action. However, it is more complex, subtle and radical than this. Popular education has a dynamic, dialectical view of how knowledge is created (Aristotle, 1976). It sees knowledge as an evolving thing (Carr and Kemmis, 1989). Part of these dynamics is that knowledge needs to be applied in particular ways in particular situations and is therefore a result of dialogue between those subject to the experience the potential knowledge relates to. As Freire put it, we need to 'come to see the world not as a static reality, but as reality in process, in transformation' (Freire, 1972, p.71). As we say in 'How we teach'.

> Knowledge is not static, it is dynamic. It is created through dialogue. In a very real sense I cannot tell you what is right, for there is rarely a 'right'. Common sense is rarely common, as in everyone agrees, or makes sense in that it's logical. Facts that were 'known' 100 years ago are now discredited. Those in power might tell you that it is 'common sense' that things stay as they are. Knowledge is power and rarely neutral. (Newman, 2015, p.1)

Furthermore, knowledge creation is not a one-off process, as most situations are multi factorial and happen in particular contexts and time. Consequently, as already discussed, most knowledge about people is similarly particular and contextual. While we may draw on wider universals, we are seeking to determine what is the appropriate action, in this particular context and in this moment of time. As Mao says, 'the development of each particular process is relative, and that hence, in the endless flow of absolute truth, man's knowledge of a particular process at any given stage of development is only relative truth' (Mao Zedong, 1937).

Principles of popular education: democracy, developing critical thinkers and consciousness raising

Democracy and equality in learning environments

Popular educationalists view knowledge, as well as being able to be created by all, as social. We create knowledge through dialogue with each other. Cho (2010) describes knowledge as 'democratic, context-dependent, and appreciative of the value of learners' cultural heritage' (Cho, 2010, p.315). The creation of this evolving knowledge is an active democratic process that entails interrogation of the world by all parties, rather than by an educated elite. However, this means not simply acknowledging the diversity and multiculturalism in the room, accepting people's own views of their cultures as monolithic. Indeed, popular education may well entail challenging and changing cultural norms as the aim of critical pedagogy is 'reflection and action upon the world in order to transform it', (Freire, 1972, p.12). However, learners have their own theories and ideas about the world, and this needs to be our starting place. As Bolton describes, 'paying critical attention to the practical values and theories which inform everyday actions, by examining practice reflectively and reflexively' (2010, p.56). We try and capture the spirit of this in 'How we teach', declaring.

> We try, in what we teach and how we teach, to create these dialogical spaces. We want to create a debate about a topic which will inspire you to go and find out more about it. We will try and make these spaces democratic – that you can challenge us, and each other, and even change what we are learning.

This can be difficult for some educators as it means, as Foley notes (2007) that they need to challenge the structure they operate within, including 'rejecting long standing cultural expectations' including their own teaching approaches and, fundamentally, the 'power which is given to them through their titles' (Foley, 2007). My doctorate is in critical pedagogy and I am a 'reader' in critical pedagogy. Yet this does not mean I know everything about critical pedagogy, let alone anything else, and I continually learn from students about that subject. In fact my titles often get in the way and I rarely use them, although I should not deny the privileges they afford me. As we say in 'How we teach', we need to be explicitly humble and challenging of our own privilege 'Sometimes you will know more than we do, and we should acknowledge this and let you educate us' (Newman, 2013 p.1).

To be a critical educator can also mean challenging the illusion of power the 'teacher' has in the educational spaces they inhabit. That many learners have years of experience of education in its narrow school form means that the 'teacher' gets a certain level of authority, though not necessarily respect, that derives from this common cultural experience. An aspect of this is that the teacher is 'in charge' of both the educational experience and the classroom itself. Learners are to be passive receivers of information. As Joldersma (1999) notes, there is a certain familiar complacency in this for learners, they do not have to make much effort, or take responsibility for their learning, let alone the learning environment. Learners can also be consumers, taking what they want and ignoring what does not immediately resonate. They can also passively resist, as they may have done at school, taking small chances to undermine the authority of the teaching, but often in a non-constructive way, or a way that can in turn be infantilized by the teacher. For the learning to be real this 'play' of accepted roles again needs to be challenged.

To be democratic means that we all have responsibility for these spaces. We have heard students say that it is the tutor's 'job' to 'control' the class. Where is the democracy in that? – There are 30 of you and only one of us. Also, if we control the class through our perceived power, either of our personality or status, haven't we all fallen into the same old traps again?

I have taken this further to discuss with students what they can do if they really do not like the education they are getting, from complaining, to voting with their feet – if they all walked out, the institution would certainly react. This means that teachers have to admit their vulnerabilities in an educational environment – they are exposed and not all knowing and their 'power' is an illusion. I have had colleagues who have found this difficult, fearing losing authority and fear mongering what learners would do with these spaces (often infantilizing their experiences of what resistance they have encountered).

However, at the same time, we may need to counter some constructions when people say they do not like the education they receive. Many of the students I work with construct democracy in education as consumerism, mainly because this is how they have experienced it. They pay for a product that they consume, often embodied in comments about 'what do I pay my fees for'. Education needs to be delivered in a way that they like, and by saying the things that are familiar. But this is not popular education, which can be very challenging. As we say in 'How we teach':

While we are trying to provide stimulus, we are not entertainers. It is not our job to perfectly match your 'learning style' – how many learning styles are there in one room? It is all too easy to fall back into being a consumer of knowledge: 'Give me what I want in the way I say I want it. Remember, we are creating knowledge together, and at times there will be clashes, conflict and, worst of all, apathy and boredom – it is the responsibility of all of us to work these things through.

Developing critical thinkers
The most important thing we are doing as educators is enabling people to become critical thinkers – knowledge creators, able to apply and synthesize new ideas and information into new ways of thinking as situations change and evolve. Our experiences are not exceptions if they do not fit current

ideas. Such experiences should become a part of knowledge creation, challenging existing theory and becoming new knowledge. The break between experience, practice and theory needs to be challenged and students need to see how they have a right and duty to create new knowledge. As we say in 'How we teach':

> We hear a lot of students say that they are not academic, they are practical, they learn by doing. There is a lot of truth in this statement, but for all of us. Much learning is experiential and all knowledge creation is – we try things out and discover for ourselves how they work. You do not learn to ride a bike through a book, you do it by trying it out – and sometimes the instructions are wrong and need to be challenged – by you.

However, this is not an easy process, as Joe Strummer from punk group The Clash put it: 'You go to school so they can teach you to be thick.' Learning to be critical is, and should be, challenging, particularly as the first thing we need to do is challenge our own assumptions about learning and re-evaluate our previous experiences of it. Capitalism is clever in that it distances people from their natural critical thinking skills and at the same time encourages them to think individualistically about their views as though they are commodities to which they have a right. Both sides of this need to be challenged, as we say in 'How we teach'.

> Some say the essentials of education are reading, writing and arithmetic. This comes from Arabic education and was originally reading, writing and logic. Logic being how to reason and argue and for us this is crucial. Schooling has forgotten this. Often students say, after asserting something, 'well, that's what I think', quickly followed by 'I am entitled to my opinion', as if your views are a commodity. Sorry, but in our spaces, this isn't good enough – you have to defend your opinions, be open to change, and sometimes have the bravery to stand alone.

Consciousness raising

> *Critical pedagogy challenges any form of domination, oppression and subordination with the goal of emancipating oppressed or marginalized people.* (Aliakbari and Faraji, 2011, p.77)

More fundamentally, as Aliakbari and Faraji (2011) go on to state, popular education aims to 'transform oppressed people and to save them from being objects of education to subjects of their own autonomy and emancipation'.

It aims to get people to 'think critically and develop a critical consciousness which helps them to improve their life conditions and to take necessary actions to build a more just and equitable society.' Fundamental here is the idea of developing critical consciousness, the process of which Freire calls 'conscientization'.

Drawing on Gramsci, it is the aforementioned idea that people need to unlearn the received wisdoms that society wishes them to believe, particularly about the naturalness and inevitability of their oppression. Popular educationalists work to encourage students to 'develop a critical consciousness of who they are and what their language represents by examining questions of language, culture, and history through the lens of power' (Brito et al, 2004, p.23). Freire (1972) names three levels of consciousness: intransitive, semitransitive, and critical consciousness. Those with an intransitive consciousness accept their lives as they are and take the view that any changes are either for reasons beyond their control, are seen as fate, or occasionally divine intervention. If I reflect on my own involvement in the union movement at this stage I was antagonistic to the idea of a union, believing received views from management about what unions were. This alternated with a belief that things couldn't be changed anyway, so why engage in the 'struggle'.

Those with a semi-transitive consciousness are aware of their problems and still think of them as inevitable, but they may think they can change things at a local level. Actions are often localized and short term. This is where an activist might involve themselves in local union actions, but will not make the connection between these actions and wider actions. They may not see that the struggle at the local level is paralleled in wider social struggles or that the oppressive forces they face are expressions of wider social forces. It is only when people have a critical consciousness that they see the structural dimensions of their problems, making connections between their problems and the social context in which these problems are embedded, both in terms of analysis and actions that will challenge their structural oppressions as well as addressing some of their immediate concerns.

There are potential issues with the idea of conscientization, particularly the idea of false consciousness. It is in danger of presenting those who are oppressed as not having agency, in that they need an outsider to enlighten them. It can also underestimate the working class, who can be only too aware of their oppression.

Do ordinary men and women need to be conscientized before they recognize that they lead desperate, oppressed lives marked by hunger, disease, and the denial of dignity? They know the score and do not need middle class do-gooders to tell them. They acquiesce in their oppression because they have no other choice. (Zacharia, 1986, p.123)

However, I do not think it negates some of the ideas of critical consciousness, just who is able to take responsibility for this development. Jaques Ranciere may help here. He was a disciple of Althusser, the Marxist theoretician, but famously broke with him in 1974 when he published 'Althusser's Lesson'. He accused Althusser of having authoritarian tendencies, and of preserving the teacher/student power relationship in that he said that those students who involved themselves in the 1968 revolution were misguided in not acting under the authority of their enlightened Marxist teachers. Rancière similarly critiqued Bourdieu's notion of reproduction for privileging the role of the intellectual, and condemning the masses as unknowing and in need of liberation. Instead, akin to Zachariah (1986), Rancière views the working class as inherently capable of learning and developing intellect. However, they have been led to believe that they are not intelligent by a hegenomic system that deliberately undermines their self-belief. In addition, they may have lost the will to use it, in the face of seemingly monolithic social forces compelling them to prioritize short-term material survival that grinding poverty necessitates.

Rancière thought that many forms of pedagogy were designed to keep people ignorant, or at least make them dependent on others for their acquisition of knowledge. Ranciere asks us to imagine what the social world would be like if we assumed a radical equality of intelligence. The educator should act under the assumption that we are all intelligent enough to understand the world, and that, given access to resources, we can discern the knowledge that will enable this understanding. He invites the educator to become 'ignorant', not denying their knowledge, or hiding, but revealing it when the time is right for others to understand their insights. Instead, they should not privilege their knowledge – we should become ignorant, not in that we pretend we know nothing but that we should 'uncouple our mastery from our knowledge'. A true educator 'orders them (the student) to venture into the forest of things and signs, to say what they have seen and what they think of what they have seen, to verify it and have it verified.' (Rancière, 1992, p.96). The role of the educator is two-fold. Firstly to act on the students' will, their self-belief and efficacy, the will to engage and challenge themselves and others, and to learn.

We have heard some students groan when we don't give 'answers', and ask us why we are making it hard for them, can we not just tell them what is right.

This is not us being awkward. In a very real sense I cannot tell you what is right, for there is rarely a 'right'. We have to create and contest knowledge together.

Secondly, an educator's role is to attend to the content of what argument people are creating (only in terms of ensuring people's arguments have logic and internal consistency) and that they attend to, understand and deconstruct the language behind those arguments and the concepts behind the language. This entails gaining access to resources, often intellectual resources, but it does not mean we determine the content of those resources. This is not always an easy process, or unchallenging, as we say to students:

> The language we use, for this is our major medium, is laden with concepts, ideas and assumptions, and it needs to continually be unpacked and re-packed. Avoid the trap of asking for things in 'plain English' as it does not exist. We do not try to be obscure, but it is equally not our job to translate everything for you. Some ideas are hard to understand sometimes because they are trying to look at difficult things – they are not obvious because they are trying to get beyond the obvious. However, sometimes ideas are deliberately made hard – those with power trying to keep power by using long words to silence you – the onus is on you to not let this happen.

Characteristics and techniques of popular education

Some of the fundamental techniques within popular education that flow from these principles are having a flexible curriculum with authentic materials, finding teachable moments and discovering generative themes.

Flexible curriculum and using authentic materials

A fundamental within critical and emancipatory education is that no single methodology can work for all cultures, populations and situations (Degener, 2001). This is because all decisions related to curricula, including the material to be studied, should be based on the needs, interests, experiences and situations of students (Giroux, 2012; Shor, 1992). Furthermore, students, as Giroux (2012) puts it, should be active participants in designing and correcting the curricula – a fundamental part of curricular decisions and determining areas of study and the associated reading needed to understand them (Degener, 2001). Most fundamentally the curriculum needs to relate to the lived social and economic lives of the learner and help them move from the micro of their situations and crises, to see the wider socio-economic forces behind them, and their contradictions.

However, learning needs to be rooted in the experiences of those undertaking it. As Mao says, educators who do not do this 'alienate themselves from the current practice of the majority of the people and from the realities of the day, and show themselves adventurist in their actions.' (Mao Zedong, 1937). Several authors note that the materials used for education should come from and have resonance with people's everyday lives and include books poems, films, adverts etc (Ohara, Saft, & Crookes, 2000; Kessing-Styles, 2003; Kincheloe, 2005). They can be equally brought to the table by tutors and students, and especially students as their consciousness develops. It is in linking people's everyday experiences and crises to wider socio-economic forces that people start to see 'both the reproductive nature and the possibility of resistance to problematic content.' (Aliakbari and Faraji, 2011, p.80).

Teachable moments
One of the characteristics of critical pedagogy is the ability to think in the moment and improvise. (Seal and Harris, 2014; Smith, 1994). This can mean recognizing that a particular session plan is not working or having resonance, and adjusting it accordingly. At another level it can mean spotting and seizing an opportunity to relate a discussion to wider issues. As an example I seized a teachable moment in a discussion at the last GFTU conference. We were discussing how trade union branches organize their meetings and conferences, with minutes, agendas and motions. I moved it from a discussion about how we should induct new trade unionists into these practices to a much wider discussion about why we do it in this way, covering debates about exclusion, replicating old power structures, responding to changing working conditions and replicating bureaucratic tendencies of capitalism. This was simply done by asking, at the 'right' moment, 'but why do we do it like this anyway – whose interests does it serve?' Interestingly, we concluded that most of these structures had validity, but it made the group see the importance of explaining their rationale to new people so they would buy into the process.

Generative themes
Taking this further is the idea of generative themes (Aliakbari and Faraji, 2011). This is where the group, in deciding the curriculum and theme to be explored, is seeking themes with certain characteristics. Firstly, themes should be a galvanizing force for the community, something about which there is passion and feelings. Secondly the theme must have tensions and contradictions within it, things that do not add up that need to be worked through and have a potential to create something new that resolves these tensions. These tensions should not be allowed to become negative, but

their energy turned into a positive incentive to change. Generative themes should also open up discussion about, and relate to, wider social issues. In doing so they can lead to the opening up of other generative themes (i.e. a generative theme has the seed of other generative themes within it). Finally, generative themes must have the potential for action, that something concrete can be done about them.

Within my own union we have sought in recent strikes, ostensively about pay, to educate other union members and students about the general state of higher education, and seek common ground between parties. On the picket lines and beyond, discussions are held about the pressures that are put on both lecturers and students, both financially and in terms of workload, leading to student-union support of disputes. This has led to discussion about how education is being commodified and stratified and reduced to employer-based training. In turn this led to students boycotting new government 'quality' regimes that were reductive.

Conclusion

I hope this chapter has served as an introduction to the key concepts of popular education, and has shown how these two traditions can inform each other. Many good trade union educators are already educating in this way, but may not have a name or structure to frame their approach. If this chapter gives them that, then it has served its purpose. For others we hope it goes further and allows educators, learners and activists to discover or rediscover an approach to learning that is so necessary to counter ever pervasive neoliberal and neoconservative forces that have convinced us that education is not necessary. I will leave you with a vision from the GFTU statement mentioned in the introduction that encapsulates the vision of what education can and needs to be:

> Education liberates the mind, challenges injustices, teaches you to think critically and to act collectively. It unlocks mysteries and enables you to question the lies of the powerful and to propose alternatives. It enables you to ultimately govern and control your own destiny and challenge the hidden hand of the market. It stops you from being a slave and a victim of circumstances and be a creator of our own social destinies. (GFTU, 2015, p.2)

3
History and context
of UK trade union education

John Fisher

It is important to realize that the early history of trade union education is intimately bound up with what was meant by 'trade union education', and questions of control and purpose, and appropriateness in the face of economic and political change were central to this fascinating history.

In those first years, at the local level the movement built and renewed itself through informal procedures, where local leaders would spot likely young men and women and guide them into taking leadership responsibility. If the 'mentors' (as they would now be called) were Liberals, members of the Social Democratic Federation (SDF), members of the Labour Party or, later, members of the Communist Party, then no doubt these views would be urged onto the newcomers. Just because there were no classrooms, it did not mean there was no education!

At the higher level, the Trades Union Congress (TUC) first of all concentrated on the struggle for mass education in the society as a whole (Griggs, 1983) and encouraged the universities to widen their 'extra-mural' activities by reaching out towards working-class adults (Griggs, 1983; Goldman, 1995). However, at the start of the new century the TUC became involved in the establishment of Ruskin College, Oxford. Ruskin Hall had been founded in 1899, the same year as the foundation of the General Federation of Trade Unions (GFTU), by three Americans, with the object of encouraging students to 'increase their usefulness to the Labour Movement in general, and to the societies who sent them to the College through training in subjects which are essential for working-class leadership' (Millar, 1979, p.1).

The adoption of Ruskin into Oxford University was partly as a result of the ground-breaking report *Oxford and Working-Class Education* (University of Oxford, 1908), which said essentially that if the working class was to come to power through universal suffrage, then they had better be 'Oxford Men' (sic) as all the earlier rulers had been.[1] But what was the college for? In the minds of the young trade union students, it was to learn about politics, economics and sociology, to strengthen their arms for the class struggle to come, but for the university it was about imposing Christian morality, temperance and middle-class values. Matters soon came to a head with the dismissal in March 1909 of the Principal, Dennis Hird, a Christian socialist and member of the SDF (Atkins, 1981; Craik, 1964; Holford, 1994).

The result was the famous Ruskin College students' strike, which led to the establishment of an umbrella body, the Plebs' League, and the establishment of the Central Labour College, whose objective was to prepare leaders for the future of the trade union and labour movement, and the rejection of (it was said) Ruskin's imposition of establishment values (Atkins, 1981; Craik, 1964; Millar, 1979).

WETUC versus the NCLC

At the local level, this division between Ruskin College and the Central Labour College was replicated in the ongoing conflict between the Workers' Educational Association (WEA) and the National Council for Labour Colleges (NCLC). The WEA was founded in 1903, and its trade union education section, the Workers' Education Trade Union Committee (WETUC), in 1919. The NCLC was founded in 1921 and the two organizations immediately came into conflict. The WEA essentially saw itself as making up for the defects of state education and providing opportunities for individual advancement (Simon, 1990). As part of this activity, it was in receipt of state funding, which the NCLC was not. The NCLC, being completely dependent on the unions, claimed that its purpose was to build the labour movement, not to provide opportunities for individuals to move up and out. The NCLC referred to WETUC as 'a sheep in wolf's clothing'.

In early 1925, the *TGWU Record* published a 'debate' between representatives of the two bodies. J.P.M. Millar (1925) stressed that the NCLC represented *independent* working-class adult education, with the implication that the WEA, by being subsidized, was in the pocket of the government and the ruling class: 'One group of workers' educational organizations stands for the extension of university education to the workers, which in my view is employing-class education, while another – the NCLC – stands for *independent* working-class education' (Millar, 1925).

G.D.H. Cole, on the other hand, entitled his piece 'Thinking for Yourself', implicitly characterizing the NCLC as a propagandist rather than an educational organization. He argued that WETUC

> does not start out by saying to the trade unionist: 'This is how you ought to do it; this is what you ought to believe.' It comes and asks the trade unionist what he wants to learn, and, when he has stated his need, does its best to make him – not believe any particular set of doctrines – but think for himself, and make up his own mind. (Cole, 1925)

At the local level, trade unions ran courses under the aegis of either the WEA or the NCLC, mostly using university extra-mural tutors. These were often around subjects of general interest such as 'Transport Policy for the UK' or 'Fascism in Italy', but were not directly linked to trade union organization. There were some excellent local exceptions, including courses aiming at the development of women as trade union tutors (Cohen, 1990a), and the NCLC established a formidable pattern of correspondence courses dealing with subjects ranging from basic literacy to economics (Millar, 1979). Both the Labour Party and the Communist Party also ran their own schools (Cohen, 1990b).

Philosophical differences between the providing organizations mattered less at the local level, and many of the student debates on WETUC or NCLC courses would have been very similar. In the early 1930s Jack Jones was Secretary of the Liverpool Labour College, but in his view:

> The difference between Labour College classes and WETUC ones was that the WETUC had more university and professional people as tutors. For the rest of it they were almost the same…We weren't concerned to talk about music and history and art and all that sort of thing. We wanted to talk about industrial law, the structure of trade unionism and what Socialism meant, international affairs, international labour politics, international economic matters…So in that sense these classes attracted good trade unionists who wanted to see just beyond their own individual job. (Jones, 1984)

At the local level, activists like Jack Jones would attend both Labour College and WETUC classes.

The TUC, education and the General Strike

At the 1921 TUC Congress a resolution was carried that the TUC take over both the Central Labour College and Ruskin, but nothing came of it. In 1922, the TUC's view of trade union education involved a fairly wide-ranging definition:

- Training in the management of trade union business – mainly branch administration
- Training for positions as Labour representatives locally and in the House of Commons
- Industrial management and workers' councils
- The training of teachers from among trade unionists. (Simon, 1990, p.45)

A scheme was adopted at the 1925 TUC Congress which provided for representation of the TUC on the governing bodies of the providing organizations, and allowed the General Council to develop its own initiatives in the field of education. It was also suggested that the two colleges, Ruskin and the Central Labour College, should be taken over and transferred to the same site. Later that year Lady Warwick offered her home, Easton Lodge, to the TUC as a venue for a residential college. The TUC required £50,000 (£1.5 million at today's values) to place the college on a sound financial footing.

The defeat of the General Strike led to the abandonment of this scheme. Another casualty of the consequent financial crisis was the Central Labour College. The college's main supporters, the South Wales Miners and the National Union of Railwaymen, were not in a position to take over or continue supporting it, and in 1929 the college closed.

The objectives set out in the 1922 report were abandoned for 40 years. After 1926, the weakness of the movement and the onset of the Great Depression meant that trade union education entered the period which Simon calls 'the triumph of liberal education' (1990, pp.49-70), where unions had to rely on external providers for their education programmes. By the 1930s the WEA had about 60,000 mainly working-class students each year studying subjects like politics and economics, but about 20 per cent of these were on longer courses in partnership with universities. The NCLC reached a peak of about 30,000 students in the 1920s, but by the end of the 1930s this number had declined to around 13,000 students in 728 classes (Brown, 1980, p.109). Like the labour movement as a whole, by the late 1930s trade union education was fairly stuck in the doldrums.

The war and its aftermath

The Second World War marked a crucial turning point in the history of trade union education. The 'People's War' gave new strength and confidence to the trade union movement. While Churchill ran the military aspects of the war, the 'home front' was completely under the control of Ernest Bevin, the Minister of Labour, previously the first General Secretary of the Transport and General Workers' Union (TGWU), and Clement Attlee, the Deputy Prime Minister and Leader of the Labour Party. Bevin used his enormous power to establish institutions in the workplace which brought the trade unions into centre stage, and he began to develop a key role for local representatives. He insisted on Joint Production Committees in manufacturing industries, laid the basis of the National Dock Labour Scheme and the National Coal Board, and prepared for nationalization of the railways, steel, road transport and other industries, using a model which gave a key role to the trade unions.

After the Labour victory in 1945, unions like the GMWU (General and Municipal Workers' Union), NALGO (National and Local Government Officers Association) and the NUM (National Union of Mineworkers) were firmly in place in the newly nationalized industries, and even in the private sector, unions like the TGWU, the AEU (Amalgamated Engineering Union) and the ETU (Electrical Trades Union) were strongly organized in the automotive, chemicals and food and drink industries, and in many others.

New methods

This growth threw up new demands for the training of representatives, and it also became clear that new education methods would be needed to meet the needs of this new generation. WEA and university extra-mural classes had been very much 'talk and chalk', with an expert lecturer and passive students, but the new circumstances demanded a different approach. The American trade unions produced a practical handbook called *Union Leadership Training*, which circulated amongst British trade union educators and went far beyond 'talk and chalk' methodology (Liveright, 1951). It set out the objectives of trade union education as (1) Facts and Information – linked to roles in the workplace; (2) Skills such as problem-solving; (3) Understanding, including the wider role of the union; (4) Attitudes, including in the British context what would be called 'political views'; and (5) Action, including stronger unions and greater democratic involvement of union members. This was a world away from top-down liberal education.

Some unions began to train shop stewards using active learning methods under a programme called 'Training Within Industry'. This had been introduced during the war by Bevin, and was aimed primarily at supervisors and foremen, but after the war it was extended to shop stewards at technical colleges, primarily in Leicester, Nottingham and Birmingham. Training Within Industry included education methods which we would now recognize as fundamental in trade union education: targeted objectives and measured outcomes; role-play and other active learning techniques, team-teaching, interactive course materials and other 'props' such as slide-rules. In particular, it advocated a military 'drill' approach to handling industrial relations problems:

- Get the facts
- Weigh and decide
- Take action, and
- Check results. (Corfield, 1969, p.106)

These new developments were music to the ears of a new generation of trade union tutors, who were willing to respond to the demand that education should be focused around the unions' needs. However, the movement lacked a systematic approach. The bulk of unions' education expenditure was still on bursaries and grants for longer courses. Although the TUC and the London School of Economics established longer courses which were mainly focused on national leadership education, the provision on the shop floor remained limited and patchy. In 1957 the WEA held 239 weekend schools attended by 7,085 students, and 332 one-day schools attended by 5,952 students (Clegg and Adams, 1959). This fell far short of demand amongst the thousands of shop stewards.

In 1957 the WEA established three 'pilot areas', in which an attempt was made to develop a systematic approach involving a partnership with local unions in Cleveland, Tyneside and Port Talbot, mainly with the TGWU, USDAW (Union of Shop, Distributive and Allied Workers), ISTC (Iron and Steel Trades Confederation) and the NUM. The report concluded that active learning methods were only rarely used, that the partnership with the unions was uneven, and that on the ground the establishment of a systematic, integrated scheme was very far from the theory (Clegg and Adams, 1959).

In the face of this, and the lack of leadership from the TUC, some unions began to take matters into their own hands. The TGWU had been the first union to appoint a full-time Education Officer, in 1940 (Fisher, 2005), and established a comprehensive programme of summer schools with courses provided by the WEA but based on its own agenda. The POEU (Post Office Engineering Union) had a similar programme. Unions like NALGO, the GMWU and the NUM, strongly entrenched in nationalized industries, began to run their own programmes from the early 1950s, with objectives and methods set by the unions rather than an outside educational body.

However, as the WEA report (Clegg and Adams, 1959) showed, provision was still uneven, and it became clear that if trade union education was ever going to reach down to the mass of union representatives (let alone members), then paid release from work (Paid Educational Leave, PEL) was an essential requirement. Salaried staff and stewards from very well-organized workplaces had ways to gain financial support, but unions like NUPE (National Union of Public Employees), which represented low-paid and often poorly organized workers, saw PEL as an essential requirement (Mace and Yarnit, 1987).

The importance of day release

In the immediate post-war period, the great majority of union members attended courses at weekends, in their own time, or were supported by their union with a 'loss of time' payment. Those granted paid release were very few. However, during the 1950s a number of developments took place which brought paid release into centre stage and set the scene for a significant expansion of shop stewards' education. The most extensive schemes were those drawn up between the National Coal Board, the NUM and Nottingham, Sheffield and Leeds Universities, and the dockers of the TGWU and Hull University, which provided courses of up to three years based on day release (Coates and Topham, 1970; Malling, 1955; Mitchell, 2000; Topham, 1970).

In industry, innovative officials also put pressure on individual employers to introduce day release. Jack Jones first suggested day-release courses in 1958, specifically for shop stewards in the British Motor Corporation. Courses began in Birmingham and Coventry that year as a result of his proposal. During the 1950s and early 1960s a number of trends came together to create a new government approach to training policy, the most important being the continuing influence of the Training Within Industry programme and its training methods, the demand for qualifications, and the joint support of the CBI and the TUC for a more deliberate training system. The result was the Industrial Training Act of 1964, which included the establishment of a National Industrial Training Council which included trade union representation. This Act introduced the practice of day release for apprentices and trainees, and the principle was easily extended to shop stewards.

The TUC scheme

After nearly 40 years the principles of an education scheme were agreed at the 1961 TUC Congress, and the scheme was launched in 1965. WETUC and the NCLC were subsumed into the TUC, which retained exclusive control over the three education programmes that were formerly separate. The scheme led to an enormous increase in day-release courses and to the entry of the technical colleges and universities into the system of trade union education on an unprecedented scale. It also enlarged the scope of union education and led to the unions and the TUC expanding their services. The basis of the scheme was day release of one day per week, usually for 10 weeks. Most courses were mixed, with a range of unions participating, though sometimes courses were held separately for private- and public-sector unions. Course materials were standardized by the TUC, and tutors were required to follow them to the letter. The courses were almost exclusively based on active learning methods, group work and role-play, with contextual content kept to a minimum.

Up to the 1980s the scheme was a great success in terms of the increase in the numbers of students and courses, but not everyone was happy. J.P.M. Millar of the NCLC opposed the elimination of postal courses, especially those with political or international content,[2] and both WETUC and the NCLC opposed their dissolution into the TUC scheme and the almost complete handing over of TUC courses to technical colleges and universities (Millar, 1979, pp.160-174). Millar commented that 'the less the members know about Socialism, the more the TUC like it' (Millar, 1979). John McIlroy summed up this criticism:

> Since 1964 the TUC has developed a provision which has limited itself to training in the techniques of collective bargaining. Moreover...it was, within a decade, receiving not simply a direct subsidy from the state but a subsidy whose disbursement was specifically limited to training courses with the objective of 'improving industrial relations'. The rounded conception of the active trade unionist requiring an education both theoretical and practical... has been ignored by the TUC Education Department. (McIlroy, 1990, pp.234-235)

The structured approach to trade union education was given a boost in 1968 with the publication of the 'Donovan Report' (Dept. of Employment and Productiity, 1968). Taking a line similar to *Oxford and Working-Class Education* (University of Oxford, 1908; see above), Donovan argued that 'stability' in industry rested not with confronting the unions but with incorporating them, and that 'educated' shop stewards were much more likely to behave 'responsibly' than those simply left to agitate with their unions:

> The need for shop steward training is immense...Additional resources are undoubtedly required. They should be used...with a view to using training of stewards as part of a planned move to more orderly industrial relations based on comprehensive and formal factory or company agreements. This is where shop steward training will be able to make its biggest contribution. (HMSO, 1967 Para 712, pp.190-191)

While a wide-ranging and government-supported programme based essentially on representative skills and role education should be encouraged, 'strategic' developments in the workplace should be left in the hands of employers (Holford, 1994, pp.173-174).

This strengthened the hand of the TUC and consigned political content and the idea of a trade union *movement* to the margins. One of the problems with having a mixture of unions on TUC courses was that not all of them were affiliated to the Labour Party, or saw themselves as having the objective of changing the wider society, so you might have the NUM, the TGWU, Civil Service unions, musicians and managers together on the same course. As the 1970s economic crisis and Thatcherism loomed, these structural problems were to become more important.

Health and safety at work

By the 1970s an expansion of union-only and joint company-union shop stewards' courses, which had begun in the 1960s, continued apace. Companies like Ford, ICI, Shell and Courtaulds, as well as universities and local authorities across the country, were happy to grant paid release for 'in-plant' courses, even if these were run and controlled by the trade unions, as they recognized that the subject-matter was almost exclusively internal to the company or organization and linked to collective bargaining. From the unions' point of view, such courses were linked to organizing drives and increasing the strength of local shop stewards.

The biggest boost to trade union education in this period came from regulations on health and safety at work, and the beginning of the systematic training of union safety representatives. Before the 1970s, although 'safety' was always a trade union issue, such training did not specifically feature in union education programmes. Unions began to argue that joint safety committees and safety representatives were the key to effective health and safety policies.

The issue of health and safety came to prominence with the publication of the Robens Committee's report in July 1972, and the Health and Safety at Work Act came into force in 1974, followed by the Safety Representatives and Safety Committees Regulations in the autumn of 1977. The Act gave safety representatives a legal right to time off for training, and also the Employment Protection Act came into force on 1 April 1978, which gave trade union representatives the right to paid time off for industrial relations duties and activities and union training. Thus the scene was set for the massive expansion in courses on health and safety at work, and for the establishment of health and safety as a key element in union education.

Thatcherism and 'New Labour', 1979–2000

As we entered the 1980s however, this edifice began to crumble. 'Role education' for shop stewards and safety representatives had been based on the assumption that the trade unions would continue to grow and be strong, and also that companies were prepared to maintain collective bargaining indefinitely. When Margaret Thatcher began her assault on the unions through mass unemployment and legal restrictions, and employers moved from collective bargaining to 'total quality management' and 'human resource management', the neglect of politics in the core programmes began to be exposed. Some unions, like the CWU (Communication Workers Union), used educational methods in campaigning against the privatization of the Royal Mail and against 'human resource management', and the GFTU and larger unions like UNISON (public-service workers), the TGWU and the GMB (a general union, formerly for gas workers) ran campaigns to defend their members against various attacks and to widen agendas, but the core TUC programme remained centred on colleges teaching introductory courses for shop stewards and safety representatives.

A key issue was funding. Throughout the Thatcher years it was ironic that the government continued to fund trade union education, so long as it did not include 'political' courses, at the same time as striking at the heart of trade unionism. The weaker the unions became, the harder it was to argue for internal funding for education. By the end of the 1980s, trade union membership had declined from a peak of 11 million in the late 1970s to 6 million in the early 1990s.

The character of the movement had also changed. 'Equality at work', identity politics, ethnic diversity, the shift from large manufacturing plants to small units, 'self-employment', agency labour and, later, globalization and the 'gig economy' all led to new demands for unions to meet.

UNISON had taken the lead in making equalities part of its core programmes, and local unions had co-operated with adult education providers in trying to reach out to union members who might not be shop stewards through 'second chance to learn' schemes (Tace and Yarnit, 1987; Kirton, 2006). This approach was given new support when Labour came to power in 1997. Under the guidance of David Blunkett, who worked closely with UNISON, the NUM and Northern College, the new government produced a Green Paper, *The Learning Age*, which promised support for adult learning across the board, and rejected a narrow 'skills' agenda (Department for Education and Employment, 1998).

> To achieve stable and sustainable growth, we will need a well-educated, well-equipped and adaptable labour force. To cope with rapid change we must ensure that people can return to learning throughout their lives. We cannot rely on a small elite: we will need the creativity, enterprise and scholarship of all our people. Learning enables people to play a full part in their community and strengthens the family, the neighbourhood and consequently the nation. It helps us fulfil our potential and opens doors to a love of music, art and literature. That is why we value learning for its own sake and are encouraging adults to enter and re-enter learning at every point of their lives as parents, at work and as citizens (Department for Education and Employment, 1998).

Although the promises made in *The Learning Age* were watered down, many unions were able to establish workplace learning centres and appoint local 'learning reps', and the TUC introduced its 'University for Industry' as an umbrella body for individual learning, of which most was centred around self-improvement. This was enhanced as state funding became available if courses were accredited, and although popular with union members, the emphasis was more and more on personal skills, meeting learning outcomes and individual development.

Conclusion

So what can we learn from looking at this history? In the early years the first stage was to fight for control over the objectives of trade union education, in circumstances where the TUC and individual unions had neither the resources nor the infrastructure to run their own schemes. It was certainly not the case that WETUC and the NCLC were not supportive of the objectives of trade unions, and the WETUC manifesto of 1925 still impresses:

> The foundation of trade unionism is organization. Its method is collective bargaining. Its object is the control of industry by the workers in the interests of the workers. Education can do much to help all three and want of it much to hinder them...For this reason the development of education is of vital importance to trade unionists. Trade unionism stands not merely for an improvement in the conditions of workers within the limits of the existing systems, but for the creation of a new and juster social and industrial order. (Corfield, 1969, pp.32–33)

However, in practice WETUC and NCLC courses were about bringing an external agenda of self-improvement and revolutionary socialism from outside the movement, and rarely linked to strengthening organization on the shop floor, even though they inspired and motivated thousands of trade union students to build the movement.

After the war, trade unions were in a much stronger position to demand control of union education, and some appointed their own education officers and ran their own programmes following their own agendas. But what were these agendas? In circumstances where membership was 100 per cent or thereabouts, in large manufacturing companies or the public sector, it made sense to concentrate on 'role education' and basic subjects like representation and health and safety. Membership education was covered to the extent that in those circumstances any active member could easily stand for steward or safety representative, and organizing was almost automatic and often encouraged by managers. The wider role of the union in society could be left to those local and national leaders who might be members of the Labour Party or the Communist Party. Active learning methods built self-confidence among active members, but also often encouraged an inward-looking perspective.

By the 1960s union control of education was established, but lack of paid release and the unevenness of provision were still major problems. This was the situation when the bulk of union education was taken over by the TUC in 1964. The dilution of political content opened the way for government funding, and this became the core education provision, based in colleges and universities.

It has been argued that such an emphasis meant that unions were ill prepared and unable to resist the fundamental challenge of Thatcherism, 'human resource management', industrial and technical change and globalization, but it could also be said that these attacks were so fundamental as to reach the core of trade unionism, beyond areas where trade union education could have helped, whatever agenda it followed.

Since 2000, as trade unionism has failed to recover its strength, union educators have been left with many more questions than answers. What role can education play in organizing the new workforce? How can trade unions link with identity politics? How do we cope with globalization? How do we link unions into communities which may be diverse and fragmented? This book will show how today's trade union educators, building on the best work of the past, are responding to the new circumstances and playing their part in recovering the strength and depth of trade unionism.

1 A look at recent Labour cabinets shows that this was not too wide of the mark, although it has come through the mechanisms of the grammar schools and comprehensive secondary education.

2 NCLC courses dropped by the TUC after 1964: Britain's Tasks Today, Electioneering, Labour Party –Yesterday And Today, Nationalisation And Social Control, Parliamentary Candidates' Course, Britain's Future, Socialism, Towards The Welfare State, Trade Union Movements Abroad, Western Europe's Struggle For Unity (Millar, 1969, pp.168–169).

4

The development of popular, informal and community education, and youth and community work in the UK

Alan Smith, Christine Smith and Jo Trelfa

'We are all in this together.'

I'm sure it is no surprise to readers of this book to hear that in the UK today we have entered a profound period of change mirrored in the shift from 'a social democracy to a neoliberal system of organizing' that prioritizes 'the individual' over 'the collective' and 'performativity over empowerment' (Smith and McAdam, 2017). It is arguably a time of democratic deficit, in which there is a fundamental breakdown of trust in political and social institutions and professionals. This is matched by a wholesale transformation of our social-welfare systems, in which citizens are being repositioned as consumers subject to the principles of the market, not care.

In particular since the election of the Coalition government in 2010 and the subsequent election of a Conservative government in 2015, there has been an ideologically informed assault on public services, underpinned by neoliberal policies, striking at the heart of many impoverished communities. Adopting the mantra 'We are all in this together', the Conservatives, as the dominant partner within the Coalition government, began a radical programme of cuts to public services, leading to an unprecedented period of austerity (Taylor-Gooby and Stoker, 2011), which has continued since their re-election. It resulted in a stark rise in social inequality, which became headline-grabbing news following the tragedy at Grenfell Tower in June 2017. The UK is one of the wealthiest economies in the Western world yet it has one of the highest levels of child poverty, and this Conservative government is presiding over an exponential growth in the number of food banks in the UK. This highlights a growing gap between those with and those without. Schools, along with other social institutions, are implicated as reproductive sites that, far from creating the conditions in which young people can learn to think critically and develop a sense of agency, are subject to educational processes designed to 'reproduce knowledge and the social relations required' in a neoliberal society. Thus it is argued that the social practices of education ensure what Freire called a culture of silence (Freire, 1972; Giroux, 1985, p.11) and which Bourdieu (2010) termed symbolic violence meted out against working-class young people. These produce a range of inequalities that follow them through their life course, including worse health and lower life expectancies (Dorling, 2011).

The rise of the 'gig economy', the suppression of wages in the public sector and zero-hours contracts turn young people's transition from school into an increasingly fragile relationship with the labour market characterized by risk and uncertainty, matched by a disillusion with the political and social institutions meant to represent them. Yet this disaffection and disillusion have not translated into an increase in trade union membership. In 2016 the Department for Business, Energy and Industrial Strategy produced a statistical analysis that signalled not only an overall reduction in trade union membership but also a sharp decline in membership among younger workers, with two in five members being over the age of 50 and only 9.3 per cent of 21- to 30-year-olds in the low- to middle-income earning bracket being members. There are a number of possible explanations as to why trade unions in the contemporary context appear no longer to speak to the labour experiences of young people, not the least of which is the role of education in engaging with their lived experiences.

In the midst of all this, there have been some slight glimmers of hope: a growing engagement by young people and traditional working-class communities with the political process for both the 'Brexit' referendum and the 2017 General Election, and an emerging interest in models of popular education and critical pedagogies. It is against this backdrop that the work to develop a new, and transformative, education strategy for trade union education, based on models of informal education, has developed, which shapes and underpins this book.

Overlapping histories

Throughout history, approaches to the role and purpose of trade union education (spanning functional education, worker education and labour studies) have been subject to struggle and contestation (Cunniah, 2007). Similarly, informal education, youth work and community work have overlapping histories, where the transformative potential has been squeezed to the margins and instead the government is expecting all young people to conform to their employability agenda, even down to the creation of a National Citizen Service. In fact, the UK Lifelong Learning policy symbolizes this state colonization of 'cradle to the grave' in nearly all aspects of informal education activity – adult education, community education, play, youth work – all of which have been subject to formalized shifts and a conditionality of engagement, marked by payment by results and other market-driven funding models. Nationally and regionally this has also resulted in the wholesale closure of some established Local Authority provision alongside a rise in market-driven forms of youth work and a shift from educational to more performative and managerialist objectives that impinge on practice. In this context the historical local and community organizing structures have become both atomized and fragmented.

Similarly, UK models of government funding have successfully engineered trade union education 'into a form of low-level training and functional skills to survive immediate circumstances. Much of it has been state funded and the politics, philosophy and economics that we used to debate in the movement have been taken out' (Nicholls, 2015), mirroring the shift in the de-professionalizing of youth and community work. What the strands of trade union and informal education hold in common is that the government has used its funding of them as an influencing mechanism so that they have become aligned to progression and outcome, mapped to economic needs. The unintended consequence of this has been to render irrelevant the advancement of workers' rights in the same way as it corrals young people to become 'better citizens' at the expense of rights-based approaches that enable human flourishing. In following this funding route, both risk losing the transformative potential of trade union organizing or informal education as well as any opportunity for achieving greater social justice and equality.

What is informal education?

In contrast to the formal education of schooling, informal education is the domain of youth and community work. While 'youth work' and 'community work' share common ground, and some history and traditions, there are distinctions, and frequently a professional worker or educator will tend towards a specific interpretation – thus 'youth work', 'community work', 'community action', 'community development' or 'community education'. All of these, however, embrace a model and practice that seek to challenge inequality, to foster learning and to promote engagement through dialogue. This same philosophy underpins the teaching of youth and community work within the higher-education sector, and forms the basis of degree-level and postgraduate study throughout the UK and Ireland. The most recent attempt to bring the teaching of these disciplines together more effectively was the Quality Assurance Agency's *Subject Benchmark Statement: Youth and Community Work*, published originally in 2009 and reviewed in 2015. This document opened with an acknowledgement that youth and community work…is rooted in a range of overlapping traditions which have developed in the different contexts of local, regional and devolved national governments in the United Kingdom…and that the term 'youth and community work' encompasses the different traditions in the four countries. (QAA, 2009, p.5)

The Subject Benchmarks go on to recognize and define a set of overarching principles. In summary these state that

[y]outh and community work is a practice of informal and community education that involves the development of democratic and associational practices, which promote learning or development in the communities or individuals who choose to take part in the programmes that youth and community workers facilitate and support…Its pedagogic practice is based on the identification and responses to needs through dialogue and mutual aid and aspirations. (QAA, 2009, p.9)

It is in this interplay between contested academic knowledge, practical experience and the wider social, political and historical context that youth and community work can be understood. Youth and community work in all its varied guises engages people in recognized processes of learning and development which have an emphasis on social justice and challenging inequality.

In order to further develop understanding it is necessary to make a distinction between the 'art' and 'craft' of practice and the 'profession' of youth and community work. In itself this habitus (Bourdieu, 1990) also reflects the historical phases through which youth and community work have passed thus far. These include: Socratic dialogue and its place in developing moral philosophy; the 'conversations with purpose' that inform and extend the 'practical, reasoning and rational judgement by autonomous human beings – that is, people capable of acting in accordance with reason and from their own free will, voluntary as opposed to acting 'under compulsion or from ignorance'' (Aristotle, 1987, in Banks, 2010, p.98); Victorian philanthropic endeavours located in the social welfare tradition; and, more latterly, being recognized as an educational process.

Taking it a stage further, it is appropriate to recognize that significant youth and community work practice has existed, albeit without that title, ever since the Industrial Revolution, although the dominant phase followed the creation of the concept of 'youth' as a point of transition between childhood and adulthood. In most cases this focused on the age-specific experience of working-class boys. Such examples, while not labelled as 'youth work' or for that matter 'education', no doubt created the opportunity for young people to gain their education for life, through conversation and shared activity with adults. Despite this almost naturalistic process of 'informal education', little exists that can be, or has been, named 'youth work'. It is only in 1844, when the Young Men's Christian Association advertise a job vacancy for a 'missionary' and T.H. Tarlton is appointed that we have any record of youth work as paid employment (Shedd, 1955). Tarlton was tasked with making contact with young men and 'making himself generally useful among the class to which his efforts will be developed' (p.25).

From Victorian philanthropy to government intervention

With the appointment of the first youth worker, in 1844, we start to see a proliferation of youth-work activity, marking the birth of this new, as yet underdeveloped, profession. For many authors, youth work was born in the period between 1870 and 1900, when the earliest pioneers of our practices started to catalogue their work, describing its distinctive mode of practice: educational but located within a social-welfare tradition. These accounts were clearly located within the youth-work tradition, while community work remained fettered by the imperialist traditions of the British Empire, as opposed to anything that resonates with modern, more politicized definitions of community work (Spence, 2006). It is from these earliest accounts of practice that a body of knowledge and technique emerged, leading to a recognizable professionalized occupation and an increasing presence in the policy fields of education and social welfare. As Booton (1985) suggests, 'without access to an efficient historical analysis the practising awareness of the occupational group is inhibited. When faced with a new problem in their practice professionals are often inclined to suppose – or worse, led to believe – that they have encountered something wholly unprecedented' (p.1). This lack of engagement with the historical traditions, or lessons learned, means that policy develops in an ad hoc fashion, responding to crisis after crisis, and without reference to context or critique. Booton goes on to say that 'one special problem with modern youth work (sic) is that it appears to present itself almost as an ahistorical entity...as a consequence our present understanding of youth work history is a piecemeal compilation of individual agency or organization biographies, usually commissioned by the agencies themselves' (p.3). Such examples, while lacking critique, show the early beginnings and trajectory of this emergent profession, and the parallel developments that responded to the differing needs of young boys and girls.

One of the earliest accounts of youth-work practice, a paper produced by the Rev. Arthur Sweatman in 1863, entitled *Youth Clubs and Institutes*, was first delivered to a meeting of the Social Sciences Association at their conference in Edinburgh. It is seen by many as the earliest account of a specific youth-work methodology, and the driver behind the creation of youth clubs and institutes. It is firmly rooted within the philanthropic tradition, and gives a sense of the emerging reformist movements that were tackling the social conditions of the poor and working classes, and in particular the experiences of working children following the Industrial Revolution. As Engels described at the time, it is the impact of the steam engine and machines for spinning and weaving that drive the Industrial Revolution, but this in turn has 'a social as well as an economic aspect since it changed the entire structure of middle-class society'.

Sweatman's paper focuses on evening classes and night school as a means of supplementing education for the 'working man', yet questions their value to working-class boys:

> To be either useful or welcome, [the content of evening classes] must be associated with some work of a more social and recreational character: not only because lads so newly emancipated from the restraints and work of the school-room very naturally shy at anything which seems to threaten a return to the old bonds, but because their day's work fairly entitles them to reasonable recreation at its close. (Sweatman, in Booton, 1985, p.41)

In locating youth work as an educational and recreational activity outside and beyond schooling, those early definitions start to emerge. A similar, and parallel, account, by Maude Stanley (1890), exists of the creation of 'Clubs for Working Girls', although its aims and intentions are perhaps less about education and recreation, and more about keeping 'the young girl virtuous...that will make life a happiness instead of a drudgery' (Stanley in Booton, 1985, p.53). Stanley goes on to assert that 'rude, vulgar, untidy disreputable habits, uncorrected during childhood and youth, will need very patient and continual correction, before we can see the manners of the working girl become refined, polite, unselfish, and thoughtful for others' (Stanley in Booton, 1985, p.54).

Early responses to 'youth' as a problem

With the emergence of a more educated working class, at the turn of the twentieth century, numerous social movements emerged for the furtherance of social reform and an increasing re-balancing of power. At a national level, this manifested in the fight for women's suffrage, but also in the 1902 Education Act. This saw the creation of Local Education Authorities, which included the provision of secondary and technical education, and encouraged grammar schools to provide free places for working-class children, although this had limited impact in the short term. Subsequent legislation sought to enable working-class children to engage more fully with secondary education and, in 1906, as part of a more general concern, 'needy school children' had access to free school meals, under the Education (Provision of Meals) Act. Around this time, Dr T.F. Young, giving evidence to the Inter-departmental Committee on Physical Deterioration, said: 'Our young people have no idea of discipline or subordination. They would not subordinate themselves to anybody. That is, I think, a very great evil.'

By 1908, and following the publication of *Scouting for Boys* by Robert Baden-Powell, a new emphasis on harnessing the energies of youth emerged, whether as a result of soldiers returning from their military campaigns, and seeking to instil militaristic values in young boys, or a response to the growing levels of unrest seen amongst young men at the turn of the century, which itself resulted in the creation of the borstal system from 1902, bringing together care and punishment, alongside education and training. Baden-Powell, through his six-part edition of *A Handbook for Instruction in Good Citizenship* became the first writer of a youth-work manual, detailing the how, why and when of youth-work practice, as well as guidance for staff, delivered as 'Hints for Instructors'. This was followed in 1910 by the formation of the Girl Guides, or Girl Scouts, by Lady Baden-Powell, which followed many of the traditions of scouting, but with an emphasis on virtue and endeavour.

While the war years failed to generate any significant policy impact on youth work, it was obvious that the physical health, access to education and behaviour of young men were causes for concern. Certainly, in a later Government Circular in November 1939, reference is made to the fact that 'The Government are determined to prevent the recurrence during this war of the social problems which arose during the last'. In the period that followed, women's suffrage, social unrest, increased unemployment and the rise of industrial action amongst the working classes meant that the focus on youth diminished, and little exists from this time by way of historical accounts of practice.

The re-emergence of 'youth' as a policy concern

It is in the lead-up to the Second World War that we once again see the focus return to 'youth' and young people more generally. This period of government focus commenced in 1937, with the Physical Training and Recreation Act, 1937, which permitted Local Authorities to provide grant aid, staffing, equipment and facilities to youth organizations. It was followed shortly afterwards by the Board of Education Circular 1486 (1939) *In the Service of Youth*, seen by many as the 'birth' of the modern-day youth service. This circular tasked Local Education Authorities with forming Local Youth

Committees, predominantly made up of representatives from voluntary youth organizations, to support the establishment of 'constructive outlets for leisure'.

Soon after came Circular 1516 (1940), *The Challenge of Youth*, which placed emphasis on social and physical training, and on the relationship between public authorities and voluntary organizations. What was perhaps most striking was the government's belief that there needed to be a 'Variety of approach with a common purpose' (Board of Education, 1940, p.1) and this idea was further developed to identify the 'common elements in training', which included an emphasis on social facilities and opportunities to participate in leisure-based opportunities with their peers. The circular also emphasized the importance of opportunities that nurtured young people as future leaders, since this was identified as the basis upon which 'the foundations of democracy rest' (pp.2-3).

This theme of leadership returned in 1944, with the 'McNair Report', *Teachers and Youth Leaders: Report of the Committee Appointed by the President of the Board of Education to Consider the Supply, Recruitment and Training of Teachers and Youth Leaders*, which starts to identify the nature of youth work and the features that distinguish it from teaching, something which a parallel report was also seeking to do. This report was *The Purpose and Content of the Youth Service. A Report of the Youth Advisory Council appointed by the Minister of Education in 1943* (Ministry of Education, 1945). In combination, these reports stress that youth work is, by its very nature, non-vocational group work.

The decades that followed the post-war period saw an emergence of governmental 'machinery' that contributed to a growth in 'institutionalized and increasingly professionalized formations of community and youth-work practice' (Jeffs and Spence, 2008). These developments were notably, but not exclusively, shaped by the policy of successive governments in the post-war period. Policy documents included the 'Albemarle Report' (Ministry of Education, 1960), with its emphasis on the recruitment and training of youth leaders and mass building of youth centres; the 'Fairbairn Milson Report' (Department of Education and Science, 1969), widely regarded as a policy vehicle for the incorporation of politicized informal educational trends more commonly associated with community development and notions of community activism (Spence, 2006); and the 'Thompson Report' (Department of Education and Science, 1982), which highlighted the need for improved services for young adults and pointed to the problems associated with growing youth unemployment as well as the urgent need for more attention to the particular needs of the age group. In recent decades New Labour's *Transforming Youth Work* (2001) and *Resourcing Excellent Youth Services* (2002) represented an attempt to modernize youth services with a significant injection of funding into Local Authorities to do this. More recently the Coalition government renewed youth policy through the publication of *Positive for Youth* (Department for Education, 2010).

In recent times the landscape for public-sector youth and community services has been subject to unprecedented change. In 2015 the community and youth-work sector arrived at a symbolic tipping point when the Local Government Association set in motion a policy direction that finished the job of dismantling Local-Authority-led youth services. The removal of the requirement to adhere to Joint Negotiating Committee (JNC) terms and conditions, set out in the 'pink book', without genuine consultation with the field, represented a damning blow that will leave a scar on professionalized community and youth work. This decision also seriously undermines the employment rights of those community- and youth-work practitioners who continue to be employed on JNC terms and conditions. The flip side of this erosion of rights is the more general erosion of rights-based approaches to community- and youth-work practices, and this replicates the challenges faced within unions. In recent times, and particularly since New Labour, such practices have increasingly beenused as a means of domesticating new generations of young people and subjugating communities to new formations of global power (Braidotti, 2013). However, in this hiatus comes what Titmuss (1963) describes as the unintended consequences of social policy. It offers the opportunity to re-think, reclaim and widen the conceptualization of community and youth work, recasting it as an educational practice with emancipatory possibilities, and to reimagine what alliances need to be fostered to enable that. It also provides an opportunity to think with Derrida about community- and youth-work education strategies that attend to the idea of 'democracy that is yet to come'.

A central strand in the historical development of informal education practices and thinking has related to both social and political movements. In this regard trade unions have consistently recognized the value of youth and community work as an informal education practice and its contribution to a 'long democratic process of strengthening the voice of young people and empowering them to challenge injustice and develop their knowledge of themselves and their world' (Nicholls, 2016, para 4). Specifically, through conversation and collective activity, informal education 'fosters self-confidence and ability to remove discrimination and oppression. It gives support, comfort, safety, advice, friendship and help to young people when they need it when other services do not and are not designed to do so' (Nicholls, 2016, para 5).

In recognition of this, trade unions have played an important role in safeguarding the terms and conditions of youth and community workers and those of the academics who are providing an education for those workers. They have also mapped cuts to services and campaigning locally and nationally via movements such as the anti-racism, disability rights and women's rights movements, and more recently Choose Youth, to protect and extend youth work and to maintain healthy workplaces. Trade unions have also been proactive in undertaking research to capture perspectives from the field and in working with higher education to capture perspectives about the need for a register of youth workers (this work was undertaken by Unite with Yorkshire Regional Youth Work Unite). By recognizing that we are all under attack from this neoliberal onslaught, and from the cancerous impact of austerity, we can start to build new alliances and contribute to shared successes. Trade unions have played a key role in protecting the rights of youth- and community-work practitioners and in safeguarding what it means to be professional, in relation to status, pay and terms and conditions of employment (Bradford, 2007/2008). This relationship between trade unions and youth- and community-work practitioners has provided a shared understanding, and common starting point, for seeking to challenge the inequalities within society.

As noted by Spence (2006), a renowned youth-work author, in her writing about the history of work with girls and young women, education can serve as either a process of domestication or one of liberation. There is a long history of educational engagement in rights-based campaigns, stretching back at least to Victorian times, resulting in, for example, the Factory Act 1833, which saw an improvement in children's rights. Contemporary movements that campaign along these lines include the anti-racism movement, the women's movement, disability living campaigns and identity politics. The overlapping interests of trade unions and youth and community work are evident in contemporary movements pushing for an end to injustice and improve worker rights and recognition while also seeking to use popular-education approaches to raise young people's awareness, open up spaces to explore the nature of social injustice and find strategies to create greater equality. Beyond these local movements is the wider international context, which will be picked up in other chapters in this book though it is worth highlighting here the role of popular education and the long tradition of resisting education when it is used as a process for domestication. Organizations such as the International Federation of Workers Education Associations work to pursue '[a] world where all working people have access to lifelong learning opportunities which enable them to claim and exercise their inalienable democratic rights, responsibilities and freedoms as global citizens'. Such associations provide important opportunities to awaken critical consciousness using popular-education approaches.

Remaking alliances

The themes outlined thus far show how the move from social democracy to neoliberalism has necessitated a shift in the relationship between citizens, the state and the market. This opens up questions about what it means for a society to educate its citizens and indeed about the type of society we want to live in. In this context education becomes a democratic and political issue; indeed Ball (2013, para 2) urges us to recognize the centrality of education to larger projects of democracy and community-building. This poses a key challenge and opportunity for informal educators and trade union activists: of remaking alliances and questioning what education should be seeking to achieve through the trade union movement. Nicholls (2015, p.6) calls, in a similar vein, for political trade unions to ensure that the focus of organizing is not limited to reducing inequality but extends to creating democracy.

Against this social and political backdrop, trade unions have been thinking about the role of trade union education in the future, recognizing the limitations that a state-funded and essentially vocational approach brings. Such an approach, which Paulo Freire would term a 'banking' concept of education, seeks to domesticate and silence the vast majority, something we referred to earlier as contributing to a culture of silence. Its purpose is to disconnect young people and activists within the trade union movement from their histories and their lived experiences, and fill them instead with technical knowledge related to employability or specific trade union roles. But Freire offers an alternative, a model that uses education to liberate, and gives all people a voice, enabling them to share their lived reality and make it the basis for action in pursuit of a more equal and socially just world. It is this approach which underpins the General Federation of Trade Unions' education project, as well as the teaching on youth and community work professional courses.

Extending from Arendt (1958), and rather than merely defending informal education practice colonized by the state, trade unionism could develop a strategy to produce informal education practices designed to engage and inspire young people using grassroots approaches. Its potential, as argued by Arendt, is one of replacing individuality, a 'conformable body politic' dependent on 'citizens remaining restricted' (1958, p.49) and being 'predictable members of a herd' (Arendt, 1950, cited in Canovan, 1992, p.25) with action. Cornish (2014) is useful here in describing pre-figurative politics as 'a conceptual touch stone' with the potential to instantiate radical social change by building capacity to critique the status quo and produce alternatives through radically democratic practices in pursuit of social justice. Shaw and Crowther (2017), community education academics from the University of Edinburgh, offer a practical look at strategies that can be put to work by community and youth-work educators in pursuit of this. They have examined the utility of the concept of community engagement in shifting educational practices from education for citizenship to a deeper, wider 'learning for democracy' approach. They usefully frame learning for democracy as being concerned with

> extending how citizens can actively shape the type of society they want to live in – as compared with the society they currently live in – and how deepening democracy through active participation is a resource for moving towards a more democratic future. (Shaw and Crowther, 2017, p.9)

In summary, the role of informal education in reinvigorating the democratic deficit offers the potential to 'lay the foundations for participative democratic processes by engaging communities in creative processes of re-seeing and re-naming their world ' (Beck, 2016, p.1). In relation to the argument here, this will mean cross-fertilizing informal education with trade union activity in new and different ways. The proposal, then, is to push at the boundaries and borders of what commonly can be understood as constituting either informal education or trade union activity.

A shared journey of understanding

Giroux (1985) reminds us that Freire's theory of education was predicated upon the principle of historical relationship between the 'present as it is' and 'the present that creates conditions for emancipatory purposes'. If informal education is to be put to work as a strategy orientated to reinvigorate the labour movement, it must start from a shared understanding and shared history, and this in turn has implications for the way in which trade union education is organized. This chapter, so far, has examined what constitutes informal education through a historical lens and has perhaps hinted at why it offers a meaningful way of re-engaging a generation of young people who face a future of precarious employment and who focus on their individual trajectories rather than on that of the collective. But if we can reflect on our shared histories, it is so much more possible to move beyond the world as it is and to consider the world as it should be.

Informal education, and specifically youth and community work, has had at its core a desire to help change society through collective action, despite a policy agenda that is geared to changing (or blaming) the individual and expecting them to conform. This change is achieved through education – not the formal education of schooling which seeks to perpetuate the ideals of the middle classes and the capitalist dream, but an education of those oppressed by that same capitalist agenda who have little or no access to the social capital that comes from a middle-class education and the 'old school tie'. Bourdieu (2010) describes education as a symbolically violent process that perpetuates inequalities and hardship through the life course of working-class young people. The evidence of symbolic violence is writ large when we note that the UK, one of the richest economies in the Western world, in 2017 has, relatively speaking, one of the highest levels of youth poverty. The gulf is widening in financial, human and social capital, between those who are doing well and those left behind (Dorling, 2011). Schools, along with other social institutions, are implicated as reproductive sites that, far from creating the conditions in which young people can learn to think critically and develop a sense of agency, instead subject them to a process which 'reproduces knowledge and the social relations required' in a neoliberal society. Thus it is argued that the social practices of education ensure what Freire called a 'culture of silence' (Giroux, 1985, p.11). This perpetuation of social inequality is also common within the labour market through suppression of wages in the public sector and zero-hours contracts, which in turn reinforce an increasingly fragile relationship between workers and a labour market characterized by risk and uncertainty.

Concluding thoughts
The impact of neoliberalism has torn deep into the heart of already impoverished communities. Those who work to resist rising inequalities, poverty and injustices have been subject to formalized shifts in working practices that have in turn marginalized them and cast their transformative potential to one side. Against this backdrop we consider that the potential alliance between trade unions and informal educators as critically political and reflective practitioners has never been more urgent as a strategy to re-engage young people. In particular we advocate reimagining alliances between universities and trade unions in generating rights-based approaches to practice, including community and youth-work education. We contend that there is a need to develop a reflective practice that is no longer based on the 'solitary business of thought, which operates in a dialogue between me and myself' (Arendt, 1958, p.200). We advocate working creatively with the concept of pre-figurative politics to develop knowledge-based approaches that are systemically and politically capable of resisting new formations of social injustices. Finally, in this chapter we advocate informal educators playing their part in asserting ways of working that are explicitly anti-oppressive, egalitarian and are capable of creating lines of flight through which social-change agendas can flourish (Deleuze and Guttari, 1987).

Section Two

Contexts and challenges

Introduction to Section Two

Doug Nicholls

When the GFTU visited Australia to consider the survival strategies of the Australian and New Zealand trade unions I was very struck by the fact that one speaker described the decline of trade unionism as meaning that some unions had completely disappeared and many were only known these days through the sale of their memorabilia in flea markets.

The work to rebuild the trade union movement in Australia and New Zealand has been fantastic and inspirational and we begin this section – which examines the new contexts in which we are operating and the challenges these present to us – with a look by Jane Parker and Ozan Alakavuklar at how unions, and particularly their leadership bodies in the UK and New Zealand, have had to widen their vision and scope and forge new alliances. Community coalitions can help sustain strikes, engage otherwise neglected groups, campaign for legislative changes and deepen understanding and support for wider political and social campaigns. The trade union movement is a lead part of social movements and cannot work in isolation. It has more durability, organization and resourcing than any other social-movement element.

The implications for future trade union education work of this approach are huge, and again point clearly to the need to associate with youth and community learning, the expert area in building youth and community organizations and campaigns. Why doesn't the community activist become the trade union trainer? Why, as the GFTU believes should happen, don't arts and cultural workers become more engaged in the organizing, campaigning and education programmes of unions? The GFTU's 2017 festival Liberating Arts sought to promote the unionization of arts and cultural workers and the deployment of more arts and cultural workers in the work of unions.

This brings us to the heavy lifting of actually transforming a major national trade union's education programme. Moving away from past practices, the functionalism of much union education is not an easy task. Britain's biggest trade union, Unite, has been involved in precisely this process and M.J. McGrath accounts for the rationale, plans, and sheer dogged hard work that had to go into making this step change.

The development of student-centred, discovery modes of learning, infused by enquiry into the political and economic factors which shape daily lives, is not plain sailing. It challenges concepts of education within unions and the ancient stereotypes of what is 'normal' politically. Adopting this approach means a union includes within its organization a strong debate about its future as a social entity and the way it will enlighten its membership and educate them for what is in fact a higher purpose. M.J. McGrath's article is essential reading as it takes us through the necessary challenges to the ideological laziness that has mouldered away in the unions. It is also a practical lesson in what can be done.

Looking again at the creative potential of union alliances with community organizations in the context of a repoliticized union purpose, Joel Lazarus takes us to the heart of Oxford and the elite's pet subject – Politics, Philosophy and Economics (PPE) – and shows how he and colleagues deliberately set out to popularize quality education to a wider community. This trend is burgeoning, with many academics around the country fed up with the neoliberal academies they are working in and seeking to share really useful knowledge in practical community contexts. A people's university is developing in embryo throughout the country. Joel provides an honest analysis of this pioneering project and draws out its strengths and weaknesses.

Above all, he lays down a challenge to the unions to become more sustainable bases for projecting this kind of work. Joel demonstrates how the deliberately constructed decline in working-class hope and self-belief has paralysed that other central human essence, the imagination so vital to social change.

In his chapter, 'Reconnecting trade union education, politics and self-reliance', Dave Spooner presents a powerful and entirely convincing case for re-politicizing trade union education as the central driver for the organizing agenda. It could be argued that much of the rush to the organizing agenda has been shallow and temporary. At the heart of the organizing agenda more truly is the requirement to develop an informed, capable, self-reliant union membership. Organizing to win, organizing to campaign, organizing to grow, organizing to express a louder collective voice are all rather short term, ineffectual operations unless they are deepened and sustained by critical thinking and reflective practice and above all a sense of transformative objectives. Such enriching factors are provided by education and education alone. Importantly, too, Dave reminds us of the international solidarity and co-operation that are essential to a revitalized trade union movement and a renewed approach to trade union education.

5

Social-movement unionism in New Zealand and the UK: the need for contextualized engagement

Jane Parker and Ozan Alakavuklar

Introduction

Trade unions across the globe have faced significant challenges to their bargaining power and political influence from a complex mix of socio-cultural, economic, legal and political factors. They have pursued revival strategies to improve their organizing and recruitment methods and to seek legislative developments, but with limited success. While the impacts of these strategies interact to an unknown degree, this chapter focuses on the efforts of the labour bodies in New Zealand/Aotearoa and the UK in building alliances with campaigning civil-society organizations. Drawing on recent empirical evidence and scholarship, it compares the contexts and nature of the efforts involving the New Zealand Council of Trade Unions Te Kauae Kaimahi (CTU) and the UK Trades Union Congress (TUC), and the extent to which they have informed union revival and other aims. These two peak bodies[1] are suitable for comparison because their labour movements have both haemorrhaged members in recent decades and experienced strong challenges to their function and powers, amid legislative changes and neoliberal economic policies, themselves influenced by the forces of globalization, deregulation and institutional change. The findings have shared and unique implications for union federations interested in advancing both their workplace-focused work and their activities related to social justice, both generally and with regard to training and education initiatives.

Union context

Statistics on union membership in New Zealand/Aotearoa are bleak, reflecting long-term decline. New Zealand/Aotearoa's union membership nearly halved between 1991 and 1994, following the de-collectivizing effects of the Employment Contract Act (Jess, 2016; Parker, 2011). After rising slightly to 20.9 per cent by 2011, the percentage of employees who are union members fell to 17.7 per cent in 2016 (ie from 384,644 members down to 357,120), while the number of employees in the national labour market grew (New Zealand Companies Office, 2016; Ryall and Blumenfeld, 2015). More than four-fifths (81.5 per cent) of union members belong to the 10 largest unions, emphasizing the small size of the other 20 or so CTU affiliates, and reflecting union amalgamations, as well as legislative developments.[2] Union membership is also concentrated in the public services and women constitute around three-fifths of members (Statistics New Zealand, 2016). In terms of influence, Blumenfeld (2016) details how, although the economic downturn that happened in New Zealand/Aotearoa as a result of the global economic decline (2008-2013) was one of the 'shallowest' of those experienced by the world's industrial economies, it caused to the country's economy to contract by 3.3 per cent between December 2007 and June 2009 and also brought about a shift in bargaining power away from unions and towards employers, which in turn impacted on wage and non-wage outcomes.

In the UK, the hallmarks of union decline have been somewhat similar in nature if not scale. Union membership fell to 6.5 million in 2015, or half its peak of over 13 million in 1979, and J. Kelly (2015) observes that the most dramatic, rapid declines in union density occurred in the wake of anti-union legislation introduced by Conservative governments in the 1980s (as in the 1990s, alongside the dismantling of arbitration machinery, in New Zealand/ Aotearoa – see Barry and Wailes, 2004). With growing employee numbers in recent years, the 24.7 per cent of UK employees who are in unions reflects the lowest rate of membership recorded since 1995 (when it was 32.4 per cent). Again, female employees are more like to be union members, and a higher proportion of UK-born employees are in a union than employees not born in the UK (Department for Business, Innovation and Skills, 2016).

Furthermore, as in New Zealand/Aotearoa, there has been a growing concentration of union membership in the public sector (e.g. J. Kelly, 2015), and older workers account for a larger proportion of union members than younger workers (ibid.; Ryall and Blumenfeld, 2014) though those who signed up several decades ago and are retiring have not been replaced fast enough to make up for the decline in numbers. Moreover, the scope of collective bargaining in the private sector in the UK and New Zealand/ Aotearoa has been declining over time in the face of extensive legislation on individual employment rights 'which may erode the incentive for employees to join unions' (J. Kelly, 2015, p.533; Foster et al., 2009; Estlund, 2013). Forth and Bryson's (2015) analysis of Labour Force Survey data also indicates that, while union membership still leads to better terms and conditions for the average employee, the size of this advantage seemed to diminish slightly in recent years, though Workplace Employment Relations Study survey data suggest that unions are judged by employees to be as effective now as they were in the late 1990s, while managers have become less convinced of unions' importance for representing employees' perspectives.

Union revival efforts: a focus on coalition-building

Fuelled by long-term decline in the context of neoliberal state and workplace regulation, New Zealand/Aotearoa and UK union revival efforts have spanned a range of initiatives. They vary in their emphasis and level of strategic intent, and include US-style organizing and recruitment approaches, enterprise-level partnerships, organizational restructuring and reactions to relevant collective labour law[3] changes (e.g. Heery and Adler, 2004; Waddington et al., 2003; Martinez Lucio and Stuart, 2002; Hamann and J. Kelly, 2003; H. Kelly, 2015; Rosenberg, 2016; Parker, 2008, 2011).

A qualitatively different yet related strand of union response concerns the development of alliance-building with civil groups and movements outside the workplace. Some scholarly attention has been devoted to coalition-building, alongside growing, if patchy, union efforts in recent decades (e.g. Frege et al., 2004; Tattersall, 2005, 2010; Briskin, 2007). Alliance- or coalition-building has also been variously conceived. Scipes (1992) regards it as a 'third type' of unionism, distinguished from economism and political concerns, which takes a broader perspective, in which workers' struggles form part of a wider effort to qualitatively change society (Tattersall, 2010). Dibben (2004) suggests that this can entail internal grassroots democracy; reaching out to other social groups and pursuing broad, social-justice aims (see Moody, 1997); and a struggle against the excesses of international business and its neoliberal hegemony.

For their part, Frege et al. (2004) describe coalition-building as a 'secondary union method' that can be used to support (1) unilateral regulation of the labour market (for example, to provide training for low-wage workers); (2) collective bargaining (for example, mobilizing community support of strike activity to increase a union's bargaining power); (3) legal regulation (for example, around a Living Wage campaign to secure a higher statutory pay floor); and (4) the reach of union activity, extending it from job regulation to wider social and political change. 'As such, it can reinforce a broad conception of union purpose, seen particularly in the labour movements of continental Europe, and allow unions to engage as civic actors' (p.4). Frege et al.'s (2004) cross-national framework also stresses two dimensions: (1) the relationship between unions and their coalition partners, which can reflect a call for solidarity, shared interests and/or the adoption of the coalition partners' aim(s) – which, arguably, could encourage critique of a union's fundamental purpose amidst public concern about union strength[4] – and (2) the extent to which the coalition is integrated into state policymaking, whether as a coalition of interest or of protest. In respect to (1), Tattersall (2010) distinguishes between positive sum coalitions which build the power of unions and community organizations while also achieving social change, and more 'transactional' coalitions.

Union alliances with civil groups may also be defined by various features, including the level at which they occur, their duration (for example, one-off, continuous), and how far they are framed and sustained by single or multiple issues (e.g. Luce, 2004; Tattersall, 2005; Wills, 2001; Reynolds and Kern, 2002; Frege et al., 2004). The political position of the union leadership has also been observed in relation to unions' openness and contribution to alliance-building. For example, Fletcher and Gapasin (2008) distinguish between three ideological stances within the labour movement – traditionalist, pragmatist and leftist – recognizing that a range of views are contained within each. Each has its own response to three questions: (1) Who are the union movement's constituencies? (2) Who are its allies and 'enemies'? and (3) What is the geographic scope of its concern for workers? They suggest that each is also likely to be ambivalent about linking with organizations outside the organized labour movement; ideological differences within the leadership, and within wider activist and membership constituencies, may inhibit the development of a consistent alliance-building programme. These problems might be compounded for peak union bodies by a lack of power over affiliate members (Bean, 1994), with implications for the roles a peak association might play in coalition arrangements.

Union coalition-building in New Zealand/Aotearoa and the UK

Alliance-building with non-labour and non-governmental organizations and bodies 'has long formed part of labour's repertoire' (Frege et al., 2004, p.137) though such activity, defined here as unionism which extends beyond concern with matters of job regulation to reaching out to other groups to emphasize social-justice aims, has never been a central characteristic of New Zealand/Aotearoa or British unionism. Notwithstanding this, a small but rich body of empirical work has examined alliance efforts in the UK, largely at the local/community level and often involving a large union (e.g. Wills, 2001; Wills and Simms, 2004; Greer et al., 2007; Holgate, 2009; Martinez Lucio and Perrett, 2009; James and Karmowska, 2012). By comparison, union-level research for New Zealand/Aotearoa is smaller but similarly qualitative (e.g. Newman and Jess, 2015; Newman et al., 2013). The case-study basis of much of this scholarship underscores the importance of not overstating unions' engagement in alliance-building, but where it does occur, coalition-building has been stressed as a strand of and support activity for wider union revival endeavours. For instance, Wills (2001) observes that even in the most innovative 'community unions' in the UK, 'the community is being used as a means to strengthen workplace organizing efforts rather than to propel the union into a new form of trade unionism' (p.475). Conceptualization of and efforts to undertake the latter, more transformational project have been inhibited, and a survivalist mode encouraged, by factors both within and external to unions, including neoliberal economic and regulatory conditions; declining employment in industries where private-sector unions have traditionally been strong; a restructuring of employment, with the rise of precarious work; and unions' struggle to engage younger workers and expand into growth sectors.

Broad-brush analyses of activities undertaken by the labour movement tend to concur that, where unions have relatively weak political and institutional support, as in New Zealand/Aotearoa and the UK, they have moved towards organizing and rank-and-file mobilization, as well as alliance-building in civil society (e.g. Baccaro et al., 2003; Hyman, 1999) though the relative significance of their scale or impact is seldom specified. Alliances involving the TUC and CTU have received little consideration in the revival literature despite these bodies being in principle well placed to promote shared learning and good practice among constituent unions and to act as a conduit between the union movement and civil groups. Where they have engaged, again, an instrumentalism on the part of unions is often assumed, with alliances conveyed as a facet of organizing, recruitment and political strategies, with the last of these reinforced by the context of shrinking union membership, resources and political influence.

The chapter gives an overview of the nature of these two peak union bodies, before drawing on a scant body of literature and publicly available documents to chart how and to what extent these union 'parliaments', think-tanks, brokers, exemplars, guides, leaders and possible coalition partners (Bean, 1994) have engaged in civil alliances, and what this has meant for advancing both job regulation and wider social-justice concerns.

Peak body profiles

The TUC was established in 1868. Its policy is set annually by Congress, but between congresses, this responsibility lies with the General Council. Affiliates meet every two months at Congress House to oversee the TUC's work programme and sanction new policy initiatives. Each year, after the Congress, the General Council appoints the Executive Committee from among its own members. The committee meets monthly to implement and develop policy, manage the TUC's financial affairs, and deal with urgent business. The TUC President, elected in the same session, is consulted by the TUC General Secretary on all key issues. In addition, task groups and committees are established by the General Council to deal with specific areas of policy. These committees (for example, Women's, Race Relations, Disability and LGBT) are permanent bodies. There is also a Young Persons' Forum and a body representing local Trades Union Councils (trade union bodies), who both report to the General Council (TUC, 2013). There are currently 50 union affiliates (TUC, 2017) with a total of 5.6 million members, down from 76 (with 6.7 million members) in 2000. At the 1996 Annual Congress, John Monks (General Secretary, 1993-2003) launched the 'New Unionism' initiative, establishing an Organising Academy in 1998 (Lyddon, not dated). Following Brendan Barber, in 2013, Frances O'Grady became the TUC General Secretary, the first woman to hold the post.

For its part, the CTU was formed in 1987 by a merger of the long-standing private-sector Federation of Labour and the public-sector Combined State Unions. In the 1990s, it became more accountable to its larger union affiliates in a process of centralization (for example, its Executive ceased to be generally elected but was instead appointed by sector representatives from unions with over 20,000 members). Under the leadership of Ross Wilson (President) and Paul Goulter (Secretary), from 2000 to 2007, there was a move towards a more professional organizational approach. This approach was further developed after 2007 by the late Helen Kelly, elected as president on a platform of 'social movement unionism' (Brookes, 2009), and subsequently the late Peter Conway, the CTU Secretary. Richard Wagstaff was elected as President in 2015 and Sam Huggard as Secretary in 2014. Although the CTU is the largest union confederation in New Zealand/Aotearoa, the number of its affiliates has shrunk from over 50 (445,116 union members) in 1991 (Gardner, 1995; Industrial Relations Centre, 1998) down to 30 (360,000 members) (CTU, 2016a; New Zealand Companies Office, 2016), making it just 6.5 per cent of the size of the TUC in these terms.

Neither peak body can be considered independent of the wider socioeconomic changes that have taken place in the last 30 years. While a snapshot of these macro-changes highlights neoliberalism as a common context for the UK and New Zealand/Aotearoa, it can also be acknowledged that both countries have witnessed increasing diversity, change in their industrial bases, private-sector growth but with shrinking union membership, and other emerging social-justice issues, including global warming, environmental destruction, and housing and refugee crises. Although unions are 'workplace-centric', social movements expect them to give voice to social justice issues. Alliance-building can thus be viewed as a response to these dynamic changes and not merely as an instrumental tactic to gain members.

The TUC and alliance-building

Research conclusions from semi-structured interviews conducted in the mid-2000s with senior TUC personnel found that most of its civil alliances were seen as a 'tool' for other union revival strategies, notably recruiting, organizing and political engagement, although some showed elements of the labour movement's capacity to act as a 'sword of justice' (Flanders, 1970). Revitalization efforts up to then had not generated much union net growth, with little known about the relative contributions of alliances and other activities. Notwithstanding this, and despite the fact that civil alliance-building was not its main focus, the TUC's interest in it was viewed as gaining momentum because of a complex mix of internal and external factors. Its role as an alliance partner was unfurling, particularly in respect of issues around international development and environmentalism, as well as quieter but essential matters such as the availability of learning services to all. The TUC demonstrated limited but important and varied engagement with alliance-building with a diverse range of non-labour partners, reflecting its multiple roles (Parker, 2008).

A decade later, Holgate (2015, p.432) observed: 'While it is important not to exaggerate the extent to which UK unions are engaging in community organizing', the TUC and a number of affiliate unions were 'taking significant steps to broaden their base and engage with communities outside their normal spheres of operation'. She describes the initiation of the TUC's 'Active Unions, Active Communities' project in 2008, as part of which it funded various trades union councils undertaking organizing work with communities and community organizations, with an eye to assessing the advantages of successful community engagement by unions and publicizing 'best practice' examples. The TUC (2010) concluded from the initiative that more community engagement and partnership between voluntary and community organizations and British unions was needed in the context of the somewhat vague Big Society agenda (see Cameron, 2009). Alongside individual union efforts to counter the impacts of the long-term neoliberal agenda and the global economic crisis on employment and workers' terms and conditions, in 2012, the TUC recruited four community organizers so as to raise the profile of union campaigns and build community coalitions in the regions. These initiatives suggest that, at the community level, nascent and longer-term civil alliances involving the TUC directly or via its support of affiliate initiatives have continued, albeit in a relatively low-key and non-linear manner (for example, the project to build community coalitions via the four organizers was disestablished after eight months); Holgate (2015, p.448) notes that this may have been related to 'fraught negotiations around affiliation fees' and other factors such as 'debates around where the political direction of the TUC should be currently focused, or whether this community organizing initiative was concentrating its efforts in the right area, or even whether community organizing should be a strategy at all'.

This conclusion, of continued but constrained activity, seems to be borne out with regard to more broadly based alliances involving the TUC in the development of balanced policymaking around single and baskets of complex pan-national concerns. A decade ago, for instance, there was relatively little mention of climate change or the environment within the peak body although transport and energy were seen as priorities. However, the TUC Policy Officer (Philip Pearson), whose brief included the environment, recognized that what unified these areas was increasing awareness of the importance of tackling climate change through a new energy strategy (Parker, 2008), in the context of the wider agenda of the Trade Union Sustainable Development Advisory Committee, itself the basis for a multi-stakeholder approach. A TUC pamphlet, *A Green and Fair Future: For a Just Transition to a Low Carbon Economy* (TUC, 2008), sought to evaluate the impact of moving towards a less carbon-intensive economy on jobs, skills and employment opportunities, and to explore 'how the transition itself can be rendered *socially just*' (p.14, emphasis added). It recognized that support and cost allocations for environmental change were required from all sections of society. The TUC argued that 'just transition' entailed consultation between government, unions, industry and communities at global and national levels.

As Hampton's (2015) book chronicles, a plethora of climate change materials and events have since been generated by the peak body or by bodies it is working with. They include the joint demand issued by TUC officials and NGOs that Owen Paterson, the new Environment Secretary in 2012, should say whether he was a climate sceptic, in a context of austerity measures that have been hollowing out central government budgets. Latterly, some alliance-building appears to reflect a more 'joined-up' and deeper coalition agenda. On 11 February 2017, the TUC and a range of affiliates, including Stand Up to Racism and Black Activists Rising Against Cuts UK supported the Campaign Against Climate Change's (CACC) sold-out conference, Climate Refugees – The Climate Crisis and Population Displacement: Building a Trade Union and Civil Society Response. Alongside speeches and a panel debate, this London-based event involved afternoon workshops led by union and non-labour group representatives. Its ongoing nature was emphasized by the closing session, where it was agreed that the strategic priorities that had emerged in the workshops were to be used to inform the development of a Climate Refugee Coalition (CACC, 2017).

Looking also at the TUC's current stated roles, these very much emphasize workplace issues and conventional social partners (i.e. employers, employees, unions and governments). Nowak (2015) also acknowledges this emphasis. However, he also argues that this has not been enough since rising inequality has remained a serious issue for workers. However, the TUC's campaign priorities for 2016 to 2017 include the following: ensuring that working people do not pay the price of the vote to leave the EU; standing up for abandoned communities; pursuing great jobs for all; reaching out to young workers; and building a stronger movement after the Trade Union Act 2016 (TUC, 2016), suggesting an intertwining of economic and wider social-justice roles. For example, on abandoned communities, it is noted that

> [t]he [EU] referendum campaign gave a voice to communities who feel left behind by globalization, de-industrialization and the pace of change...We cannot stop globalization, but we can demand that politicians shape it to work for working people, their families and communities...[O]ften, but not always, outside London and the southeast – good skilled, unionized jobs that pay enough to raise a family have gone. De-industrialization and the hollowing out of local labour markets has been decades in the making, and has only got worse since the financial crash in 2008. The average wage is still £40 per week lower than it was before the crisis. During the referendum campaign, many voters cited the pressure that they feel uncontrolled immigration has put on wages (especially in some industries), on housing and on public services. The trade union movement is clear: blame for underinvestment in public services and an economy where wages are stagnant and good jobs scarce lies with government policy. Trade unionists are the natural spokespeople for these communities – and it is vital that we acknowledge their concerns, renew the ties that bind us and together demand accountability from a political and business class that for too long has failed them. (TUC, 2016, p.6)

The TUC proposes a dual approach for 'behind' communities, involving (1) a relaunch of its campaign for practical solutions to deal with pressures caused by migration (for example, calling for action on poor employment practices and bogus self-employment; demanding equal pay for workers doing the same job in the same company; extending sector-wide collective bargaining, and reasserting union values of hard work and respect for one another; emphasizing acceptance of difference and opposing racism and extremism to once again help workers fulfil their aspirations within the workplace and their community); and (2) demanding that the government set up a proper industrial strategy to bring back 'pride, good jobs and opportunities across the country, and revitalize manufacturing – [w]e will make the case for trade agreements that create wealth and distribute it fairly, opposing those deals which would undermine good jobs and good wages' (TUC, 2016, p.7).

On its plans to ensure that working people do not bear the brunt of the vote to leave the EU, the TUC references the need for the union movement to spearhead opposition to racism, xenophobia and all forms of prejudice in the workplace and communities, and to banish them from public discourse. It also seeks to defend the rights of EU migrants who have made the UK their home 'but feel the vote to leave the EU has put their right to live and work here in doubt' (ibid., p.6). Throughout, the TUC will demand a seat at the table for working people as decisions are made, and for unions to play a full role in negotiations around Brexit. The wider context of Brexit and the referendum debate, which has heightened long-term tensions around immigration, national identity and inequalities; legislative change that constitutes 'the biggest assault on working people's rights to organize and to strike in a generation' (ibid., p.4); and, as in New Zealand/Aotearoa, the movement's challenge to engage young workers appears to be galvanizing the peak body to

> be a showcase for a modern confident trade unionism that is in touch with the concerns of trade union members and their communities – and we should seek to put trade unions back at the heart of British civil society and public life…We are internationalists.' (ibid., p.5)

The extent to which this confidence has translated and will translate into meaningful action and achievements is likely circumscribed by the TUC's resources, including funding for its alliances, which is often stretched and sometimes provisional, constraining its capacity to develop frameworks or engage more deeply or speedily in certain forms of coalition work (Parker, 2008). Furthermore, its statement of intent seeks to chart a brave course that draws on a repertoire of new and old strategies, whose intertwined effects are difficult to predict in the highly dynamic context of Brexit and the presidency of Donald Trump; a globalizing economy; the peak body's varying levels of direct authority over affiliates (Behrens et al., 2004); the complexity and longevity of the issues to address and stakeholders involved; and thus the extent to which the TUC's own behaviour is path-dependent. The implications of the tension between the industrial assumptions/ aspirations of unions and the need for new perspectives in response to wider societal challenges are also needed (for example, the revitalization of manufacturing comes with the burden and cost of environmental pressures, global warming and outsourcing to developing countries). That said, the TUC's plans suggest more mature thinking around work and non-work concerns, which could inform future alliance-building and other strategies, and thereby widen its base of support among disenfranchised quarters of the workforce and wider society.

The CTU and alliance-building

A study of the TUC's smaller New Zealand/Aotearoa counterpart, involving interviews with senior CTU officials, unionists and industrial relations academics, found that alliance-building (along the lines of Dibben's (2004) second conception of social-movement unionism) was beginning to percolate the union movement but to a much lesser extent be implemented as a plan of CTU and union strategies (Parker, 2011). Informants were 'under no illusion as to the considerable constraints on the CTU's capacity to shift itself or affiliates towards a wider role via civil alliance-building' (Parker, 2011, p.400) though there was a 'growing sense of urgency in the union movement of the strategic need to widen the CTU's relations with outside groups' (p.401). Two key examples of multi-stakeholder alliances concerned (1) the International Labour Organization's (ILO) (1999) Decent Work agenda, whose four elements – creating jobs, guaranteeing rights at work, extending social protection, and promoting social dialogue – conjointly emphasize better work, workplaces and societal cohesion (with José Manuel Salazar Xirinachs, the ILO Regional Director for Latin America and the Caribbean, recently commenting that 'work is directly related to peace');[5] and (2) the environmental agenda has been problematized by different affiliate and partner positions (see also Obach, 2004; Hampton, 2015).[6]

However, much of the movement's alliance activity examined in the study was characterized as reactive and ad hoc. For this activity, the CTU's small size and environment had disadvantages (for example, union defensiveness and reduced resources in the face of conditions also experienced by the TUC: falling membership and hostile legislative changes; internal political heterogeneity in the peak body; a 'culture gap' between union bodies (at once procedurally bureaucratic and organizationally efficient) and the more informal *modus operandi* of other bodies). However, advantages were also identified (for example, the CTU's tight leadership and cohesion; its greater agility, as per Michels' (1949) iron law of oligarchy; the concentration of networks in New Zealand/Aotearoa). As in the UK, the CTU's continued engagement with civil-society organizations around work-centred issues such as pensions and part-time working, stressed coalition-building as a strand of and support activity for wider union revival endeavours.

Since then, there has been little specific focus on alliance-building with non-labour entities. However, a small body of literature and anecdotal evidence help to construct a recent picture of the level and nature of and factors driving such activity. Regarding the Decent Work agenda, whilst the last Labour government (1999-2008) enthusiastically promoted the initiative, the current administration voted against an ILO convention to establish fundamental rights for domestic workers at the ILO in Geneva in 2010, and has reduced state support for Decent Work programmes, including at international level. Thus, efforts by multiple agencies, including the CTU, for the programme remain subject to politics and diminishing resources (Parker et al., 2012).

Nonetheless, the CTU continues, and has encouraged others, to engage with the programme. It recently issued a comprehensive report about the Decent Work initiative in New Zealand/Aotearoa with regard to insecure work (CTU, 2013). The peak body recommended, among other things, that the principles behind the Decent Work agenda should be supported through certain measures: locally derived measures that reflect the culture, aspirations and resources of a given region or industry; improvement of income-support mechanisms for insecure work; reform of government procurement to promote decent work; and strengthening of union campaigns and bargaining to support secure work. Regarding the last of these, the report's recommendations included the promotion of 'community campaigning to break down the barriers between work and community and to promote unions as social-justice organizations' (p.62). It also called for employers to recognize employees' commitments outside of work, noting that 'demands being made on workers' time on a 24/7 basis are harming society' and for employer organizations to promote employers' 'recognition of the value of social inclusion and participation' (p.66). It observed that the issue of insecure work 'needs the full attention of a wide range of stakeholders, *including* unions, employers, and government' (p.5, emphasis added). Moreover, the CTU has helped to fortify multi-party support for the New Zealand Labour Party's Future of Work Commission, which involves political, academic, union, employer, industry and consultancy representatives. A major plank of the Commission's work concerns the Decent Work agenda, with its report referencing the *CTU Vision for the Workplace of the Future,* which recognizes the significance of life outside work via an array of interrelated issues, aims and proposed initiatives (CTU, 2007).

Indeed, New Zealand/Aotearoa faces an environment that is familiar in the UK in terms of an increase in precarious work and under-employment (Statistics New Zealand, 2014; CTU, 2013) and the weakening of key employee protection provisions (for example, the latest batch of changes to New Zealand/Aotearoa's cornerstone Employment Relations Act, 2000, in 2015 allows collective bargaining to end with no agreement between the parties rather than go on indefinitely for fear of breaching the requirement of 'good faith' – see New Zealand Ministry for Business, Innovation and Employment, 2016a). These developments in turn reflect globalization and deregulation pressures that have driven more competitive markets and more uncertain economic conditions. A prime example of union-led activity is a successful campaign led by Unite Union (to end zero-hours contracts), which was endorsed by and involved other unions and opposition political party leaders (Treen, 2015). It attracted considerable media coverage, and helped to build pressure for the Employment Standards Legislation Bill which came into force on 1 April 2016 and seeks to prevent unfair employment practices, including zero-hours contracts (New Zealand Ministry for Business, Innovation and Employment, 2016b). Somewhat differently, New Zealand/Aotearoa's campaign for a Living Wage – the income needed to provide workers and their families with the basic necessities of life and to enable them to live with dignity and participate as active citizens in society – has been spearheaded since 2012 by the Living Wage Movement Aotearoa New Zealand (LWMANZ), with its governance body and membership comprising three streams of civil society (faith-based/religious groups, community/secular groups, and unions and employers – (LWMANZ, not dated). The CTU and unions have supported the campaign (for example, the CTU has backed the fight against insecure work by advocating a Living Wage with greater security of hours; the Service and Food Workers' Union, now part of the E tū union, has engaged with a vision of union renewal via coalition-building through their participation in the LWMANZ (Newman and Jess, 2015). In the UK, unions have been more in the vanguard of a longer-running Living Wage campaign (e.g. Prowse and Fells, 2015, 2016a, 2016b; Parker et al., 2016).

Returning to the global-local issue of climate change, it is clear that here, too, the CTU, like the TUC, has stepped up its policy development, support of alliance work and emphasis of the connection between key workplace issues and wider issues and responses. In February 2016, it made a submission on the priority issues of the New Zealand Emissions Trading Scheme Review 2015/16 (CTU, 2016b), commenting that it was 'gravely concerned at the effect of climate change and [does] not believe that the Government is doing enough to contribute to world efforts to combat it' (p.1). It also noted that the effects of climate change and measures to combat it would 'impact working people in their jobs and their communities unfairly', and stated that 'measures must also be taken to address this' (p.1). The CTU outlined the impacts it anticipated in terms of falling real average wages, a consequent fall in consumption, slowing investment and a slowing economy, and the uneven and unfair effects of these for households and industries. It recommended a set of policies to combat climate change that include measures to address its social and economic effects, stressing the need for 'an integrated approach to the climate-change issues, emissions reductions, labour, economic, industry and social issues rather than the current piecemeal approach' to the new environment (ibid. p.2). The necessity of such an approach (known internationally as a 'just transition') was noted in the preamble to the Paris COP21 Agreement signed in March 2016 and ratified by 129 countries including New Zealand/Aotearoa and the UK, with New Zealand/Aotearoa ratifying the Kyoto Protocol to the UN Framework Convention on Climate Change 1992 in 2005 (New Zealand Ministry for the Environment, 2007).

However, a recent study highlighted a disconnect between different unions and non-labour parties. Based on interviews with leaders from 11 CTU affiliates (representing three-quarters of all affiliate members), Douglas and McGhee (2016) reported that all of the respondents saw the CTU and wider union movement as important stakeholders and leaders in this sphere but none of the individual unions was in a strong position in terms of developing policies regarding climate change. Some unions had not begun to address climate change within their formal structure or register it as an issue; their memberships had shown little interest in raising related issues. Unions' lack of preparation, the authors suggested, reflects the socio-political environment in which they operate, with neoliberalism from the 1980s and subsequent legislative changes precipitating union membership decline and, since 2008, a sustained undermining of rights such as access to workers in the workplace narrowing the role that unions play in the lives of workers. They added that union leaders were also concerned that a shift towards long-term social issues like climate change could affect membership numbers if it wasn't perceived as a 'core' union concern, '[t]he irony being that the continued focus on the short gains of wages and conditions will be pointless if in the middle to long term members' jobs ceased to exist' (ibid.). This contrasts with US research findings that indicated union members were more likely to embrace their union engaging with climate change mitigation strategies (Vachon and Brecher, 2016).

Discussion and concluding remarks

Peak union bodies enter into coalitions for various reasons. Alliances can help sustain affiliates' strikes, organize minority groups, push for legislative change and make progress on multiple or single-issue agendas. They can also express broader social-justice and political views, and enable engagement with non-labour groups. Frege et al. (2004) maintain that, at heart, they are union attempts to access the resources controlled by their coalition partners, including physical and financial resources, networks, expertise, legitimacy, and the capacity to mobilize constituencies and popular support.

Indeed, our analysis of recent empirical work and publicly available documents reveals that the UK's TUC and New Zealand/Aotearoa's CTU have remained primarily focused on job regulation, workplace issues, and staving off further membership decline. Their capacity to provide leadership, guidance and support on such matters has been increasingly vital, with a number of pressing challenges: workers facing an onslaught from legislative changes that go to the heart of unions' capacity to effectively collectivize, represent and keep members; production and work design changes, themselves linked to sectoral, technological and skill-set shifts; increasing and largely employer-driven flexible use of labour (e.g. Rasmussen et al., 2012); and the individualization of much of the employment relationship. Such changes are themselves reflective of longer-term globalization and deregulation in an increasingly uncertain economic and institutional context. In this setting, neither peak union body has been a 'strong centre' with regard to its influence over or on behalf of affiliates but, all things considered, both have demonstrated a relatively prodigious level of activity, suggesting that they punch above their weight and bureaucratic tendencies to help guide, advocate for and frame unions' activities to protect members' interests and improve wages, hours and working conditions.

On a more modest scale, the same broad conclusion might be reached about the peak bodies' recent engagement with and support of alliances with civil-society parties. A decade ago, empirical work suggested that, whilst reaching out to other groups to emphasize social-justice aims had never been core to New Zealand/Aotearoa or British unionism, such activity simmered away in areas of the movement, particularly among large affiliates. The TUC and CTU's respective civil alliances were largely seen as a tool for furthering other union revival strategies, though some showed their capacity to profile or actively pursue wider goals. Furthermore, their role as ally on such issues (for example, the environment) gained a modest level of momentum despite resource constraints and tensions between the leadership and members around shifting towards long-term social issues during a period of growing economic uncertainty.

More recently – during and following six years of global economic decline, the negative impacts of which were more keenly felt in the UK than New Zealand/Aotearoa – the economistic purpose of these union movements has been heightened for workers, themselves increasingly diverse in character and circumstance. This is against a backdrop of intensifying use of flexible labour; growing job insecurity, precarious work situations and under-employment; retreating social-welfare protection; in the UK, the uncertainty engendered by its withdrawal from the familiar institutional infrastructure and relationships of EU membership; and both union movements' struggles to maintain their numbers and influence amid state backing of substantive and procedural regulatory changes that have further girded employer power. Civil alliance-building has thus remained an ancillary characteristic of New Zealand/Aotearoa and British unionism.

But remained it has, with our exploratory analysis suggesting that the peak bodies' recent interest in coalition over wider matters of social and economic justice has held its own. Shared areas of concern for the peak bodies, and their more nuanced attention to some longer-term matters (for example, again, climate change; the Living Wage; decent work in relation to wider quality of life) reflect increasingly informed, multi policy-aware approaches that recognize different stakeholders' positions, contributions and goals, whilst retaining a national flavour (for example, whilst Living Wage campaigns are led by the union movement in the UK, in New Zealand/ Aotearoa and the US they are more reflective of unions joining with a wide range of community and other alliance partners – Hurd et al., 2003). Ongoing external challenges have stimulated both peak bodies to think about their identities and new opportunities, including 'reaching out' activity with new parties outside their usual areas of operation in various ways; union memberships and leaderships' own increasingly diverse characteristics and circumstances may also have this effect. As Piven and Cloward (1992, p.314) observe, 'breakdown is often prerequisite to breakout', though impact analysis of alliance-building activity remains scant. The CTU and TUC's resilience and adoption of multiple coalition roles reflect, as Gumbrell-Mc-Cormick and Hyman (2013, p.205) discuss more generally, a capacity to '[embrace] alternatives to their time-honoured traditions' and make hard choices although they will need to continually reinvent themselves if they are 'to survive as effective 'continuous associations' '.

Such debate also highlights the question of whether the role of traditional unions in prioritizing economistic gains must come to an end. Given that contemporary political and economic organization of society is dominated by neoliberal, individualized assumptions conditions are, arguably, ripe for challenging the atomizing power of neoliberalism by engaging with other collectives (Clawson, 2008). In particular, new and alternative civil alliances could be imagined with those sidelined as a result of the unions' focus on the workplace. As Fairbrother (2008, p.218-219) contends, 'only by defining themselves in relation to and demonstrating their capacity to connect with life experiences under capitalism, will unions be in a position to renew and move beyond a narrow economistic focus'.

The peak bodies have engaged with civil alliances on different scales and levels. In absolute terms, 'reaching out' activity has occurred more modestly as part of CTU and TUC strategy plans. This reflects, *inter alia*, their respective size, the quality of their alliances with civil partners, their priorities regarding wider concerns, affiliates' own priorities and access to their resources, and the peculiarities of their social, political, economic, cultural and institutional settings. While the CTU's small size and both peak bodies' environments have put constraints on such activity, advantages have also been identified (for example, a combination of institutional and size effects, which concentrate networks). Furthermore, the added complexity of and uncertainty engendered by recent changes, including those around the post-Brexit institutional and political terrain, make the nature and extent of subsequent TUC alliance activity difficult to predict, particularly given its non-linear trajectory to date (as the TUC's short-lived foray into building community coalitions with organizers emphasizes). However, the tensions between the leadership and members in both movements around the peak bodies' political direction and strategies might provide shareable lessons about future union purpose that resonate less with the recent experiences and developments of union movements elsewhere.

Ultimately, the local impacts of international socio-economic and political developments may help to force unions' hands in terms of engaging more in civil alliance-building. For example, the intensification of international crises, including more than 65 million people around the world being forced from their homes, among them 21.3 million refugees (UN High Commissioner for Refugees, 2017), stresses the need for a fundamental examination of the contemporary purpose of labour movements – and other parties. A key project for the peak body and their affiliates thus lies in pursuing (shorter-term) economic aims for workers, whilst convincingly conveying their interdependence with wider diversity and social justice goals.

Indeed, the twentieth century showed that unions could benefit from the widespread surge of people being mobilized for social justice in countries such as the US (in the 1930s), and the UK, Germany, France and Italy (in the 1960s-1970s). With the impetus of social movements including but not limited to anti-war, civil rights, women and the environment, established institutions were challenged in favour of an emphasis on workplace issues (Turner, 2003). However, the dynamics have changed because of the global wave of neoliberalism and austerity measures which have directly impacted on communities' daily lives. Communities in different locales now strive to protect not only their labour but also their lands, rivers, oceans and life forms – which some refer to as the 'commons' (Caffentzis and Federici, 2014). Under social-justice issues, in addition to global refugee crises, both the UK and New Zealand/Aotearoa are experiencing deepening inequality, housing crises, lack of access to healthy food and the destruction of the natural environment. And social unease within different groups is apparent with regard to a new order where disagreement and critique are subsumed beneath the discourse of consensus and politicization, and political demands for change are suppressed through various mechanisms (Boltanski and Chiapello, 2007; Rancière, 2004). In this ongoing struggle, social movements and other actors can thus open up a space for discussion and engagement; the qualitative and quantitative impacts of civil alliance-building need to be clearly delineated in terms of their individual and collective work and non-work meanings. Unions might recall that they are already 'social movements' aiming to challenge the power of the state and capital, and seeking social transformation (Fairbrother, 2008).

The impacts of peak bodies' alliance activity must also be considered in relation to their other development activities. In the Australian context, McAlpine and Roberts (2017) recently asserted that the amalgam of challenges faced by unions has been 'uniquely bad', and that the concentration of union strategies on improved organizing and recruitment methods is misplaced. Resonating with the UK and New Zealand/Aotearoa, however, they note that, '[a]t the micro-level, organizers, officers and delegates simply have to fight their battles under the current regime of anti-union laws, and there is little time to consider the broader questions of what a better system might look like' (p.5) whilst, at the leadership level, there is a failure to articulate that unions cannot rebuild under the current legal regime, let alone have a discussion of what changes need to be made. Seeing the legal framework in which unions operate as 'the central determinant of their limited success in recent years' (p.1), they propose a minimum legal framework, based on collective bargaining, to encourage union recovery.

As a precursor to or alongside other strategies to aid union revival, struggles for workplace change and actions that reflect a broader 'sword of justice' role, this is a key consideration. It also raises challenging issues about how peak bodies can join others to guard against the repeal of labour law that empowers workers and unions. A response to such becomes particularly urgent in the face of New Zealand/Aotearoa's 'fast-track' system of litigation (Palmer, 1987); and with the growing need for world-wide labour standards that offset the excesses of globalized capital. And even if unions receive legislative and state support, as Edwards (2016, p.1) observes, 'the ground has moved so far underneath [them] that a fundamental shift in how unions operate and who they represent may be needed'.

We thus argue that alliance-building and social movement unionism need to become more important as the near future does not promise much to labour and other disadvantaged communities, given the rise of conservatism and racism (for example, Trumpism in the US, Brexit in the UK and rising nationalism in the EU), and increasingly automated work and new forms of economies using online platforms (for instance, Uber) create precarious working conditions. Alliance-building may become less an option than a necessity, for unions and for workplace struggles as well as to cope with the detrimental consequences of such changes.

One key implication of this analysis concerns the challenges that it presents to existing union training and education programmes, particularly around whether they can be orientated to incorporate social-movement unionism as a key, if not the central, approach to understanding union purpose and development in terms of deep multi-stakeholder engagement. Such an approach to learning could help inform the identification of nexus points between various parties' priorities and practices, including unions' own, with a view to assessing the strategic and operational feasibility of their coordinated pursuit at a single point in or over time (e.g. Holgate, 2015). Education initiatives involving stakeholder representatives as tutors and/ or participants are likely to take such an approach forward more readily than those populated exclusively by unionists, for instance. Activities will also likely require a nimble approach in terms of using a wider array of venues, timeframes and teaching modes (for example, online and via apps, as through well as more conventional delivery), working closely and flexibly with communities, and learning by doing to maximize participation by parties which may diverge on complex issues and *modi operandi*. Union bodies, as brokers, guides and thinktanks, even if not strong or well resourced, can still help inculcate greater adoption of wider issues. Whether this approach can fully function alongside existing initiatives or whether, via its need to coalesce and critique current activity and aims, it might eventually render traditional training approaches obsolete, is a moot point.

1 This is an Australian term for an advocacy group or organization that represents an entire sector of industry or the community to the government or trade association.

2 The number of unions in New Zealand/Aotearoa fell markedly in the late 1980s and early 1990s, largely because of the Labour Relations Act 1987, which required unions to have a minimum of 1,000 members.

3 Labour (or employment) law regulates the relationship between workers, employers, unions and the state. Collective labour law relates to the tripartite relationship and processes between the employee, employer and union while individual labour law concerns employees' rights at work and through the contract for work.

4 Although union numbers and strength have been in decline, New Zealand/Aotearoa Election Study survey data indicate that, in 2011, 32 per cent of the public felt that unions had too much power – up from 18 per cent in 1999 (Edwards, 2016).

5 In a speech he made at the 16th Nobel Peace Prize Laureates' Summit, at which he represented the ILO (which was awarded the prize in 1969). See http://www.ilo.org/global/about-the-ilo/newsroom/news/WCMS_543589/lang--en/index.htm.

6 A useful document by the New Zealand Department of Labour (2009), *Decent Work New Zealand: Towards Decent Work – Charting Our Progress*, which overviewed New Zealand/Aotearoa's involvement in the programme across government and other agencies, can no longer be located on the web.

6

Backstory – a Unite approach to political education

M.J. McGrath

Educate yourselves, because we will need all your intelligence. Agitate, because we will need all your enthusiasm. Organize yourselves, because we will need all your strength.

Antonio Gramsci, in the first edition of his newspaper,
L'Ordine Nuovo (The New Order), 1 May 1919

Introduction

As Richard Ross ar gues: 'Trade union education needs to be seen against the backdrop of the wider world of workers' education, itself a part of the even wider world of adult education' (2005, p.1). Ross's paper is such a useful, concise account of the growth and development of trade union education from before the Second World War to the mid-1990s, that its contents will not be reprised here. Instead, the starting point for this chapter shall be Ross's conclusion, which questions the tensions between the provision of independent trade union education in the context of state funding and the resultant strictures as to content. This tension is summed up by John Fisher, former Director of Education for the Transport and General Workers' Union (TGWU), one of the two components of today's Unite:

> In the latter 1960s and '70s the style of trade union education became dominated by TUC courses. On the positive side, this meant the use of active learning methods and a clear focus on role education rather than theory or academic study. On the negative side, it meant the virtual elimination of politics from the curriculum, so that by the end of the 1970s a generation of shop stewards had been made to feel that it was acceptable to be a shop steward and have no link with politics or even combine the role with voting Tory. (2005, p.227)

While the disparagement of 'theory' and 'academic study' is unfortunate in that, as Marx remarked, echoing Kant, 'Practice without theory is blind, theory without practice is sterile', we may attest to the validity of Fisher's observation. Ross concludes his piece as follows:

> What is the purpose of workers' education? Who should control it? Who should provide it? How can Independent Working Class Education be achieved? The Plebs League[1] wanted 'neither crumbs (nor) condescension' but control of their own destiny. That should surely still be the objective. (2005, p.7)

Such is our starting point.

Political education in Unite national courses
In 2007, a new Director of Education was appointed within the joint Amicus-TGWU. A former TUC Regional Education Officer and full-time officer with the TGWU, one of his first acts was to commission the rewriting of national core provision for health and safety and workplace representatives. This provision comprised four five-day modules for each of these workplace union officials, totalling eight five-day modules. In addition, today Unite has a wide range of provision encompassing equalities and lifelong learning, along with a range of specialist courses. The challenge confronting the writers of this provision was to ensure retention of what was positive in the TUC model, in the form of high-quality materials delivered in student-centred, discovery-learning mode, but, crucially, to couple it with investigation and interrogation of the political and economic contours which condition, if not determine the effectiveness of a labour organization operating in a capitalist, neoliberal global economy. It could be remarked that the inhibiting tension between the desire for independent working-class political education and the strictures imposed by government funding may well be resolved with the withdrawal of public funding, in England at least. The contours of this task became clearer with the adoption, in December 2011, of the Unite Political Strategy document, which commits the union to, among other things, striving for 'a socialism for the 21st Century' (Unite, 2011, pp.3 and 7).

'Sunny Jim', Dr Faustus and that contract
History is not without its ironies. At a time when the post-war settlement was in the process of disintegration, paving the way for the ascendancy of a resurgent Right, the Social Contract between organized labour and the Labour government of James Callaghan delivered not just positive employment legislation, but a comprehensive package whereby trade union education could be delivered through the use of public funding. Thus, when we should have been mobilizing all our forces to resist the ideological

onslaught of reactionary forces, we were bequeathed a Faustian pact which meant that the provision of publicly funded trade union education, while permitting access to provision for thousands of workplace representatives over the years, disabled educators from engaging in political and economic analysis. A signifier of the Left's inability, which extended well beyond the trade union movement and educational provision, is that the so-called Winter of Discontent, at the end of that decade, has been widely attributed to the actions of too-powerful labour unions. The objective facts of this are that organized labour was simply reacting to the effects of one of the periodic crises of capitalism, which stemmed from the multiple dysfunction of Western economies from 1973. So it is that the proscription on the opportunity to dissect and discuss the real causes of the Winter of Discontent and all that followed, has led to significant numbers of workplace union officials and members voicing the belief that trade unions in the 1970s were 'too powerful' and, consequently, the authors of their current weakened state.

For the last half-century or so, awareness, understanding and discussion of those economic and ideological forces informing and shaping the configurations of the free market and economic liberalism, including the Right's use of the 'Overton Window' (Jones, O., 2014) has been largely off limits in much of trade union educational provision. Where discussion of the configurations of capitalism and economic liberalism, their nature and their effects on working people and our organizations has taken place in mainstream courses, it has been because the tutor has managed to create the opportunity to explore such issues. The result has been at best, a haphazard, ad hoc and minimalist interrogation of the seismic shift in politics and economics, resulting in the Right's revanchist smashing of the post-war settlement.

Education as a site of struggle

Informed by Unite's political strategy objectives and guided by the union's 'three pillars' – organizing, politics and international solidarity – Unite education works hard to embed and integrate the analytical with the practical through ensuring we start from and constantly refer back to the material experience of participants. When our tutors explore such issues as power and authority, ownership and control or discipline and grievance processes, these are not treated as abstractions but are related to how work, society, politics and the economy are structured and how they function to embed and perpetuate exploitation and inequality.

There is awareness, however, of what trade unions and trade union education can and cannot do in the political and economic sphere. Overarching the dichotomy between the TUC education model derived from the 1970s and what is asserted to comprise the current, more progressive Unite practice, is therefore consideration of the tension between trade unions' industrial function and those wider political aims which some (e.g. the Fire Brigades Union and the National Union of Railwaymen, as was) still retain. As Perry Anderson put it, some years ago: 'As institutions, trade unions do not challenge the existence of society based on a division of classes, they merely express it. They can bargain within society, but not transform it' (1978, p.334). While those adhering to a syndicalist vision of the role of trade unions might well disagree with Anderson, the logic of this argument appears sound. This does not mean, however, that trade union education has no role to play in what Gramsci described as the necessary development from 'an incomplete and deformed variant of class consciousness which must…be transformed by the growth of political consciousness' (Anderson, 1978, p.334).

Education can be conceived as a site of struggle in which reps are equipped to undertake their day-to-day organizational and representational functions along with developing their understanding of the economic order as a construct which operates in the interests of the few and to the detriment of the many. In Unite education it is understood that ideas constitute a material force. A guiding principle is, therefore, the requirement to challenge the political justification that depicts the contours of free-market, economic neoliberalism as naturally occurring phenomena, in respect of which, its proponents assert, there is neither logical nor practical alternative and, if there was, that such would be undesirable. As Pierre Bourdieu argues:

> As the dominant discourse would have it, the economic world is a pure and perfect order, implacably unrolling the logic of its predictable consequences… One that, with the aid of the economic theory that it proclaims, succeeds in conceiving of itself as the scientific definition of reality. (1998, p.1)

In this, care is taken to start from and to mesh the material experience of participants so that investigation of such explanatory frameworks can make sense. Following some preliminary remarks, we provide examples of how we do this, along with excerpts taken from the Unite publication which represents both a discussion document and tutor guide as to both our methodology and political purpose.

The importance of the backstory

Before examples are provided of some of the activities and resources we use to combine skills and knowledge development with the creation and furthering of political understanding and commitment to Unite's objectives, the relationship between tutor and backstory requires attention. Thus, in respect of discipline and grievance procedures and processes, tutors are required to be proficient in understanding all aspects of what, how and why these operate in the workplace: from legislative provisions and case analysis to how to interview and represent members. But we also require our tutors to have a well-developed understanding of the history and context of the subjects they are teaching. As well as understanding this body of knowledge, tutors need to be able to convey the relevant linkages between it and the issues under consideration. These linkages are described as the backstory. By backstory, we mean an account or set of accounts that illuminates the contours and process of how we have got to the current situation. Discipline and grievance is a staple and very important aspect of the workplace reps' course and is dealt with in the first module and returned to in various forms throughout this provision.

The backstory as antidote to reverse amnesia

It is a curious fact that our reps and members, along with workers in general, often display what might be termed 'reverse amnesia'. So it is that, while those suffering from various forms of dementia can, quite often, remember the more distant past in great detail, the events of the present can escape them. With workers, the opposite can be the case. Acutely aware of the deficiencies of the present in the form of austerity, wage stagnation and falling living standards, the past is often only vaguely perceived. Part of our task, through the backstory, is to ensure reps and members understand the past so as to appreciate how things are, as they are, in the present. Only in this way can it be appreciated that the struggle for progressive values has been a long time in the making and has encountered the persistent hostility of elites throughout the ages. Using the device of the backstory helps people to understand that the way things currently present is contingent on many factors, few if any of which can be said to have been inevitable.

The backstory and the application of discipline – an example

The functional and skills-based aspects of discipline and grievance are not discussed here. Suffice to say these are fully covered in the course activities and resource material. What is at issue here is the contours of the body of knowledge necessary to make sense of employer application of discipline. These are discerned by engaging the backstory as the mechanism that assists an understanding of how these procedures and processes come to be as they are now. Michel Foucault's work on the history of discipline as a mechanism used to subjugate, oppress and control not just workers but also the citizen is useful, as is Bentham's panopticon and the similarity of its design to that of the prison, factory, shipyard and, more recently, the call centre. Such analysis explains the need of the employer (along with others) to ensure that discipline is internalized by the worker (Foucault, 2006; Bentham, 1995 [1787]). Moreover, we can relate these constructions to current and evolving management developments and techniques, such as the increasingly managerialist function of human resource management and performance appraisal in today's workplace, as comprising measures designed, in too many instances, to intimidate, instilling discipline and inhibitory self-discipline in the workforce (Taylor, 2013). Recent developments in human resource management include seminars in which, according to a growing number of reps, work teams are encouraged to identify 'angel' and 'devil' words. No prizes for guessing which category the following fall into: 'can' and 'but'.

In what ways tutors choose to extend such analysis is for them to decide. However, failing to move beyond an instrumental view of discipline, which accepts employer entitlement to exercise such, and simply developing defensive skills devoid of any critical analysis, is not an option. Before moving on to consider some activities and their accompanying backstories, it is worth mentioning how an understanding of the development of thought on the subject of discipline, as an example of the backstory, can illuminate the imposition of austerity and accompanying attacks on and denigration of the working and non-working poor.

The backstory and the creation of wider understandings

The work of Michel Foucault and Jeremy Bentham has been mentioned in the context of discipline and control. Allied to this, in the tutor guidance, consideration is given to the current attacks on welfare and the poor along with the systematic denigration of the latter, exemplified by the work of Owen Jones (2012). Thus, the ideological orientation of those antecedents of today's denigrators of the poor can be clearly traced in this extract from recent Unite guidance for tutors:

> It is important to understand the ideological justifications advanced through history in respect of work, work discipline, ownership and control. If resonances of current government attacks on welfare and on 'lifestyle-choice welfare scroungers' can be discerned in the following account, this is as it should be. Thus, from the seventeenth century the increasing need of capital to ensure a disciplined workforce is demonstrated through constant attacks by the rich, powerful and – be it noted – idle, on the capacity of the poor to work: 'On one hand labour was the source of wealth; on the other, the wages of the poor were to be kept as low as possible' (Linbaugh, 2006, p.4).

As Bernard Mandeville, the eighteenth-century writer who regarded self-interest as the means through which society progresses, said of the poor: 'They have nothing to stir them up to be serviceable but their Wants, which it is prudent to relieve, but folly to cure' (Linbaugh, 2006, pp.54-55). Money must both excite and hurt; there must be equilibrium between paying wages which allowed the poor to subsist but not so much as to encourage idleness (cf. Labour Theory of Value and Socially Necessary Labour Time). Too much money in the hands of the working class and, as Daniel Defoe noted with alarm: 'There's nothing more frequent for an Englishman to work until he has got his pocket full of money and then go and be idle,' while Josiah Child noted that 'When corn was cheap the poor would not work for more than two days a week…while Roger North found that the poor preferred not to work if they did not have to, than to work to accumulate and save' (Linbaugh, 2006, p.4). The equation of worklessness and vagrancy with that of deviance and madness is further explored by Foucault (2006). As ever, capital and its apologists require ideological justification for the persecution of the many their system disadvantages. This criminalization of the poor had characterized labour policy from Tudor times with the Punishment of Vagabonds Act of 1572, the first of many enactments to deal with those whom the ruling class feared might be idle.

This passage, providing tutors with a set of historical contours, might raise the question: why should our tutors have an understanding of this body of knowledge? The answer is, so that they can provide the backstory showing the continuity of physical exploitation of the class which produces the wealth but must be denied access to it, justified by ideological denigration, to be a constant historical feature of exploitative, class-divided societies though time.

Leitmotif

If there is a leitmotif in Unite educational provision it relates to Bourdieu's observation (1998) that neoliberalism and its ideological justifications are not facts of nature: they are human constructs which serve the interests of corporations and elites. Looking at the history and development of discipline from historical, sociological, economic and cultural perspectives enables us to question the assumption that one class is historically entitled to exert discipline in the workplace over another through ownership of the means of production, distribution and exchange; and that this histori-cally derived entitlement, in respect of the attacks on welfare and working people, is contingent on but sanctioned through the enduring sanctity of private property in class-divided societies. The making and re-making of contemporary consciousness through the enduring 'private good, public bad' mantra, requires constant challenge. The drive to privatize everything, from transport and public utilities to health and welfare (what there is left of it), and its impact on working people, provides key linkages in this backstory.

It is important that reps understand where the inequity in employment relations originates that means that whereas a worker can lose their livelihood through some (real or imagined) infraction of a workplace rule, often the worst that can happen to a corporate entity is that they receive a rebuke from an employment tribunal and a trivial fine. Such consideration lays the groundwork for a subsequent activity on industrial democracy, with the question as to why democracy stops at the workplace threshold being posited. Eddie Cornick's (2011) thought-provoking piece on the relationship between industrial democracy and the transition to a socialist society is useful in this regard.

The backstory: an outline of some indicative activities

The union's core workplace and safety rep provision comprises over 250 activities in 8 five-day modules. It is contended that in almost every activity there is the opportunity to access the political and economic reality underlying it. What is presented here are outlines of some of these activities, along with an indication as to the nature and scope of the backstory. The overall purpose in all of this is to move workers from trade union consciousness to class consciousness. This is our contribution to that process. The following are selected, if not at random, then in order to demonstrate that however diverse the nature of the subject matter, it is always possible to mesh the functional and political through the engagement of elements of the backstory.

Understanding the union: how our stories are the Unite story

In this activity reps are invited to put the words 'Unite the Union' in the centre of the flip chart and to write the words best able to describe Unite and its purpose around it. So, for instance, they may have put 'fairness', 'equality', 'justice' or something like that, and the group is then asked to describe what each word means, providing examples from their experience as reps. In addition, they are asked to say whether the things they have described are apparent in the workplace and society and why it is that our union should be based on a system of values. Finally, groups are asked to 'tell us a story' from their own experience, in which one or more of these values has been realized as the basis of an action or actions undertaken by a group member or members.

The importance of this introductory activity is to get reps thinking about what abstract concepts are and how they are reified in the things that Unite reps do in the workplace and beyond. One resource for this activity contains a description of how facts convey information but stories involve emotion, empathy, understanding and commitment. The other resource is Brecht's 'A Worker Reads History', which requires little elaboration. Except for this: we need to emphasize that one of the best ways of getting our message across is to make sure people understand that it is the workers of the world that create wealth. The engagement of analytical formulations like that of the Labour Theory of Value (LThV) must always be preceded by investigation of reps' own experience. Through interrogation of the LthV is uncovered its incendiary nature, demonstrated by the fact that, as has been remarked by left-leaning academics, it is seldom, if ever, taught in university economics courses but is located in departments of history, politics or sociology, thus diminishing its status as a valid economic theory. The theory's relevance is easily highlighted through, for instance, investigating company profits at a time when wage restraint is normative and examining the issue of shareholder dividends, interrogating from where the latter are derived. Paul Mason's (2015) account of the theory is a useful starting point, particularly his explanation of 'socially necessary labour time', which can be one of the trickier aspects of the theory.

This is a fairly gentle introductory activity for reps, but one which is important in setting expectations as to the nature of the journey on which they are embarking.

Good work and the good society

A theme which runs through and unites our National Workplace Rep and Safety Rep provision is the nature of work, its location and its relationship to society. A taste of this can be gained from consideration of some activity titles from both strands of provision: 'Work-Life Balance and Family Friendly Policies'; 'Inequality – the Good Society and the Bad Society'; 'Bad Work – Cause and Effect and Good Work – Dignity, Respect and Fairness'. In respect of the last of these, the struggle for Decent Work is an ongoing Unite campaign. Again, the focus is on what the labour process comprises and its relationship to life beyond the workplace. One activity in this process invites reps to list those things they do outside work on one side of a flipchart, with workplace activities on the other – typically evoking such responses as gardening, DIY, caring for the family, playing and watching sport, walking and exercise, and so on. They are then asked to identify any activities that people choose to do which are not, in some other respects, paid activities in the labour market. Very few, if any, of the things that people choose to do are not employment-related activities. A debate then normally develops: beyond the necessity to engage in the labour process in order to sustain themselves and their dependants in life, what is it about work that is important for people and why does democracy stop at the workplace threshold? Braverman (1989) is a useful source for the backstory as are Marx's views on the relationship between work, the labour process and what he describes as our species nature. What work is, and what it should and could comprise, even in a system geared towards profit maximization above all else, provides the arena for exploring Unite's Decent Work initiative. Also of importance for the backstories to this and other activities are Robert Donkin (2010) on the history of work and Wilkinson and Pickett (2009) on the effects of inequality.

Universal Basic Income (UBI)
UBI is becoming an ever-more debated subject. Arguments for and against are presented in the resources and reps are asked to debate the issues, taking opposite sides of the argument. This activity on UBI complements other modules as it deals with the economics of capitalism and capital accumulation. It covers the inherent instability of capitalist development from the second half of the eighteenth century to the present, using Kondratieff's formulation of Long Wave Cycles. We also examine how these cycles are called 'Long Waves of Prosperity' by Allianz Global Capital Investments, exploring how a change in language obscures the devastating downturns, which are good news for those able to use devaluation and crisis as a means of further capital accumulation. Consider the website that appeared shortly after Greece's bankruptcy entitled 'Buy Greece', along with the privatization of many state assets and the sale of three sovereign Greek islands to a Saudi billionaire. Rich pickings for the super-rich. In addition, work already undertaken on the validity of the LThV adds currency to this debate on rights and entitlements, obligations and duties in respect of the ownership and control of productive capacity and resources. Clarke (2014) provides some interesting views on UBI, amongst other things.

Past, present and future
This activity invites reps to work in small groups to develop a narrative, organize and make a presentation on the past, present and future of the trade union and labour movement. Reps are encouraged to access the internet for information and for the presentation, but not to use images from it. Instead, groups are encouraged to go outside, take pictures or make drawings of things – buildings, artefacts, people working or at leisure – that represent aspects of the story their presentation tells. In this way, reps are encouraged to think about where our class has come from, what it now

comprises and what the future could and should hold for working people. Along with a number of other activities (for example, 'Workers? We are More than Just That!'), it affirms our identity as members of a class with a rich culture and a story to tell.

Doing something different

This activity extends the previous one, inviting reps to organize to do something which they might not have thought of doing. The evidence-gathering outings considered might include – depending on course location and circumstance – a planned walk where reps are encouraged to take notes/ pictures of buildings, transport, canals, factories, shopping malls and so on. Consideration is given to why things are as they are, who built, designed and financed these things, and so on. Alternatively, a visit to the local library or art gallery or cinema might be planned. Whatever form the activity takes, the tutor is expected subsequently to lead a discussion whereby the different thoughts and the shared experience of participants can be interrogated as to why leisure and recreation (literally re-creating ourselves and looking back to the aforementioned activity) are important for us. Apart from Braverman (1989), another useful source for the backstory is Beynon (1975) although there are many more useful resources in this area. Part of the backstory for this is the following, by Thomson (1963, p.120):

> R.H. Tawney is quoted as stating that 'the New medicine for Poverty' with its denunciation of sloth and improvidence in the labourer, and its convenient belief that – if success was a sign of election – poverty was itself evidence of moral turpitude,

who goes on to quote Max Weber on the crucial aspect of work discipline: 'Wherever modern capitalism has begun its work of increasing the productivity of human labour by increasing its intensity, it has encountered the immensely stubborn resistance of...pre-capitalist labour' (Thomson, 1963). See also Brown (1977) for the persistence into the twentieth century of 'St Monday' as an act of resistance, originating in the pre-industrial age.

Creating a code for life

This activity introduces reps to the 'Ten Commandments' of the Socialist Sunday School. Throughout the course, we have explored and examined our values as part of the industrial wing of the labour movement, often in the context of constructing and telling 'the Unite Story'. The latter is designed to permit reps to contextualize abstract ideas – for example, fairness, justice, equality – through concrete examples that mesh with the material experience of workers. Creating a code for life provides further opportunity to locate our heritage, as a class, as an ethical force for good within society. In so doing, reps can counter the view of the elites and their representatives in the political and business sphere that, at best, trade unions can be tolerated when they are weak but that they should be denigrated and attacked when they are able to do what they are meant to do: represent the interests of their members and communities. Creating a code for life can expose much that is wrong with class-divided society, through investigating what could and should comprise the ethical bases of a good society.

So, we all know what equality means – right?
Although it is mainly concerned with the nature of equality and equity, this activity reprises and extends consideration of such issues as contribution and entitlement. As such, it explores the many facets of the idea of equality, exposing not just the unworkable principle that everybody should be treated equally (which can gain traction if not challenged) but also questioning what the principle means in a number of different circumstances. Thus, if the simple proposition of treating everyone equally is absurd, how should people be treated? Does this mean we need to treat people unequally for the sake of equality? And, if so, what has equity got to do with equality? Brief case studies are provided for each.

In terms of access to goods and services, what should be available to all? Thus, it can be argued that the founding of the NHS on the principle of collective provision for individual need, with access free and equal to all, at the point of delivery, constitutes a set of 'goods' of the kind considered in the case study. What other goods should be considered as worthy of equal access for all? And, if not all goods and services, why some and not others? Does distributive justice apply only to those goods commonly produced, i.e. through social and economically fair co-operation, or to other goods as well, in respect of, for example, inherited wealth? And what about natural resources, in the form of, for instance, land ownership? In addition, further areas are considered: identifying the arguments used to defend inequality; investigation of the proposition that if everyone could have enough of what they needed and wanted, would the excessive wealth of some, say the minority, be a problem and, if so, why? This activity clearly links with others in the provision which calls into question the deficiencies of capitalism in the promotion of a better way of organizing society for the benefit of all.

Modern Britain and the logic of capitalism
There is only one resource for this activity: a cartoon strip from the magazine *Viz*. Now, while *Viz* is not to everyone's taste, the single-page strip cartoon

of a young male worker on a zero-hours contract speaks volumes for what has come to be known as the 'precariat'. Inspired by a phone conversation overheard on the bus by the cartoon's originator, which apparently featured a thinly veiled threat that the recipient of the call was free to refuse a request to come into work, in which case he would 'not work again that month', the cartoon chronicles the subject getting such a call, being told to wait in the canteen for a period, working for 37 minutes, then going 'off the clock'. He then has to wait around for a further period before being told to go home, as he is not needed. On arriving home, he receives a phone call saying he is needed for an hour and a half, in an hour and a half's time, before being told to wait in the canteen for an hour. Then he is told he is not needed at all. The activity asks reps to consider in what ways the cartoon format gets the message across in a way that an analytical narrative on zero hours might lack. Reps are then invited to use two of a number of techniques to get their message across about modern Britain. These include a cartoon storyboard (like the example in the resources), a short play involving characters and dialogue, a poem or rhyme, a drawing or set of drawings, photographs, jokes, stories, mime, dance, or anything else they can think of. Reps are then asked to use another two of these techniques to illustrate what life and work could and should comprise in modern Britain. The results are sometimes strikingly imaginative, not to say entertaining.

Work – what if we were able to start from scratch?
The point of this activity is not to create profiles of desirable societies (although this can be a part of the discussions, cf. Morris, 1908) but to create the opportunity for participants to consider Unite values generated in previous activities (and re-visited throughout) and their consonance or dissonance with the way work and the labour process are presently organized. It also allows consideration of the development of the differing forms of social and economic organization in the Western world; from primitive communism, through slave-owning society to feudalism and the stages of capitalist development – commercial, industrial, financial and global. Again, the message is that work has not always been organized in the way that it is now and, as a social construct, need not be so organized in the future. Speculation as to the increasing impact of technological systems, which are diminishing the need for human labour, provides many linkages with other activities (for example, on UBI), and helps to bring out one of the major contradictions of capitalism in its tendency towards over-production and under-consumption. Rob Harrison's thoughts (2014) on people over capitalism are a useful resource for this activity. The Culture Matters website also provides some very useful insights.

What is to be done?

Unite education is committed to putting politics and political understandings at the heart of our educational provision. This is not to neglect the functional, skills, knowledge and attitude development of participants but to ensure that when politics and political formulations are accessed, the discussion always starts from the material experience of our reps and members. We need to assert the validity of the claim that since things have not always been as they are, they could and should be different. We do this principally through the backstory.

While the de-politicization of trade union education from the 1970s hasn't caused all the ills of working people or organized labour, it certainly hasn't helped. The task of creating an understanding that how things present now is not an immutable fact of nature but a set of economic, political and cultural constructs, to which alternatives exist, must intensify. As trade union and labour educators we need to make certain that while assisting in delivering the policies of our respective unions, we ensure that this is meshed with understanding of the bigger picture. In Unite, as demonstrated, we strive to achieve this through the backstory.

The initiative of the General Federation of Trade Unions (GFTU) in promoting this book is, therefore, long overdue and to be welcomed. At a time when the wealth of the economic elites bleeds over into political power, and media owners determine what thoughts and ideas comprise 'common sense', the Left needs to use every mechanism at its disposal to counter a set of narratives that interpret global hunger and poverty, food banks and homelessness as naturally occurring phenomena and to replace such with our own positive vision of how things could and should be. In respect of corporate power and its effects on the democratic process, Chrystia Freedland (2012, p.38) quotes Scott Turow as writing: 'Everybody patting himself on the back because the Reds went in the dumper is going to wonder who won when Coca Cola applies for a seat in the UN.' If we have learned one thing from developments in the recent past, it is that the absurd can quite quickly become the just possible, before morphing into the probable; unless we stop it happening. The neoliberal project, as the latest manifestation of an increasingly rapacious capitalism, while largely neglected for analysis in news and broadcast media, is eminently understandable when approached in the manner suggested in this chapter.

We need to build on the GFTU initiative and involve the TUC, the WEA, our sister unions and other providers in sharing ideas and best practice, and debating the contours and mechanisms of embedding political education throughout our provision. And if there is dissent to the proposition that such political education is needed, let's have that discussion in a comradely fashion. In this, Unite is ready to take the lead in facilitating a wide-ranging discussion involving all relevant parties.

1 For more on the Plebs League, see Chapter 3, p.53.

7

The future of community education: what role for trade unions in promoting the co-production of knowledge and culture and supporting democratic institutionalization?

Joel Lazarus

In the summer of 2012, four friends with academic and activist backgrounds, myself and three others, came together to set up a community education project in Oxford. Two of us, Neil Howard and James Sevitt, had helped establish the 'Tent City University' at the Occupy London site the previous autumn. Our project, initially called 'Political and Economic Literacy' was later renamed 'People's Political Economy', shortened to PPE. Since PPE is also the short name for Philosophy, Politics, and Economics, Oxford University's infamous elite-producing conveyor-belt degree, the choice of these initials also constituted an act of reclamation, a direct, subversive challenge to the elitist model of education associated with Oxford. Our goal was to set up learning groups in community organizations at the sharp end of austerity. In this way, we sought to bring people together to learn about and respond to the structural factors constraining their lives and opportunities.

In this chapter, I will describe my experience of PPE, the vehicle for my ventures into the world of community education over the past five years. I will also describe a pedagogical experiment I conducted within a university setting – the 'ROSI Website Project' – which took place at the University of Warwick in 2016. I will then offer some reflections and projections, envisioning the emerging future of democratic education and the potential role of trade unions within this future. I focus on two central issues: the co-production of knowledge and culture and the institutionalization of democratic organizations and pedagogical models. I will argue that the production and consumption of knowledge is a crucial site of political struggle today, with the battle played out mainly on and through the internet, and that any models that maintain a separation between teaching and learning, teacher and learner, are essentially regressive. Instead, the emerging future is defined by the praxis of the co-production of knowledge and, therefore, the mutualized, common ownership of both that knowledge itself and the means of its production.

It is hugely encouraging that trade unions are recognizing both that they need to repoliticize their educational content and that they need to reach out and work with community partners. However, the primary message of this chapter is that trade unions need to go beyond any notion of education as a tool of personal empowerment and recognize that collective empowerment through education means not teaching and learning, but the collective production of knowledge and culture.

PPE – Adventures in community education

Prior to 2012, I knew nothing about community education. Like so many others, what triggered my move away from my academic work on international aid and development towards community education and critical pedagogy was reading Paulo Freire's *Pedagogy of the Oppressed* (Freire, 1972b). Another key moment was my experience of and participation in the Occupy London event earlier that year.

The pilot project

I set up PPE with three friends. We ran a pilot by setting up learning groups in five community organizations: a homeless charity; a mental-health organization; a City-Council-funded programme for young adults; and a secondary school. We also ran a group for graduate students at the University's Department of International Development. At the same time, we recruited and gave some rudimentary training to 10 doctoral students and academic colleagues, to help them facilitate these learning groups in pairs. We developed an initial syllabus, but soon discarded it.

The learning groups ran with mixed levels of success. The school group was small but fruitful. Our groups at the homeless and mental-health charities ran reasonably successfully, but the main factor impeding their development was the inconsistency in participation caused primarily by the very unstable and precarious nature of participants' own lives. The stand-out group was the young adult group, which ran weekly for almost a whole year. The two facilitators of this group did sterling work. Their pedagogical and ideological approach differed significantly from ours. Nevertheless, the participants expressed their excitement at learning about political and economic issues. The highlight of that year was undoubtedly a debate on education organized by the City Council between group participants and local Labour and Liberal Democrat Councillors.

When we reflected on our first year, we felt confident enough to conclude that 'PPE works and can grow...Many people want to learn about the political economy of this crisis – the political economy of their lives – and many people were attracted by our democratic, critical approach to learning'. That said, we also fully recognized that our successes were very limited in both scale and depth. This pilot phase had given us mere glimpses of the possible, and had, at the same time, revealed to us just how hard it would be to go further, particularly on our then voluntary basis.

My Life, My Choice

In reality, by the summer of 2013, PPE was becoming too difficult to sustain, let alone expand. By that time, the other three co-founders of PPE had left Oxford and, in 2014, I also headed abroad for a year. However, one learning group, set up by me in late 2013 and run by a friend, continued to run weekly for over two years until mid-2016. My Life, My Choice (MLMC) is a self-advocacy charity run for and by people with learning disabilities. The group was small – eight to ten regular participants – but its intimacy made possible significant learning experiences.

The group covered a wide range of issues, using various pedagogical, artistic and spiritual practices. In 2015, for example, we spent two months covering the 2015 general election; we looked at benefits, work, and the universal basic income; and we spent several months on the issue of power. In one session, Prof. Danny Dorling came in to explore the housing crisis with us. We used brainstorming, watched films, devised and performed role plays, used meditation and games, and employed theory to develop our learning.

MLMC's former Project Development and Training Co-ordinator, Alex Brooks, was instrumental in supporting the PPE process. Alex described how MLMC members unconsciously 'wear the labels' that society gives them.[1] She saw group participants gradually becoming able to question these labels and to reconsider who they really are and what they really think. This process was aided by myself and the previous group facilitator providing participants with the information they require and helping them to analyse it.

To give a concrete example, on the issue of benefits: by sharing their personal stories and by analysing media output, participants were able to begin to recognize and challenge the structural violence they endure as disabled people and benefit claimants. Prior to this, as Alex put it, 'there was a total belief in many members that they were the only ones in their situation'. Their work informed one of MLMC's major campaigns, its 'We Will All Benefit' campaign, which aimed to challenge the dominant narrative regarding the welfare system and those it supports. The significance of this sense of empowerment for a group of people, whom Alex describes as being 'historically very oppressed and dictated to', and who generally must submit to the 'big rules that govern their lives', is profound. Alex talks about how PPE brought a positive energy into MLMC, and about how PPE and politics are talked about in the office, in group meetings, and on 'Stingradio', MLMC's own online radio show.

The PPE process contributed directly to the political actions of MLMC members. The tragic and entirely avoidable death of 18-year-old Connor Sparrowhawk at Slade House, an NHS assessment and treatment unit in Oxford, in July 2013, triggered demands for justice, accountability and improved standards in such facilities (see Salman, 2014). MLMC members were at the forefront of this campaign, both locally and nationally.

Ultimately, however, the group came to an end in the autumn of 2016. The reasons for this are complex. A two-month period during which I was both abroad and ill disrupted our routine and numbers dwindled. Support from the charity's most senior figure waned as they questioned PPE's contribution to MLMC's strategic objectives. There seemed to be a dissonance between PPE's generality and qualitative essence and the charity's increasingly quantitative focus. Nonetheless, I look back on the MLMC experience with pride.

The ROSI website project

Project overview

In early 2016, I recruited a group of 10 University of Warwick undergraduates from across the humanities and social sciences to participate in the 'ROSI Website Project'. 'ROSI' stands for 'Reviving Our Sociological Imagination' (Wright Mills, 1959) – that essential ability to link our personal lives and problems to wider social and historical issues and structures. I invited the students to work with me for two hours each week over 10 weeks to design a website that would encourage and help a general, non-academic audience to use philosophy and social theory in order to deepen their understanding of the issues they face in their own individual and collective lives. The project also needed a narrower focus, so that participants could concentrate their efforts, so I decided to invite participants to explore the question: 'What is money?'

The ROSI Website Project was transdisciplinary and pedagogically radical. I sought to invite students from a wide range of disciplinary backgrounds into a process of genuine dialogue, mutual teaching and learning, and knowledge co-production; to offer them an opportunity to engage with and generate more diverse forms of knowledge far beyond the dominant perspectives and logocentrism of most academic study; to enable them to use their creativity and to empower them to produce not just knowledge, but culture; and to give them the chance to develop technical filmmaking and website design/construction skills. Instead of detailing a preset course of study for them to follow, the project presented student participants with a broad task to complete and a loose and fluid framework for action, thereby offering them the space and freedom to produce and create as they collectively saw fit.

The ROSI Website Project's aim of contributing to a revival of our sociological imagination can also be described as an attempt to cultivate 'mass intellectuality' (Will and Hall, 2017). This involves the democratization of social knowledge and, of course, its corresponding social power.

From the start, then, I harboured great hopes for this small project. The means were always as important as the ends. Indeed, the means *were* the ends. I didn't just want to create a great website with the students; I wanted to show how alternative, democratic ways of working within a university – ways that recognized and enabled a plurality of ways of learning and forms of intellectuality and creativity to flourish – were not just possible, but were potentially more fruitful. And, in stark contrast to the misanthropic, alienating implicit assumptions of the bureaucratized university, this project was founded squarely on faith – faith in the enthusiasm of the students for participation; faith in their intellectual and creative power; and faith in the superior power of collaborative processes of knowledge and cultural production.

Implementation

At the beginning of our work together, I presented the students with little more than a specific task (the production of a website); a broad question ('What is money?'); and a loose and fluid framework for action. The framework certainly proved to be just that, as it was adapted through an organic, unfolding process. Yet, in the first few weeks at least, the weekly sessions followed the plan I had developed.

In order to cultivate a process of genuine transdisciplinarity among a new group of scholars from diverse backgrounds, disciplinary perspectives and ideological orientations, I knew that it was necessary to begin by spending time on establishing a common language for effective dialogue. This meant building solid foundations of mutual respect and strong teamwork. A vital part of this process would be to start by bringing the scientific question we planned to explore – What is money? – back to a more primal emotional and experiential level. When we begin by listening to the personal feelings and experiences of others and by telling our own stories, we can build solid foundations of respect and bonds of affection and solidarity that are far more likely to overcome the ideological disagreements and prevent personal tensions that may emerge later than are mere good manners and tolerance. This was indeed the case.

From building strong relational foundations, we moved slowly into a more intellectual analysis of money, sharing and critiquing our personal disciplinary perspectives. I invited two deep thinkers about money – Prof. Mike Neary and Brett Scott – to lead two of the sessions. The final few sessions were devoted to designing our website.

In Week Eight, we came up with and consensually agreed upon a name for our website – 'Moneypedia'. The process by which we did so was beautifully expressive of the whole ethos of the project and the group. Although we could probably identify the individual who first called out the word 'Moneypedia', s/he would be the first to recognize that s/he would never have had that idea without the prior group discussion, during which ideas to-and-froed among us all. The idea for the name of the website, just like the ideas for the site itself, were truly co-produced by the entire group.

In the final two weeks, I began to notice the amazing degree to which I was no longer the clear leader of this project. I played my role in facilitating our activities, but the students themselves were working happily and productively under their own steam. There was an undeniably natural and playful, but serious and productive, atmosphere and energy within the group that was a joy to be part of.

We ended the project with a sense of satisfaction – that we had come up with such exciting ideas for a website called 'Moneypedia' that truly had the potential to help people develop their understanding of money and cultivate their sociological imagination – and a willingness to continue our work together the following term to bring our ideas to fruition.

Project outcomes

As I stated earlier, though the concrete objective of the project was the design of a website, there were other qualitative goals. These included cultivating transdisciplinary understandings and introducing alternative perspectives; building democratic dialogue and solidarity; facilitating intellectual and psychological development and transformation; facilitating and promoting the co-production of knowledge and culture; and, of course, cultivating our sociological imaginations. I have produced a project report, which provides evidence for these goals being met based on exit interviews with student participants. However, I will offer here three broad, characteristic endorsements of the project:

I felt that the project opened up a very creative space to express your ideas and opinions. It was a great forum for discussion that was much more open than the seminar experience at Warwick. I think this was helped by the team building and getting-to-know-each-other exercises that we did at the beginning of the project that really set the tone for the rest of the term…It was a process that was able to stimulate you intellectually as well as creatively, which is something that is missing for the general academic curriculum at Warwick…I really recommend having more projects like this, and opening more chances to students.

A fantastic experience.

This is what uni should really be like!

Unfortunately, though the design for Moneypedia remains ready to go, the site itself has not yet been built. First, the prolonged revision and examination period kicked in. Then, the long summer break arrived and momentum dissipated. Finally, most of the students then graduated and moved on and the keen and supportive member of IT staff at Warwick was just too inundated with work to get the site built. Nonetheless, at the time of writing, I am waiting for my friend, the filmmaker Ben Cook, to finish a small film using the participants' own footage. Once the film is complete, I will work with Ben to produce the website.

My experience of the ROSI Website Project has convinced me that the shift from our teaching-learning model, what Paulo Freire calls the 'banking method' of education, to the co-production of knowledge and culture can be practicable and exciting, and is also very effective. Buoyed up by these convictions, I applied to the Institute for Advanced Teaching and Learning within Warwick for funding to develop ROSI as an accredited module and to disseminate the model across the University. Unfortunately, my application was rejected.

Reflections and projections: Co-production and democratic institutionalization

In the remainder of this chapter, I will use my reflections from my ROSI and PPE experiences to focus on two key, interrelated issues that I believe are the foundations for the emerging future of democratic community education: co-production and institutionalization. By co-production, I refer to the collaborative production of knowledge and culture – the knowledge and culture that we ourselves need to understand and transform our own lives as individuals, as communities and as a society. By democratic institution-alization, I refer to the hard work we need to undertake to ensure that the temporary projects we run can grow into stable, resilient organizations and that the models we develop can flourish and be adopted and adapted across the UK and far beyond. Since the co-production of knowledge and culture raises the question of ownership, I also define democratic institutionalization as promoting co-operative organizational forms based on common ownership.

The co-production of knowledge and culture

> Political commitment, however revolutionary it may seem, functions in a counter-revolutionary way so long as the writer experiences his solidarity with the proletariat only in the mind and not as a producer (Benjamin, 1998 [1934], p.91)

Walter Benjamin, the German-Jewish philosopher of the early twentieth century, was ahead of his time. Forerunning Raymond Williams' 'cultural materialism' by decades, Benjamin recognized that culture was no mere social superstructure resting upon a totalizing economic base. Instead, he saw that the production of culture was itself a material phenomenon and that, consequently, the means and modes (ownership and practices) of cultural production had also to be democratized. This led Benjamin to hopeful, democratic analyses of his contemporary communications media – the newspaper and radio – which, tragically, fascism's rise ultimately turned into servants for totalitarianism. What we have today, however, in the internet is a communication medium pregnant, I believe, with democratic and emancipatory potential. We can assume nothing, however. Instead, we must recognize the internet as a site of crucial political struggle and consciously devise principles and practices to cultivate this emancipatory potential through the creation of websites and other online technologies that support and cultivate participatory, collaborative processes of knowledge and cultural production.

The ROSI Website Project was directly inspired by the work of Prof. Mike Neary, himself directly inspired by Benjamin. During his decade at Warwick University, Mike initiated and developed the 'Student as Producer' project, working in exciting, radical new ways alongside students, empowering them to transform themselves from passive recipients to active co-producers of knowledge and culture. Mike then ventured on to the University of Lincoln, where, as Dean of Teaching and Learning, he attempted to embed Student as Producer across the University.[2] Such a remarkably ambitious agenda achieved real successes. Yet, ultimately frustrated by the wider higher-education landscape of intensifying commodification of education, Mike decided to resign as Dean, to take a professorial post in Sociology instead, and to pursue the vision of Student as Producer through an alternative channel. In 2010, alongside other University colleagues, Mike co-founded the Social Science Centre (SCC) – an autonomous higher education not-for-profit co-operative in Lincoln that is 'organized on the basis of democratic, non-hierarchical principles, with all members having equal involvement in the life and work of the SCC'.[3] At the SCC, there are 'teacher-scholars' and 'student-scholars'. Student-scholars work through undergraduate and postgraduate courses and, though the SCC is not yet an accredited higher-education body, students are awarded the equivalent of a university degree, without, of course, a debt of £50,000!

The ROSI Website Project seeks to advance the agenda of co-production through a 'hybrid pedagogy' that combines real-world and virtual interactions. It begins with a recognition of the blurred boundaries between the 'real' and 'virtual' and of the exhilarating transformative power of networked information and knowledge, as well as the need for us to consciously design websites and applications for democratic, participatory, and dialogue-based learning.[4] In essence, the project is my initial attempt to bring the principles and philosophy of critical pedagogy (or 'popular education') to the internet. This seems to me to be an absolutely essential political move if we are to capture the political battleground of the internet for humanity from capital, patriarchy, racism, and other authoritarian forces.

This is not in any way to diminish the importance of creating real-world spaces for dialogue, learning, and the co-production of knowledge and culture. I seek only to highlight and respond to the urgent need for a conscious online strategy for radical educators.

Democratic institutionalization: space, time, money

Institutionalization has, quite understandably, seriously negative connotations. When we think of institutions, we think of bureaucracy, rigidity, stasis. We recall impersonal, dehumanizing, even humiliating memories. We feel cold, perhaps painful, feelings. Yet by institutionalization here, I mean nothing more than processes by which we can turn temporary projects into strong, resilient organizations and can ensure that the models we develop flourish and are disseminated. Institutions can be radically democratic. What these radically democratic forms look like is the question at the heart of our current experiments.

We can understand democratic institutionalization, alternatively, then, as the crystallization of combined human creative energies in particular locations of space and time. We need to emphasize that space and time are what we live and work in, but that space and time are socially constructed and relational. Consequently, capitalist space-time is what we both seek to overcome and are, of course, dramatically constrained by. Our time is taken by our need to labour to survive. Our personal and civic space is increasingly privatized for capital accumulation – rent, production, consumption. Nonetheless, 'free' time still exists, of course, particularly for those cast out and deemed unproductive or for the members of the growing 'precariat', who have to contend with 'flexible' work and/or under-employment. The ability to find convenient, safe, affordable spaces greatly depends on whether your village, town or city is situated within or beyond the scope of the UK property bubble. If you are in that bubble, such spaces are generally very hard to come by. If you are outside it, they are far more plentiful.

The third and final constraint on democratic institutionalization is the dominant theme of capitalist society, namely money. In conditions of grotesque inequality, money is becoming *the* single greatest obstacle to institutionalization. A combination of economic crisis and the state's huge cuts to funding for the arts, education and the third sector means increasing dependency – ever more hands reaching out to beg from a small, wealthy collection of philanthropic foundations, most of which are, unsurprisingly, supportive of reformist rather than radical proposals and seek to fund projects (maintain dependency) rather than support organizations and institutionalization.

One potential path beyond dependency is the kind of crowd-funding that the internet has facilitated. We can also combine crowd-funding with grants or loans from progressive donors or lenders, respectively, for mutual benefit. The promise of any crowd-funded donations being doubled by major donors attracts small supporters, while evidence of public support for an organization attracts the support of larger donors or lenders.

The combined pressures of all three factors are taking a profound toll on us all, physically, emotionally and psychologically. The toughest barrier to successfully working with oppressed and vulnerable people has been overcoming the fragility of their material situations and physical and mental health. This makes the need to support the institutionalization of organizations rather than the funding of temporary projects all the more vital. There is clearly an important role here to be played by major institutional players, particularly universities and trade unions. It is to this role that I now turn.

The role of trade unions in supporting radical education

I leave it to other contributors to this book to document the history of trade union education within trade unions and the communities they primarily represent. Instead, I will argue that, though they may be diminished, the resources that trade unions command in terms of money, space and time can make a major contribution to the cause of online and real-world community education, but trade unions will need to think and act beyond reformism.

This means thinking about ownership. That in turn means learning from and working with the co-operative movement.

Echoing a common theme throughout this book, I believe that trade union approaches to education remain far too wedded to liberal, reformist ideas of self-improvement and social mobility and emphases on the teaching of technical skills to achieve these goals. The TUC's Unionlearn, for example, seeks to 'transform workers' life chances through lifelong learning' and defines 'Informal Adult and Community Learning' as 'learning...to [help participants] pursue an interest, address a need, acquire a new skill, become healthier or learn how to support their children'.[5] The educational work 'championed' and developed by trade unions in local communities should be praised, yet the offering of courses in 'everything from computing to cake decorating' will not help steer our society away from its current terminal trajectory.

This is in no way to deny the primacy of 'literacy, numeracy, and... tackling the digital divide'. Let us not forget that Paulo Freire's first and continuing focus was on tackling illiteracy among the peasants and proletariat of Pernambuco and beyond. Yet Freire's great insight and lesson was that learning to read was not a technical skill, but a profoundly political act that, to paraphrase him, must involve not just learning to read the word, but coming to read *and to write* the world.

With reference to trade union efforts to build 'community unionism', though Andrew Mathers and Graham Taylor (2008) highlight powerful and far-reaching successes, their research also points to the dangers of 'institutional rivalries' and an 'imbalance of power and resources' between unions and community groups (p.6). Such evidence supports a belief that it will be hard for hierarchical, centralized organizations like trade unions to support non-hierarchical projects that reject a set curriculum and skills-based view of education in favour of processes aimed at empowerment and conscientization through dialogue, knowledge and culture production, as well as through local activism. Nonetheless, if influential figures within the union movement can champion this new approach, things can change.

What we are talking about is truly radical – rather than going to community groups to tell them what they need to know, the proposed process requires instead that trade unions begin by listening to what these communities have to say. As James Holland rightly emphasizes, trade unions can and should be a major force in community organization and development, 'but this will have to be gradual, respectful and take place through the individuals who are already part of the communities' (Holland, 2012). Unionlearn seems to be promoting more participatory and dialogue-based methods of teaching and learning, but the shift away from technical

125

course-based teaching and learning towards the co-production of political knowledge and cultural co-production needs to take place. Such processes could really help grassroots initiatives to emerge and flourish and '[i]f these grassroots institutions do start to gather confidence they could soon form a model that could really grow and spread' (ibid.). The rich history of radical popular education in this country and elsewhere suggests that James Holland's optimism is well founded.

As Walter Benjamin and others have indicated, the production of knowledge and culture raises central questions of ownership of its means and mode. Questions of ownership tend historically to fall beyond the more reformist outlook and agenda of trade unions, whose ideological starting point tends to accept the capital-labour social relation and, consequently, private property. Both the current information revolution and the present conditions, which I and many others believe to represent capitalism's terminal crisis, make this starting point untenable. Instead, trade unions need to learn here from their friends in the co-operative movement and make ownership a central issue. In terms of institutionalization, this means supporting groups' incorporation as appropriate forms of co-operatives. In terms of the co-production of knowledge and culture, this would mean supporting the movement for an online commons in which information (knowledge and culture) produced by trade union-supported groups would be freely available for use, development and adaptation by all other groups apart from those seeking to use that information for commercial gain.[6]

Conclusion

We face an existential crisis, which manifests itself as interconnected crises of ecology, economy, politics, society and self. Reform will not do it. Transformation is required. Transformation requires a praxis – a process of learning and action that generates the knowledge and culture that our transformation needs.

Ever since the crisis was catalysed by the global financial crisis of 2008, there has been a revival of scholar-activists across the UK and beyond experimenting with new practices of community education and development. The vast majority of this, like PPE, has been on a voluntary basis. Such endeavours are hard, almost impossible, to sustain. They take their physical, mental and emotional toll, particularly when they are undertaken on top of the already overwhelming experience of work in neoliberal educational institutions. Space, time and money are against us!

Trade unions could, in theory, play invaluable roles here. They could work alongside community education and development practitioners and use their resources to support and expand existing and new community projects. Such support could help turn fragile projects into stable organizations and experimental processes into exciting new models for adoption and adaptation. In short, such support could boost democratic institutionalization. The most exciting projects and processes being developed, in my view, go beyond mere teaching and learning towards embracing the co-production of knowledge and culture. With the emergence of next-generation co-operatives that decentralize money, production, knowledge and power, this trend will only continue, with or without trade unions. Trade unions should play a substantial role in promoting this trend. Despite evident dangers, I hope and believe that they can and I believe their contribution would be invaluable.

1 Interview with Alex Brooks, 8 December 2014.

2 See http://studentasproducer.lincoln.ac.uk/ (accessed 11 January 2017).

3 See http://socialsciencecentre.org.uk/about/ (accessed 10 January 2017).

4 See the Hybrid Pedagogy journal at http://www.digitalpedagogylab.com/hybridped/ (accessed 11 January 2017).

5 See Unionlearn, 'Adult and Community Learning', https://www.unionlearn.org.uk/ adult-community-learning (accessed 10 January 2017).

6 See Dmitri Kleiner's 'Telekommunist Manifesto' for his articulation of his 'copyfarleft' proposals. http://telekommunisten.net/the-telekommunist-manifesto/ (accessed 11 January 2017).

8

Reconnecting trade union education, politics and self-reliance

Dave Spooner

The world of trade union and workers' education is as diverse as the challenges and needs faced by the unions themselves. It includes everything from short training courses to intensive advanced courses, residential programmes and international seminars. It caters for the needs of full-time union staff in Romania, plant union representatives in Ohio, informal economy union organizers in Kathmandu, and branch secretaries in Birmingham, UK. It can be informal and unaccredited; it can provide university qualifications.

But on an international scale, trade union education in different countries faces three major common challenges: reconciling training programmes for strategic organizing with workers' education traditions of developing the curriculum democratically; responding to the new demands for political education in the new world of crisis and resistance; and coming to terms with the need for self-reliance.

The organizing agenda and workers' education

In recent decades, many trade union educators around the world have been in a dilemma regarding how to support the development of training programmes for tougher, smarter, centrally planned and more strategically focused organization, yet maintain their traditions of collective and participatory education for rank-and-file activists. Some are worried that more liberal or political trade union education is being marginalized in favour of a narrow, skills-based training agenda.

Trade union priorities have necessarily changed, affecting policy and priorities for education. The worldwide attacks on trade union rights and the associated decline in trade union membership and power over the last 20 years has forced a rethink of strategy and approach. Very few unions can now rely on the automatic delivery of trade union membership through collective agreements in major workplaces. Employers, supported by state legislation, have been on the offensive, and the workplace itself has been splintered, outsourced and mechanized: the 'hollow corporation', as some have described it (Street, 2011).

Unions have had to rethink their organizing strategies, recognizing that social and economic justice depends on the democratization of decision-making and the devolution of power to the workplace. Yet strategic organizing also requires concentrated and centralized (albeit democratically determined) decisions on priorities and resources.

Substantial numbers of unions around the world have been strongly influenced by the 'strategic organizing agenda' techniques and methods developed in the US by the Service Employees International Union (SEIU) and others. The SEIU developed a blueprint for trade union renewal: concentrated heavy investment in organizing, corporate research, strategic targeting of employers, time-limited campaigns, building sector-wide power – based on well-trained teams of organizers and activists.

This sits uncomfortably with the traditions of democratic participatory workers' education. Since the 1970s unions throughout the world have adopted educational methods rooted in 'learning from your own experience', such as student-centred learning or a 'negotiated curriculum' – influenced by the ideas of Paulo Freire, the Swedish study circle tradition, the old British TUC Education 'Red Book', and so on. These methods were focused on education as the driver of grassroots democratic union processes, culture and renewal.

Strategic organizing approaches depend on organizers and activists being trained in skills and approaches that are suitable for pre-determined priority targets, using very different training techniques, methods and language – much of which is borrowed from corporate culture. The core of this organizing methodology was adapted from community organizing ideas developed by Saul Alinsky in the 1960s (Alinsky, 1971), avowedly 'less ideological and more practical', which also became very influential in Obama's community organizing activities in Chicago. Alinsky's ideas were central to the development of SEIU organizing strategy by Andy Stern, SEIU president from 1996 to 2010 (McAlevey, 2016).

Perhaps there has always been a tension between the democratic, self-directed and participatory traditions of the workers' education movement, and the need for trade unions to provide training to achieve centrally determined strategic objectives, but in the last 10 years there have been fears that this tension has become institutionalized between union organizing departments and education departments.

New approaches – strategic organizing meets critical pedagogy?

As unions adopt a strategic organizing approach at the core of their work, the techniques, approaches and language are being adapted and reshaped to meet local or sectoral circumstances and the need for the democratic involvement of the activists at the workplace.

A key driving force is recognition that the 'classic' strategic organizing approach only works when resources are time-limited, prioritized and concentrated in certain places, sectors or companies. As Michael Crosby, the then SEIU Regional Organizing Director explained in 2003:

> When our organizing resources are so limited, we have to be honest with workers and let them know that we have a limited time – and then we must move on to the rest of their industry. That will mean that when potential members ring with a problem, we might have to say that no we can't help them organize just yet. That we have to concentrate our resources in quite another part of the industry. We will get to them later. (Crosby, 2003)

In the meantime, in what could be a very long wait, activists and shop stewards need educational opportunities to develop their own organizing strategy – without the benefit of substantial resources or teams of professional organizers. This requires learning from and adapting these strategic organizing techniques, but integrating them into a broader educational framework.

Unite the Union in the UK, for example, developed organizing courses for shop stewards in specific sectors to support the development of national and international industrial initiatives that integrate some of the strategic organizing methods with trade union traditions of critical pedagogy; in other words, practical skills in developing union power are combined with an understanding of some of the root causes, context and political analysis of the key issues facing workers.

In addition to the skills needed to map the workplace, develop workplace leaders, identify the campaign issues, build communication with members, and so on, this requires an understanding of the broader industrial, economic and corporate context – 'getting inside the head of the Corporation', as Jennie Formby, former Unite National Officer, described it:[1]

> It's absolutely essential for our stewards and activists to be fully engaged in all aspects of organizing rather than [for it to be] something done by separate Organizing Units. To do this meaningfully they have to understand why companies do what they do and how global capital operates. If we maintain an insular, reactive approach we will consistently lose. We must be better at predicting how employers are going to behave and act accordingly. It's vital to ensure that all our members, not just our stewards, are fully involved at all stages and understand the underlying motivations of transnational companies if fight-backs are going to be effective.

In the Global South, many of the traditional trade union development programmes have been replaced by training programmes for organizers – sometimes at the request of country union organizing departments within the Organization for Economic Co-operation and Development seeking to gain campaign 'leverage' over transnational employers through international solidarity action. In truth, large numbers of the education departments of unions and their respective national centres in the South and East had in effect already ceased to function in a sustained and programmatic way, having become dependent on shrinking short-term project funding from external agencies (see below).

Moreover, the numbers of workers who are in a recognizable formal relationship with an employer are in a minority in the global workforce, and even this number is shrinking. While organized labour in the 'formal economy' remains, at least for the time being, the power base and the backbone of the trade union movement, the last few years have seen a dramatic increase of interest in the need to organize precarious and informal workers. The rise of precarious work, particularly among young workers, has sounded alarm bells throughout the movement. The democratic organized voice of informal workers, precarious by definition, is becoming increasingly articulate. There is a growing realization that 'standard employment' or Decent Work is actually a relatively recent and perhaps temporary phenomenon, enjoyed by no more than a minority of workers, mostly men, even at the best of times.

Despite many challenges, trade union educators are increasingly turning their attention to programmes designed to support the organization of precarious and informal workers. The workers themselves are becoming increasingly organized – still in relatively small numbers, but growing.

New education and training approaches are being developed for work among precarious and informal workers: re-thinking the functions and operations of a union when there may be no discernible employer, constructing new models of collective bargaining, and fighting for labour-law reform to assert rights for all workers, not just those in waged employment.

Again, the response has been to develop education programmes that appropriate some of the tactics and methods of strategic organizing, but to adapt it to a very different context. Examples can be found in StreetNet International (the international network of unions and associations of street vendors and market traders) in their work training activists in collective bargaining with local governments; in home-based workers' unions and associations, or in the campaigns by the International Domestic Workers' Federation for ratification of the ILO Domestic Workers Convention.

More recently, the International Transport Workers' Federation adapted strategic organizing campaign methods when they developed new methods for the union organization of informal transport workers, and sometimes the results were spectacular.[2]

New demands for political education

There are causes for optimism: the new international agenda for strong industrial organization, evidence of increasing corporate vulnerability to well-organized and targeted campaigns, and a new generation of activists emerging from movements for democracy and climate justice.

Yet there is a political vacuum. Union members want an international political resistance to rightwing populism, and an alternative to neoliberalism and corporate capitalism, but little emerges beyond rhetoric. Many of the formal institutions of the international labour movement have retreated into a bland lowest common denominator of politics, shy of even the basic principles of social democracy, let alone any mention of democratic socialism. Trade unionists fighting to emerge from the shadow of dictatorship find their democratic labour histories and traditions destroyed and unrecorded after generations of suppression and censorship. Yet this is the time when radical political solutions are required – a new sense of political direction for the international trade union movement.

There is a growing demand for new workers' education initiatives to debate and question the politics of the international trade union movement. Programmes and events are needed to stimulate discussion on democratic socialism, radical democracy, and the political agenda of the international trade union movement, in the context of the global economy, of the general attack on the labour movement, and of financial crises and environmental destruction.

In other words, what are we organizing for?

A bit of history…

This is nothing new. From a historical perspective, the early international workers' education movement included a broad alliance of the educational institutions of socialist and social democratic parties, trade unions, co-operative societies and independent workers' education associations. By 1924 a conference was convened to establish an 'International Federation of Labour Organizations concerned with Workers' Education'. This was not agreed without considerable debate, however. The Austrian socialist party delegate proposed that the federation should be 'for the purpose of assisting workers' educational associations in the various countries and co-ordinating their activities, and the systematic awakening and strengthening of the class-consciousness of the workers of the world'. Debates on resolutions concerning the 'character of workers' education' agreed that workers' education should be under workers' control, should be considered an instrument for social emancipation, and should 'give an intelligent impetus to the demand for a new social order' (Hansome, 1931, p.43).

Today, the involvement of major socialist political parties in this movement has virtually disappeared. Trade union political education has been in decline for decades. Many of the old 'workers' educational associations' have retreated towards vocational training and leisure education. The cooperative education movement has little contact with its historical partners in the trade union movement. The more recent wave of workers' education organizations in the Global South are certainly more directly political, and many are engaged in political education work with their respective national trade union movements, but the majority struggle for financial survival.

Yet there is clearly a growing demand for political education. In 2012, for example, the Global Labour Network, based in Manchester, along with its sister organizations in Geneva, Moscow and New York, launched an annual international summer school for young trade unionists, explicitly to discuss 'What are, and what should be, the politics of the international trade union movement?'. It was an open 'safe space' for union activists from 30-35 different countries to talk politics, at a time when the relationship between unions and their 'traditional' political party allies was being stretched to breaking point throughout the world.[3]

Remarkably, these summer schools gained the support of dozens of national trade unions, along with five out of the eight major Global Union Federations. This would have been unthinkable a decade ago.

Resources – workers' education and the state

From the outset 100 years ago, there was a further internal debate in the international workers' education movement that still has resonance today, namely, whether or not workers' education organizations should seek financial support from the state. This was at a time when the growing political power of social democratic parties in some countries made grants and subsidies for workers' education possible.

Since then, the major source of finance has been (directly or indirectly) governments, particularly those committed to broad social democratic politics. In the Global North, particularly in northern Europe, this frequently meant direct financial support for workers' education associations, trade union education programmes and workers' colleges, with few conditions attached. In the immediate post-war period, state money was supporting workers' education programmes throughout Europe.

Northern government funds were also channelled to union and labour-NGO education programmes in the Global South, through national and international union federations, and specialist labour-movement or social democratic institutions such as the German-based Friedrich-Ebert-Stiftung or the American Center for International Labor Solidarity (the Solidarity Center) and its forerunners. Similar institutions were given state aid in the Nordic countries (SASK, LO-TCO, OPIC, etc.), Netherlands (FNV Mondiaal), Spain (ISCOD), Japan (JILAF) and elsewhere. While not necessarily focused on workers' education, inevitably all support programmes for the development of trade union organization and effectiveness and rely on education as the main method of delivery.

Interestingly, there have never been comparable large labour-movement grant-awarding institutions in the UK. From time to time, the TUC International Department has had access to financial support from the Foreign Office, and more recently, under the Blair government, from the Department for International Development, but the scale of funding was very small compared with what was available to the TUC's continental European counterparts, and is now practically non-existent.

Today, the most direct and practical impact of the current economic and political crises on workers' education has been the reduction of funding available – in both the Global North and South. Where funding does exist, the extent to which trade unions and workers' education organizations are free to determine their own curricula and educational methods has been considerably restricted. Resources for long-term institutional support in the development of workers' education programmes, such as there were, have by and large been replaced by short-term project funding, with increasingly strict criteria imposed by funding agencies.

With few exceptions, the budgets of the European labour-movement institutions have been cut by their respective neoliberal governments. Some institutions have closed altogether. In former decades, the European Commission was a lucrative source of support, particularly for union education in central and eastern Europe. Very little of that support now survives, and the few funds that are available are notoriously complicated to manage and administer.

Other non-labour-movement funding agencies that have supported trade union education programmes from time to time in the past have shifted position in response to the political and economic climate. Oxfam International's programme on labour rights, for example, was closed in 2010.

Where government support has continued, it has been far more conditional on specific criteria, and more tightly monitored and controlled through stringent application and reporting procedures. In some countries, the administration of project proposals and management have been contracted out to the big consultancy companies, such as PricewaterhouseCoopers – part of a larger trend towards privatization in the international development industry.

In many countries, particularly in the Global South, this has further disadvantaged trade union education departments, very few of which have the practical management skills to apply for, manage and report on funds in the format, language and detail demanded by the funding bureaucracies. The impact on workers' education organizations has been profound. With rare exceptions, long-term support for basic trade union development through broad education provision has disappeared, replaced by short-term highly targeted project activity – often with little or no contribution to core budgets.

In many northern countries, education programmes to support the work of trade union workplace representatives and provision of broader political and cultural workers' education have been eclipsed by accredited skills-based and vocational training, such as UnionLearn in the UK. In some unions, this proved to be a valuable tool in union recruitment, but there are many who fear that it was a distraction from the core purpose of union education.

Self-sufficiency?

One hundred years ago, many socialists argued that unions and workers' education organizations should not accept state finance. Maybe they had a point. Certainly, in many countries and in many unions – both North and South – there is a dependency culture in the trade union education movement that has been entrenched over decades. It is common to meet trade union education officers who explain that they are unable to provide programmes for their members, because they are 'waiting for the funding'. In some unions, 'education officer' is virtually synonymous with 'fundraiser'. Somewhere along the way we've forgotten how to run education from our own resources, meagre as they may be.

Perhaps a new sort of trade union education is emerging – rooted in the traditions of participatory learning, concentrated on building union organizing power, built around the big questions of democratic socialism in a corporate world, and based on financial self-reliance. Crucially, this would mean a renaissance of trade union education which reconnects organizing with politics.

This is adapted and updated from an article originally published in 2012 in *International Union Rights*.

1 In a personal communication to the author.
2 See www.informalworkersblog.org
3 See http://global-labour.net/summer-school/

Section Three

Implementing critical education in the classroom and beyond

Introduction to Section Three

Doug Nicholls

The chapters so far have considered macro, historical, theoretical, international and organizational issues relating to the rebirth of trade union education.

How can our lofty ideals transform the actual classroom environment or the way in which a union adapts its teaching and learning models?

The chapters in this section begin to answer this question by drawing on the actual work of skilled educators with an impressive record of achievement in their unions. These chapters will prove an especially instructive guide to trade unionists tasked with delivering learning and wanting to attend to the detail of applying new theories to the learning environment.

Nadine Rae draws on her work in the union movements in New Zealand/ Aotearoa, India, Southeast Asia, Africa, Central and South America to distil immense experience into an essential tenet that underpins the changes that must be set in motion if trade union education is to be at its very best. This sounds simple – we are all educators and we all constantly educate each other – but the implications of this for union organization are profound.

Nadine's chapter is for union organizers and activists. It therefore practises what it preaches, recognizing that learning is not just for the classroom. To be effective, all paid and unpaid organizers and activists must be better educators and must more consciously deploy the proven techniques of inclusive popular education. Developing other people, firing their imaginations, strengthening their confidence, generating ideas with them and providing guidance to them: all of these processes are deeply educational. Nadine tackles the false polarities that have developed between skills/knowledge development and personal/organizational development, between the political and the technical, and she argues successfully for a new synthesis. This new synthesis is achieved by her reassertion of basic but essential values of collectivism and solidarity as prevalent working-class mores which imbue both workplace and non-workplace organizations within our class. She gives practical examples of projects she has been involved in to make this new synthesis real. Union organizers, mentors and activists are at the cutting edge of the interactions necessary to grow and promote unions and this chapter will strike a particular chord with them.

Within the spectrum of union activity, education has generally, as we have seen, been relegated to training occurring in classrooms separate from the body of union development. Having conveyed the idea that there is education in everything, Nadine is able successfully to demonstrate that if the culture of a union is that its whole functioning is educational then people within it will constantly seek to create informal opportunities for learning in any situation.

A much-neglected terrain for learning is conversation. Trade unionists are often good talkers with a lot to say and important stories to tell. Conversations must be valued and nourished and the importance of face-to-face exchange is therefore critical to our new union learning models. Constantly asking questions is a way of constantly reinforcing the learning culture of a union – why did we do this, why did the boss do that? Trade union educators who seek to answer questions before they have been asked and who give the impression that they know the answers to all questions are not really educators.

If education is integral to organizing, which it so clearly is, and if it links to conversation and informal learning opportunities, how can it be planned? In a groundbreaking section of her chapter Nadine shows exactly how it can be and how this skill in planning is a much more onerous and valuable one than conventional lesson preparation.

The result of a plan is often a session, or what conventional language would call a class or a course. Let us call it a learning session. It is not a teaching session – the emphasis is on learning for all participants. There is no teacher and student in 'old speak'.

Carl Parker's and Martin Smith's chapter drills down into the sensitivities and nuances of applying a new educational methodology to consider the dynamics and tensions that inevitably exist within any group you work with. They ask extremely important questions which get to the heart of delivery and how to make learning sessions as exciting, useful, educational and dynamic as possible. How do you create a good discussion? How do you use a variety of learning methods? How do you manage the various expectations of learners, many of whom in the trade union context will have been alienated from the classroom at school?

Carl and Martin provide us with some options for variety in learning delivery to escape from the wretched PowerPoint or the evil flipchart. This is detailed stuff and practical suggestions are made that point us to a new curriculum method in our work. It opens a very fertile debate about how we open eyes and minds to new ways of working in the learning situation.

Reflecting further on how new education techniques can transform a national union's way of delivering learning and emboldening its members, Gawain Little and Lindsey McDowell carefully consider and reflect upon the trailblazing work they have done in the National Union of Teachers. As you would expect, this chapter locates the transformative educational work within the union to the educational context generally and how the terrifying culture of neoliberalism has grotesquely perverted public education with the ideology and organization of the hidden hand of the market. Wider educational reform has created a new educational environment and the choice for teachers has been rapprochement or resistance to the deluge of interconnected changes that have touched on the core of professionalism and the nature of the working day.

Unsurprisingly, Gawain and Lindsey reject both rapprochement with the new situation and simple resistance to it. They argue for a sense of renewal. They have revived their union's training programme to assist teachers to become more confidently active in their union and more confidently working to replace the general neoliberal onslaught. Following membership consultation, the union decided to completely overhaul its education provision. In standing up for education, teachers in the NUT developed a new education programme internally that would better enable them to stand up for themselves. A thorough, useful account of the pilot courses and curriculum to achieve these changes is given and the chapter provides excellent resource material and concepts for all unions.

The motivational examples from Unite and the NUT demonstrate that individual unions benefit greatly from a new approach to education. Sharing this new approach with many unions has been a challenge that the GFTU has faced up to in its own transformation of provision. A starting point for this was developing a youth conference into a new generation festival in its work to engage and inspire a new generation of union leaders. Galvanizing the strengths of the younger generation is not optional. Fail to do it and the movement will die. But how do you best do it? If disparate younger workers come together randomly from 25 different unions, how do you offer a relevant learning environment?

One key to success is that you involve and engage younger workers in organizing the event itself. The GFTU has enabled a group of younger workers to do this and organize an annual event. Through an interview with Sarah Woolley of the Bakers, Food and Allied Workers' Union, who has been helping to lead this work in the GFTU for the past five years, Mike Seal draws out the techniques applied to the festival and the principles behind them. This event has probably been the trade union education event most influenced by the popular-education approach and, as the chapter shows, it has an exceptionally high success rate in ensuring longer-term involvement by activists. The chapter is neither a 'how to' guide nor a blow-by-blow account of an event. Rather, it seeks to illustrate how popular-education principles are applied in an innovative way to attract long-term loyalty and commitment to unions by workers from the younger generation.

The penultimate chapter in this section may seem a strange choice within a book on trade union education, given that it is about the development of a community of learners on a Psychology course in a university. The chapter is included because it again further illustrates the applicability of popular-education theories and practice (called 'critical pedagogy' in the university context). It shows that even in the most hierarchical, formal and exam-laden learning context at a university, the authority required to skew learning into unhelpful shapes can be successfully subverted. The methods and ideas described will be useful in any adult-learning context.

The final chapter in this section touches on the rich experience of a major adult institution, Northern College, which has been committed to progressive ways of learning and progressive learning content for 40 years. Jill Westerman, the College Principal, demonstrates that the principles and practice of progressive popular education can inform a residential learning environment across a range of 'levels' of learning from short course to week-long trade union education to more sustained undergraduate programmes.

Northern is one four adult residential colleges with which the trade unions work and the cross-fertilization of learning and teaching techniques that they encourage across disciplines and student groups is a beacon within the movement. At a time when private accreditation agencies, private providers and legions of freelance 'consultants' and 'tutors' are scouring the neoliberal market, it is vital that publicly funded institutions like Northern are supported by the movement and that government funding to such valuable, publicly accountable institutions is increased. The commitment of colleges like Northern to quality face-to-face learning and to residential opportunities that enable group development forms an invaluable component of the trade union and working-class education offer.

Avoiding some of the curiously pretentious and pompously academic language that can ironically infect the dialogue about popular education, which is distinctively accessible and comprehensible, Jill's article espouses the basic advantages of this model of learning. 'Popular education,' she writes, 'isn't a prescriptive set of practices – it's a continuous moral project that enables young people to develop a social awareness of freedom.' It is this dynamic commitment to enabling group learning so as more effectively to realize freedom from ignorance, exploitation and oppression, that underpins the new learning that we need.

9

Seeing education in everything we do

Nadine Rae

Introduction

In 2010 I co-facilitated an active plenary session at the General Federation of Trade Unions' (GFTU) Union Building Conference on trade union education. My colleagues and I posed a question to the union leaders and activists present: 'Do you consider yourself to be an educator?' The results were interesting. Almost everyone at the conference considered themselves to be an educator. The work that they did, no matter in what sector or what leadership role they had, involved them educating informally, if not through non-formal classroom-based education. Most interestingly, though, very few of those present had ever thought of themselves as an educator before, or had ever identified themselves in that way, unless they had specifically held an education role.

This was a great lead-in to very engaging discussions about how as trade unionists we educate in everything we do and how important it is for organizers and activists to embrace that as part of their work and identity. As a question, it was supposed to spark conversation that led to a deeper discussion on political education in trade unions – and it did just that. It also struck me as a great example of informal union education. In this case, using conversation and questioning to provoke analysis, evoke an ideal and build further commitment to the subject at hand. While the concept that everyone is an educator could have been handed down to all, for people to really explore this and then accept it as a truth, they needed to identify it for themselves. That day, everyone present was educating each other, and my role facilitating was not to impart my expertise, but simply to help them acknowledge their own.

There is a tradition of informal education in trade union and other community movements that organize people in a collective manner. This is not always thought of as education, more as agitation, or politicization, or sometimes as propaganda. The process involved is crucial in gaining members and support from the community for workers' plight. It has always been understood that to organize workers you need to educate them on the issues at hand before you can expect them to act.

A 2007 International Labour Organization paper on the role of union education and capacity building states that union education has always been at the core of union action, with hundreds and thousands of workers taking part in formal and even more in informal education each year (International Labour Organization, 2007). In the 1800s, the Tolpuddle Martyrs met under a tree, sharing their stories, deciding together their fate and how to fight for decent wages and against oppression (tolpuddlemartyrs.org.uk/museum, 2017). Also in the 1800s, the Working Men's Clubs, originally founded by Henry Solly, provided informal opportunities for political and social-justice education through conversation, networking and leisure activities (Cherrington, 2012). The cliché of the 'soap box' became a cliché because it was a frequently used way for people to be informally educated on a topic of passion to the speaker.

In fact, the right was fought for and won by the working-class movement. In 1872 the Parks Regulation Act established the right to meet and speak freely in Hyde Park, London, where 'soapbox orators' have been speaking freely since, often at the place called 'Speaker's Corner'. Moving forward to today, the existence of large well-resourced trade unions in the UK and other developed countries has meant that the necessity of informal education as a way to grow unions and activate their members is not always acknowledged in everything a union does.

As John Fisher notes in a previous chapter, the trade union movement is often credited as being the largest independent adult education provider in the world. Whether that is proven true or not, unions certainly have the potential to reach and educate more adults than most other organizations, based on the size of union membership and the extent of their national and international networks and federations. Depending on the resources and expertise available, unions make strategic decisions about how they best provide education to their members. In many developed countries, the most recognized form of trade union education has been through structured non-formal classroom-based training (Newman M., 2007). This of course is a huge positive resource where available, in that it provides structured time and space for learning, equipping union workplace representatives and activists with the skills and knowledge they need to fulfil their roles of representing and organizing. A reliance on this form of education provision can, however, also have negative effects. It is resource intensive, both for the cost of provision and for the union member attending, who may need to dedicate a significant chunk of time to their learning that may keep them from paid work. It relies on the union member to translate their learning into their workplace context mostly by themselves and remain motivated to do so once leaving the learning environment. That is not an unusual expectation of a learner from formal education, but it can be a barrier for a union member or activist learning in their own time. Without support in translating their learning into their own context, a union member could discount their learning as not being relevant, or not know how to enact their learning into their day-to-day roles as union representatives and activists, stalling change. These negative effects can be overcome where there is support provided for the learner after the education event. That is not to say all unions who rely heavily on non-formal classroom education do not provide any support following the education event, but such a reliance has the potential to isolate a learner once they are back in their workplace.

What is the support that unions can provide for a learner after a classroom-based education event? This question is one that all unions providing such education have no doubt asked themselves at one point or another. The greatest resource available for this is the union organizer or official and other union representatives and leaders acting as mentors. These are traditionally roles that are already stretched for time and filled by busy people, so how does that work? Where a union organizer or leader is actively involved in a member's development as part of their organizing approach, this is not an additional resource that a union needs to provide for, but it does take time. To be in that position, an organizer needs to see all their interactions with a person as an opportunity to educate, effectively embedding education in everything they do.

A reliance on classroom-based education also relies on that environment being the best learning environment for trade union issues. While it always depends on the subject, sometimes a practical activity is best for learning and may require real-life experience to learn from. Recruiting a union member, for instance, might be best carried out in a workplace where an experienced union activist could demonstrate their skills and coach a new activist in the same. Equally, conversation provides educational opportunities that are often underestimated. Participating in union and community activities such as meetings, marches or rallies can lead to discussions that build awareness and analysis of our environment and context. Broadening our perspectives on where and how education can take place enables an organizer to work with the members they are developing and supporting in more flexible and meaningful ways.

I have been fortunate throughout the years I have worked for unions to have organized directly or supported campaigning and organizing in a variety of contexts globally – originally in New Zealand, then India, then working as part of a global union to support organizing in Southeast Asia,

Central and South America and in several countries in Africa. One thing that has remained true no matter the context, is that it was and is necessary to approach my organizing role with a strong education focus. I did this through a mix of classroom-based education and informal education, which might be in small groups or one to one, through a structured approach or ad hoc, casually through conversation or seizing an opportunity to use an incident or topical news to engage people. Basically, I ensured that education was part of everything I did to organize workers. This is not a new concept, of course, but an important one to revisit and refresh regularly. In writing this piece I intend to do just that, aiming to broaden our perspectives on what tools we have available to grow our unions and our movement and to overcome injustice and inequality.

This chapter is written for union organizers or activists mentoring others or considering their role in developing others, generating ideas and providing guidance. If you already consider yourself an educator and incorporate this into your day-to-day interactions with members, possibly this text will refresh your ideas or reinforce a practice you already enact. For the purpose of this chapter, there is an assumption that a union member will be supported by a union organizer, often a paid role, or another workplace representative, a voluntary elected position, who acts as a mentor. As Fordham (1993) notes, formal education is education that progresses through the state-accredited education system, such as primary, secondary and higher or further education. Non-formal education is education that may or may not be accredited to any recognized body, is independent from state education and usually classroom based. Informal education is not usually classroom-based.

In the chapter I will explore and share reflections on my practice, through the concepts outlined above, and giving examples from my personal and professional experience. I have broken down the structure of the chapter into five areas: Informal education and trade union values; The case for an organizer's or mentor's role as an educator; Informal opportunities to educate; The art of conversation; and Planning for informal education.

Informal education and trade union values
What is the aim and purpose of trade union education?
It is easy to focus on specific skills and knowledge when thinking of what a union member needs to know. Just as you need to know what your learning outcome is for an education session or workshop, or your aim for a campaign or project, we need to keep at the forefront of our minds what we are aiming to do when we are interacting with people in order to develop them. We can then identify informal opportunities to educate more readily and

better design our education courses for both the short-term and long-term needs of our unions and the movement as a whole.

In the UK context today, the Trades Union Congress (TUC) operates its education through Unionlearn and states:
'TUC Education courses are designed to achieve:
• Improvements in the performance of union reps at the workplace and in the union;
• Greater understanding of trade union policies and priorities;
• Enhanced study skills and personal confidence;
• Recognition of learning achievements through accreditation;
• Personal satisfaction and enrichment through learning.' (TUC Unionlearn, 2017b)

The General Federation of Trade Unions (GFTU) recently adopted the following principles that shape its education programme (the majority of which is currently non-formal, classroom-based training). The priorities for the GFTU are to provide in its education programme a critical analysis and understanding of context as opposed to simply providing skills and knowledge development. The GFTU aims to:
• Provide and develop an understanding of the political and economic context – political economy, labour and capital, within which Trade Unions operate;
• Provide and develop an understanding of the political and economic context which has shaped and which continues to shape the historical development of Trade Unions;
• Provide the skills and knowledge needed to develop confident and informed activists in order to build collective power;
• Be informed by our commitment to the values of equality, diversity and inclusion;
• Be informed by our commitment to social justice, empowering communities and internationalism. (GFTU, 2017)

These organizations have two different priorities in terms of their education. One focus does not negate the need for the other, indeed both organizations provide skills and knowledge training as well as political and contextual and values-based education. So what is or should be the aim of trade union education? Skills and knowledge are required to ensure workplace representatives and activists can deliver for members and their unions, whether that be through representation, advocacy and 'service' type activities, or in campaigning and organizing activities. A person capable of executing their responsibilities is what members and potential members expect of a trade union representative or leader. However, without having a grounding in trade unionism, politics and contextual issues, can a representative be fully effective in creating organization and workplace change beyond basic advocacy? How can we establish workplace democracy and broaden that to industry development if our union reps and activists remain focused solely on their day-to-day representative duties and not on building organization and union power? The answer is that we need to think more holistically about the learning and development needs of union members and incorporate informal non-classroom-based educational opportunities.

Whatever the focus of priorities of a union organizer and the union they belong to, there are potential ways to use informal methods and opportunities to educate and develop union members that will reinforce or extend learning that comes from any non-formal, classroom-based education. Informal education can be used to deliver learning outcomes that are skills- and knowledge-based, as well as outcomes that are centred on hard-to-measure concepts such as political understanding and analysis. Coombs, Prosser and Ahmed (1974) define informal education as

'the truly lifelong process whereby every individual acquires attitudes, values, skills and knowledge from daily experience and the educative influences and resources in his or her environment – from family and neighbours, from work and play, from the market place, the library and the mass media.' (p.21)

There is a dual purpose to educating a union member in these outcomes, values and union concepts: both to build their skills and knowledge and to inform and influence their attitudes and behaviours. Informal education is therefore well suited to achieving these goals. You can find many sources from within our movement that cite the values and principles of trade unionism, from the TUC and the GFTU, to individual unions both national and international. Keeping these in mind helps an organizer or workplace leader to identify education and development opportunities in their union work and in everyday situations, including values and principles such as collectivism, activism, solidarity, equality, justice. Informally, an organizer or mentor can readily explore these values and concepts with a union member as much as they can through non-formal classroom-based education. The following are some examples of union actions and activities being used for informal education within the areas of collectivism, activism and solidarity.

Collectivism
It is easy to take for granted that someone knows how to act collectively. Collectivism is one of the fundamental concepts of trade unionism, that in

acting together we are stronger than if we act alone. In an age when societies are divided and individualism is promoted, people are not used to acting together for collective gain, especially in the workplace. Looking for opportunities to teach people how to be collective – or, more importantly, how it feels to fight issues together rather than be alone – is important.

* In one New Zealand workplace that was looking to break the fear factor of joining the union, a small group of active members realized that they needed to make people feel a part of something, so that they would be motivated to join and to be prepared to fight for a collective employment agreement. They decided they would cover the staff areas of their workplace with approximately 1,000 A4 posters of union slogans and images that they designed themselves. The effect was stark; people had a sense that the union was active, visible and involved large numbers of people. Over the next few weeks the union grew its membership by over 100 members.

* In India, where unions are often based in a particular workplace or locality, security workers across four cities united in their efforts to address inequality in a dominant global security company. Determined to address significant issues faced by workers in the fast-growing private-security industry, union leaders had come together despite geographical and political barriers, to organize workers and improve the industry. They decided a meeting with the Central Labour Minister should be held. While this was politically possible to arrange, the union leaders identified the necessity to educate workers about the union campaign to build union membership and grassroots support. An activity involving existing and potential union members was devised with education in mind. A set of principles was developed and printed on a postcard addressed to the Minister. The postcards were distributed, discussed and signed by security workers and collected in a systematic approach over a four-week period. Over 10,000 cards were distributed, of which 9,000 were returned signed by individuals and were hand delivered to the Central Labour Minister to emphasize the collective support for the campaign.

Activism

Motivation to act is critical for demonstrating union power. Without active members, there are no organized workplaces. While convincing a union member to be active as a workplace representative can be hard, convincing them to lead collective action in some way can be harder. Informal learning and education can help encourage leadership. In the example below, a collective experience was used to encourage ongoing activism and leadership.

Having participated in a successful union campaign to win the first collective employment agreement in a New Zealand casino, two young women activists decided the next issue they wanted to tackle was making their casino smoke-free. As the bill to ban smoking in the hospitality industry, including casinos, was being scrutinized through the parliamentary select committee process, these two women took to the streets. Their aim was to get as many signatures as possible on a petition from workers and the general public, appealing for the major casino and hospitality leader to become smoke-free. Having experienced success first hand from the collective-agreement campaign, they knew the power of collective action and the power of engaging with the public. The result was that the casino agreed in collective bargaining voluntarily to adopt a smoke-free policy and to amend its position in the select committee hearings to one of supporting all workplaces to be smoke-free, impacting not just the casino workers but the entire industry.

Solidarity

Solidarity Forever is an anthem for unionists throughout the world. '…Yet what force on earth is weaker than the feeble strength of one, but the union makes us strong…'   Ralph Chaplin, 1915

Using chants and songs that describe solidarity, unity and collectivism is another way to informally educate people about our union past, and about the values that remain relevant today. The concept of 'Practical Solidarity' was a concept often discussed in my time working with one global union.

In the security workers' campaign in India, co-ordinated days of action were part of the strategy, designed for workers to experience solidarity and for the employer to witness it. Each union held demonstrations in each city on the same day. Trade unionists from Sweden and the US who were supporting the campaign came to India and participated in the action in several locations. These co-ordinated actions signalled a united effort to and gained leverage over the employer, which had not seen this level of co-operation or collective action before. Nor had the workers and union members previously experienced this level of solidarity and unity. As a result, company management agreed to meet with the union leaders as a collective group to address their members' concerns. This action was replicated at a global level for many years, on union-led International Justice Day, 15 June.

In the examples I have shared, most of the informal education was done in the form of practical experience and learning through debriefing, analysing and discussing these experiences one to one. What helped me as an organizer was ensuring there was conscious action made on the part of the members I was developing. Planning the campaigns, activities and actions of each activist meant they were ready to analyse their experiences. Not everything can be planned, so I was also watching and waiting for opportunities to arise where I could emphasize a point of learning through unexpected events or outcomes of their organizing.

Establishing organizing committees for workplaces, as I did in the casino campaign, or geographical areas as was done with security workers in India, enabled a collective forum for members to learn together from their experiences, without it being a classroom learning environment. Even experiencing collective decision-making through the committees reinforced learning about solidarity, democracy, collectivism and commitment to these values. These concepts can be hard to teach in a classroom, but the process of organizing provides the perfect platform to learn through doing, making my role of organizer one of guidance.

I created exposure to experiences and drew out the learning acquired through these experiences from individuals in conversations, debrief situations, etc. as described above. In all of these cases I also ensured that activists had the opportunity to participate in non-formal classroom-based education, which was also valuable. But I was able to ensure that learning in the classroom was reinforced through practical activity and that classroom learning was informed and shaped by that activity as well, especially when it came to basic trade union values and principles.

The case for an organizer's or mentor's role as an educator

Any organizer who is following the model of 'Educate – Agitate – Organize' or the organizing cycle of 'Issues-Organization-Education-Action' will already know that education is a key component of successful organizing. In these models, 'education' on the issue at hand or the bosses' agenda can be enough to get them to join the union or take part in a collective action. Education primarily takes the form of one-to-one conversations, as well as union leaflets and forms of communication such as social media and many other ways. To think separately of an education approach from these models of organizing and from the ongoing development of an activist doesn't make sense, yet, as expressed in the opening paragraph of this chapter, many union leaders do not identify themselves as being educators. However, as these models suggest, education is a way of generating organizing. When an organizer understands this not just in relation to getting a good turnout at an action, but in relation to their development of activists, the benefits of informal education become undeniable.

Where a union has an education officer or department, or utilizes centralized education in some way, often a union member's development is primarily channelled through this department and through classroom-based education courses. It can mean that the people the member comes into contact with the most are not a part of their education or development in a considered fashion. If this is the case and the interactions a member has with their organizer or other mentors are not considered with their development needs in mind, then the majority of opportunities to empower, politicize, develop understanding and commit to growing their union are potentially lost. When an organizer or mentor takes their development needs into account throughout all their interactions, a member will then find their primary development coming from the person with whom they have the most contact. Classroom-based education then boosts their development and supports all their learning.

These additional educational opportunities can be both planned and unplanned. They can be scheduled as an education session would normally be planned, or there may be a simple desired outcome identified for a conversation and a strategy as to how to get the conversation to that point. Where they are unplanned, an organizer or mentor must be able to recognize the opportunity when it arises and assess how to engage or educate appropriately given the circumstances. The learner may not be aware that this is an education opportunity in the sense of something transparently presented to them by their organizer or mentor. Indeed, the organizer or mentor may not be open about their intent to explore an idea or concept or to use a shared experience as an educational opportunity. This can be beneficial when you want interaction to be more casual. Deciding whether an education opportunity should be transparent or not would come down to the strategic choices of the organizer or mentor and their 'craft' of organizing.

Whether planned or unplanned, transparent or not, the opportunity an organizer or mentor has to develop a union member is far greater than that of a tutor or facilitator who has limited time with that member, even if that time is concentrated. Given the considerations of how informal education opportunities can be identified and utilized, an organizer or mentor who is supporting a union activist in their role is best placed to have an overview of their needs, as they are interacting with them more regularly than others involved in their development. It also follows that an organizer or mentor will be in the best position to act on the informal education opportunities that present themselves through their day-to-day support work. The relationship between organizer/mentor and union member/learner is therefore crucial to understanding a person's development needs and maximizing opportunities to educate. From the learner's perspective, having a person regularly share their knowledge and skills or shape the learner's own is valuable support.

A study of activism conducted in Australia in 2002 concluded that what determined whether someone's activism increased following an education course was whether or not the member had contact with their organizer within three months of completing the course.

'...Changed commitment was strongly and positively related to the existence of post-training contact with an organizer...Changes in commitment were also positively related to the frequency of post-training contact with an organizer. As we would expect then, contact was also linked to involvement and effort.' (Peetz, Webb and Jones, 2003, p.32)

The study had strong conclusions about the benefit of trade union education in increasing an activist's confidence, and contact with their organizer was part of building that confidence. Through my years of supporting and developing union activists and organizers I have observed this to be true. I have also found that being able to develop someone directly was dependent on the relationship I had built with them, with credibility and trust being the two most important factors. It is also true that repetition and reinforcement of ideas are more often than not required to embed new learning and transform learning into practice.

One union workplace representative I supported as an organizer had been through many training sessions with me on one-to-one communication techniques. I invited her to attend a community workshop where I was going to model the use of a common technique, 'Anger Hope Action'. Knowing she had been exposed to this technique many times, I felt she would be able to share with the other participants how she used the technique effectively in the workplace, which I had observed her doing. This was an opportunity to get her to display a skill she had learned and to pass this skill on to others. Afterwards, she told me she had done that session about 10 or 11 times, yet she had only recently fully understood how to use the technique effectively in conversations. Without that repetition, she might not have been as effective as she was in recruiting members and motivating them to act collectively. Without the relationship I had built with her and the knowledge of what she had learned and how she had used it, I might have wrongly assumed she had a skills set that she did not possess.

As her organizer, I was able to reinforce her learning and provide opportunities for repetition of the communication skill. I could do that as her development was at the forefront of my organizing work with her. The outcome of what we were trying to achieve was always balanced with the opportunity to positively affect her skills, knowledge, attitudes and behaviours. Combining the informal opportunities with classroom-based education, I could plan for her development as well as utilize informal unplanned opportunities to reinforce learning, concepts and ideas.

Informal opportunities to educate

Educating through everything we do requires identifying opportunities to educate through the course of an activist's everyday experiences and the regular contact an organizer or mentor would have with them. It may require creating opportunities, such as debriefing an activity, or attending a march with them. It requires thinking more broadly about how a person can be introduced to ideas, concepts and values and how they can explore them. These opportunities to informally educate can either be opportunistic, following events that are random or out of your control, or planned, whereby you have mapped out specific learning outcomes and decided what (informal) route you will take to meet those outcomes. In reality it is likely that a conscious effort to develop someone will involve both planned and unplanned informal education opportunities. What follows are a range of informal education methods and opportunities.

One-to-one meetings

A basic tool of organizers, meeting one to one with a member and potential activist allows you to build a relationship with that person, understand their situation and motivations, and assess their development needs. One-to-one meetings should be planned by the organizer or mentor, with a specific outcome, even if there is only one outcome sought. Such meetings are the cornerstone for community organizing, drawing on people's experience and narrative to build a relationship that will influence the person's actions. One-to-ones can be an excellent education opportunity in several ways:

- Introducing a new piece of knowledge or skill and exploring that with the activist, such as mapping their workplace, recruitment and campaign messages, etc.
- Debriefing and analysing a critical incident, event, a campaign success, even a conversation the activist had with a potential member. Use the resulting discussion to identify and highlight any learning to come from the event in question. This learning opportunity may be approached transparently by the organizer, or it may be approached casually, as if stemming from an unanticipated conversation.
- Planning a campaign, action or event, learning through the process about campaigning, organizing, planning, etc.

- Building your relationship, learning about one another, understanding what motivates the activist to be active in the union.

Modular learning

Usually done in a one-to-one session, or with a small group, 'modules' in this context are short pre-planned education sessions conducted with the activist. They would be conducted overtly and transparently by the organizer or mentor. A module may have supporting written materials and resources, or an online component. This form of informal education provides structure to the learning experience.

Stories, experiences, personal narrative

Hearing a person's story of struggle can be very powerful. The media knows this, which is why they seek stories to share from people directly involved. During a campaign, educating members and the public as to what the issues are can be done in a variety of ways, but hearing someone's story can take something from the abstract into reality. We can use personal stories to build solidarity and support, and to explain circumstances such as injustice.

Rallies, marches, protests

Rallies, marches and protests allow for education to occur informally in several ways, including educating around the issue at the centre of the protest or action, the process of conducting the protest or action and the experience of acting collectively and what can be learned from that. For this type of informal education, a debriefing session or conversation after the event is useful to draw out what the activist has learned and link this learning to what they can do in the future. An organizer can also use the debrief or conversation to bring to the activist's attention anything they didn't immediately think of or comprehend. Without a debriefing process of some sort, learning is left to chance, as with other life experiences. This is not necessarily a bad thing, but the opportunity to shape and guide learning exists through the debriefing process.

Topical news

Using current news events to spark discussions and create an education opportunity can be a great way to educate without needing to be transparent. Raising the issue in conversation and asking questions about how it relates to the activist is one way to do this. This can also be done transparently by adding the topic to the agenda of a branch or organizing committee meeting. Examples of topics that could be used are: racism in the aftermath of 'Brexit'; another union's campaign that is widely reported in the media;

local or general elections; budget announcements; or a storyline in a popular television programme.

Arts and cultural experiences

Using the medium of the arts can be a great way of exploring concepts and seeing how change can happen. Examples include theatre/street theatre, music, songs and chants, films, books, etc. Use of pictures, cartoons and interpretation of art can also be effective in exploring concepts, especially if there are language or learning barriers. Comedy and satire are also excellent ways of raising political issues and educating members (and the public) in an engaging, enjoyable way. The GFTU has incorporated the work of the Banner Theatre Company into its New Reps Course, to explore the role of a workplace rep in fighting injustice, not just negotiating better terms and conditions.

Historical places, events

Visiting places of historical importance to the union movement or reflections on historical events can be used to discuss organization, the importance of protest, solidarity, historical wins of workers' rights, injustice, etc. Ultimately these experiences can reinforce the purpose of trade unionism, struggle and solidarity, grounding an activist in their understanding and commitment to trade unionism. It is also a good way to highlight issues that exist and recur over time, such as the fight for reasonable working hours, safer workplaces, job security, decent work and living wages. The Tolpuddle Martyrs Festival – held every year in the town of Tolpuddle, Dorset, in the UK – does just that, incorporating learning from the history of the Tolpuddle Martyrs into a festival that highlights today's issues.

Coming up with ideas for informal education can actually be less difficult than incorporating some of these ideas into your organizing. Convincing members and leaders of unions to put resources into street theatre, for instance, can be an uphill struggle if it is not within the 'norm'. Deciding to incorporate union history in education programmes can mean deprioritizing other learning which may be seen in the short term as more important. These barriers are real, but if education is incorporated into everything we do, then an organizer or mentor can build experiences into a longer-term development plan that will have flexibility across classroom-based education and informal learning opportunities leading to a well-trained union representative who can make decisions and take actions grounded in union values and principles. Utilizing informal opportunities such as those outlined above can help create a new 'norm'. Planning for these opportunities is discussed later in this chapter.

The art of conversation

Often activists and organizers are taught that they need to listen twice as much as they talk ('You have two ears and only one mouth!'). Open questions are used to create that balance, opening up the person you are talking to so they are talking more than you. This is a simple skill but one that is often not applied unless it is done consciously. As organizers and union activists we need to be able to start and hold conversations with people we have never met and then influence them, so questioning as a skill is absolutely essential, though often undervalued. When mastered, it becomes more of an art, powerful for any conversation in any situation.

A personal example of the power of questions is highlighted in a story once shared with me and a group of educators in New Zealand/Aotearoa. Our colleague said that he taught a group of members about open questions in a course one day. The next day, when reviewing what they had learned the day before, a member became very emotional. He said he had gone home the night before and for the first time ever he felt he had a real conversation with his child, because he had learned how to ask questions. Professionally, in my own experience, working globally with unions in many contexts, I needed to gather information, analyse unfamiliar contexts and build relationships quickly. I found my training and experience in the use of questions helped me to do this. In short, using questions is a life skill that, when used effectively, helps us to engage with other people. As activists and union organizers we need to be able to engage with people we have never met before and to do so comfortably.

Questions have a much more powerful role to play, however. Our conversations can be used not simply to gather information, or even to build rapport, but they can be used to change opinion and motivate someone to act. Very early on in my work as a union organizer I was introduced to Socratic questioning, a skill that proved to be essential in my role as organizer and educator. Socratic questioning is a method of using questions to explore and challenge ideas, with the potential to change a person's understanding of a subject. It is often used by educators as well as therapists and psychologists. Using Socratic questioning requires some practice, balancing the nuances of what we are trying to achieve in a conversation or learning discussion and ensuring we are actually educating effectively. In organizing it provides a way of getting a potential member or activist to come up with their own analysis of their situation and conclusion as to what needs to be done. Thus, it is a tool for informal education through conversation.

Socratic questioning is useful in terms of building motivation or commitment to a course of action, such as joining the union. If a person concludes themselves that joining the union is what they need to do to change their situation, then they are more likely to join, as it is their own idea or conclusion motivating them to do so. By posing a series of questions designed to get a person critically thinking about their situation, perhaps in a way they had not thought of before, it is possible to challenge their previous assumptions as to what a union is, or have them think about why their employer is acting negatively towards the union and how acting collectively could change their workplace. Using Socratic questioning also enables an organizer or leader to do some good old-fashioned agitation. The right questions can help tap into a person's emotions, be it anger, frustration, excitement, or their sense of justice or loyalty. The stronger the emotion, the more likely a person will be motivated to act.

These are examples of Socratic questions within a union environment:

Why do you think your boss has done this?
Is that fair?
What do you think of that?
How does it make you feel?

These questions individually are designed to evoke thought and emotion. Used together, they can help deepen a resolve to act – so long as you propose a positive way to channel the anger or feeling of injustice you evoke.

Teaching the use of questions can be more difficult than it seems. In my years of experience educating union organizers and activists on questioning and other communication skills, I have found there are a couple of common barriers to using questions to organize, educate and activate. First, most people think questions are about getting answers; therefore they only ask a question if there is something they need to know. This is problematic when a person is recruiting, because they will not explore how a person is feeling or what they think needs to happen. Often, when asking Socratic questions, we already know what the answer is and are simply encouraging someone else to analyse the situation. Second, most people know intellectually what an open (and closed) question is, but often they are unaware of their over-use of closed questions. People are frequently unaware of their ratio of talking to listening and rarely use questions once they think they have an answer on hand. Therefore, while they may realize they are not as successful in recruitment as they need to be, without analysing their own skills and application of skills they will often come to the conclusion that the problem is not theirs, but the context, or the potential member is anti-union, or people are too scared, or 'the union' needs to do something before people will join. Even when presented with the idea of using questions, unless they realize they are not using questions as they could or should, they won't apply any change to their methods of face-to-face communication. Practice is the only effective method I have found to bring people's attention to their own use of questions – or the lack of them.

At a recent training course I ran on recruitment communication skills, I had the group do a simple exercise to demonstrate the use of Socratic questioning in their organizing. I started by asking them whether they had ever shared an idea in a meeting that was not acknowledged or taken seriously, but that someone else in the group had then raised enthusiastically. Most people related well to that experience. While I have experienced this to be frustrating and in some cases downright rude, I have also noted that the commitment to the idea is greater when it comes from the person themselves. It is something that can be used to our advantage. Following our group discussion of this phenomenon, I then introduced Socratic questioning as a way of helping someone reach their own conclusions, so they will be more enthusiastic and committed to joining the union.

Exercise:
1 In pairs, come up with one compelling reason why a person should join the union in your workplace right now.
2 Come up with a series of open questions that could help someone reach that conclusion themselves.

The group responded with the following examples:

Issue 1: a member had their request for flexible working turned down by their employer.
Compelling reason to join: 'You should join the union so you can fight for family-friendly policies'.
Questions:
• How do your current work arrangements fit in with your family life?
• How often do you get to see your kids?
• Is there anything you have missed out on (with your family)?
• If you appeal, how do you feel about conducting the appeal by yourself?
• How do you think we can make the company change their approach to be more family friendly?

Issue 2: job security, company restructuring and job losses
Compelling reason to join: You should join now to have a say because our employer is reducing staff.
Questions:
• What do you think of the plans for your area?
• Do you have any concerns? What are your worries? How anxious are you?
• How do you think you can influence what is happening?

The group then used this skill when practising recruitment through role-play. Through using the questions, they found that they could then engage with people more readily on collective solutions, joining the union, attending a meeting, bringing a friend. It also increased the amount of listening they did as opposed to talking.

This method of questioning, as the name suggests, is not a new idea! Named after Socrates, the Greek philosopher born in 470 BCE, the 'Socratic method' was recorded through the writings of his students, Plato and Xenophon, who wrote dialogues of conversation between Socrates and other people, using Socratic questioning to help explore and enlighten these people on moral and ethical issues (Taylor, 1994). As a tool of organizing, this provides us with a way to engage with people on issues, rather than challenging them directly or slipping into a mode of telling people what they should do. Through questions, we can draw out what a person knows and does not know, and even help them to challenge what they thought they knew. It can also aid the questioner, in our context an organizer or mentor, by deepening their understanding of a person's experience and perspective. To achieve that understanding, we must not see the process as simply talking to a script – we still need to use our listening skills and keep our minds open. If this is done too obviously, people can switch off from the learning experience, especially if they feel you as a facilitator are seeking a definite right and wrong answer. Having said that, we must not forget that trade union education is not neutral – we want people to believe in our values and principles, and to act from a belief that joining the union is the best way to create change and build power for workers.

Planning for informal education

Developing the skills and knowledge of a workplace representative or active member can be done in many ways. The first and most obvious way to approach this is through the union's education programme, utilizing courses that will cover the learning needs according to their role, activities or commitments. The learning and development required to build a stronger active union with sustainable organizing activity comes from a broad range of learning needs and can require opportunities in addition to those offered by an individual union's traditional programme. Including more informal development can be one way of continually educating through the activities and experiences of a union member, representative and activist. Once you have identified a potential active member and/or representative, starting them on that journey as soon as possible will ensure their commitment is maintained and increased. The first step is to assess their learning and development needs.

Learning needs could be assessed with consideration of the following categories:
- Perceived needs of learner;
- Organizational needs;
- Skills gaps, knowledge gaps of learner;
- Movement education.

In combination, learning from these categories will develop an activist with skills and knowledge to organize, recruit, campaign for change and represent members in their day-to-day issues.

Categories of needs	Description and factors
Perceived needs of the learner	This is what the learner thinks they need to fulfil their role as a representative or achieve their desired aims of participation within the union. It does not always include the other categories of needs, as a new activist may not have a comprehensive understanding of what skills and knowledge will assist them. In other words, they don't know what they don't know.
Organizational needs	The pool of skills, knowledge and behaviours required of representatives and active members to successfully implement the union's vision and strategic plan. This may have less focus on the day-to-day skills required for workplace representation and more to do with recruitment and organizing.
Skills gaps, knowledge gaps of the learner	The skills and knowledge (including but not exclusively for specific roles) that the learner *does not* have, that would arm representatives and active members with the tools to effectively represent members and challenge injustice in the workplace and wider community. Any learning they have already achieved would need to be assessed.
Movement education	Education that aims to provide a political grounding, historical understanding and analysis of the current context in which we are organizing. This develops free thinkers, critical thinkers, change agents, positive collective behaviours and activism, as well as leadership in the workplace and community. It aids a member's participation in the democracy of their union, the wider union movement and their community.
Other	Needs are fluid and changing, depending on the current context, the learner(s) involved, resources, priorities, etc.

It would be helpful for an organizer or mentor if the skills, knowledge and desired attitudes and behaviours of a workplace representative or active member are outlined and agreed by the organization, encompassing the categories above and any others that are required to deliver the union's vision and strategic plan. In the absence of this, learning needs can be derived from:

- Role descriptions of a workplace representative or activist;
- The union's strategic plan, vision or operational plans;
- Plans for campaigning, organizing or particular projects;
- Knowledge of workplace issues that need to be addressed;
- An understanding of the union's own education programme, what that provides and what it does not provide;
- Knowledge of the materials and resources available for workplace activists and representatives;
- An understanding of the opportunities and challenges arising in the day-to-day work of the workplace representative or activist;
- Knowledge of the legal framework that applies to the context of organizing;
- An analysis of the political and social context in which the union is organizing;
- An understanding of the individual's current skills set, strengths, areas for improvement and limitations at any given time.

Once the learning needs are identified, the process of prioritizing a person's learning needs is required and the opportunities to meet those needs will form their development plan. There will inevitably be a need to identify what must be achieved in the short term and long term and thought put into what needs to be introduced and when. For instance, just because there is a longer-term need to have someone learn about the history of the union movement, it does not mean there is not a need to prioritize some of that learning in the short term. These are strategic choices that the organizer or mentor and in some cases the union organization, will need to decide. The learner will also dictate what is possible by making choices on their own perceived needs, which is not to say those are not real needs. If the union member does not agree on the priorities, their organizer or mentor will need to influence them. Including informal education from the start of their journey as a workplace representative or activist will help broaden their perspective on what their learning needs are.

Templates are a good way to ensure an organizer or mentor is being consistent and thorough in their approach to developing workplace reps and activists. Some unions will have these designed already but, if not, it is a simple process to design one that will fit your specific organizing needs.

Below are two templates and examples that can be used and adapted to aid the education planning process.

A simple template for a development plan:
PAGE ONE – DEVELOPMENT PLAN

Name:	Contact details:
Role:	Organizer/mentor:
Date of plan:	Timeframe of development plan: 3 months / 6 months / 1 year

Area of learning: Learning outcomes required in each area	Confidence/ Strengths: 1 (low) – 5 (high)	Education method: One to one, programme, practical activity, etc	Timeframe for learning (1 month /1 year / 1 year+)
Learner-identified needs:			
Organizational needs:			
Skills/knowledge gaps:			
Movement education:			
Other:			

PAGE TWO – DEVELOPMENT PLAN

Education programmes:

Programme	Date	Learning Outcomes/Content

One-to-one sessions:

Topic/Module	Date	Learning Outcomes/Content

Other learning opportunities (including practical activities):

Learning opportunity	Date	Learning Outcome/Content

Longer-term learning needs:

Support:

A development plan helps map out what needs to be learned and when. To maximize the opportunities for learning, an organizer or mentor will need to plan for the informal education to occur and how that is brought about, determining the method or strategy for each learning need. When designing a training session, best practice dictates that you need to know what the intended learning outcomes are. The content of the session will then be based around this.

Even in an informal education context, some of the content can be explicit and planned. There may be a topic you want to engage someone on as part of their structured development and you may choose to do that informally. There may be an event or topical issue you want to use as an opportunity to engage with someone so as to achieve particular learning outcomes. The adage 'failing to plan is planning to fail' still applies to informal education, for the situations that you can plan in advance.

Consideration needs to be given to the method of delivery according to the learning outcomes:

- What does the education programme provide?
- What is the best way to teach/reach this outcome? Practical activity? Theoretical discussion?
- Are there experiences that will help the learner understand the concept, such as a union action? Event? Election? How will we debrief these?
- How will their learning be best demonstrated and measured?
- Transparent or not? Will this be through conversation? Through modular learning?
- What questions can I ask that will help the learner explore this concept?
- What are my opportunities to engage with this learner over the period of time?
- How does the learner best learn? Do they have a particular learning style or approach that suits their needs? Do they have any barriers or challenges to learning?
- Who else can support/mentor this learner?

Taking in those considerations, informal education can be planned and incorporated into the contact between the organizer or mentor and the workplace representative or activist.

Preparing for a specific learning opportunity can be extensive or basic, depending on the method. If the learning needs of a workplace representative or activist are defined, modules, session plans and other educator's aids can be prepared in advance and used time and time again. With informal education, the more familiar an organizer or mentor is with their method of delivery and the variety of ways in which they can engage on a subject, the more casual the learning experience may feel to the learner, which puts them at ease and also helps the organizer get the most out of short amounts of time. In my experience of organizing, the momentum of a campaign or even the pressured workload of day-to-day organizing can mean there is little preparation time available for one-to-one or small group meetings. Keeping the aims of that contact simple and focused and using familiar materials and methods will help to reduce preparation time. Whether the union has its own materials or not, an organizer can build their own standard set of one-to-one learning plans, modules or short learning conversations to achieve this. These can be planned very simply, identifying what the organizer needs to do and what the activist will do.

Here is an example of a simple one-to-one learning plan for an organizing outcome:

Task/skill Learning outcome	Activist to do	Organizer to do (with the activist)	Resources
Analysing Issues	Brainstorm current workplace issues	Clarify the issues with the activist	
	2. Identify which are – widely felt – deeply felt – winnable (or partially winnable) using issues checklist	Discuss the organizing potential of each issue using checklist. Question the activist's reasoning; use open questions.	Analysing issues checklist List of questions to ask the activist
	Identify one issue to act on	Help select small 'win'/ issue to build activity	
		Brainstorm an activity for members to be active on this issue (survey, leaflet, petition, etc)	

The approach in this example is that the organizer does things alongside the workplace rep or activist. In particular, something that could be given simply as a task, identifying an issue to organize around, is instead done with the activist, ensuring that learning happens and that there is also a practical outcome for organizing. Some organizers mistake successful organizing for simply shifting tasks on to an activist. An organizer who also considers themselves an educator will be part of their activist's learning experience and will be able to judge when to lead and educate and when to step back. This will change as the activist shifts their comfort zone and increases their knowledge and experience. The organizer's approach therefore will be more like waves, with peaks and troughs of control and leadership, as opposed to a gradual decline of control.

So far I have covered planning for informal learning through one-to-one structured development, but what about learning for the more experience-based opportunities mentioned earlier, such as arts and culture, topical issues or personal stories? How can these be planned as learning experiences? The more we can do without a script or agenda, the more natural the experience and more engaging we can be. Incorporating a variety of learning experiences, which these types of informal education allow, taps into different learning styles and can be fun. Many of these opportunities can be planned through campaign activities that will help educate but also achieve campaign outcomes. The more creative our thinking in terms of campaigning and organizing, the more opportunities we can create for learning.

There are numerous examples:

- The GFTU piloted a New Reps Course in 2016, which opened with a Banner Theatre piece. Also in the course was a visit to the People's History Museum in Manchester, showcasing for the new workplace representatives examples of achievement through collective struggle, highlighting the role of the representative in agitating and building power through collective action.

- To help educate employers on the benefits of employin someone who is neurodiverse (conditions include dyslexia, dyspraxia, autism and ADHD) the Transport Salaried Staffs' Association (TSSA) developed a poster campaign sharing the experience of a member who has Autism Spectrum Disorder. Often seen only as a disability, and indeed as a disability that is difficult to manage, this campaign highlighted the benefits the person brought to the team, in particular how their attention to detail was an important part of their role on the railways.

- As part of a security campaign, part of the global strategy was to engage shareholders in the attempt to pressurize the company into signing a global agreement securing collective bargaining rights for all their workers. Personal stories were used to highlight the situation of workers in various countries. This was a successful strategy to put pressure on the company, but also encouraged solidarity among workers all over the world. Through educating workers in Sweden on the conditions of workers in India, for instance, unions committed to taking collective action together to support one another and further pressurize the company. The campaign was eventually successful and has led to significant improvements in terms and conditions for security workers in some countries.

- In 2013 I developed a theme for the TSSA's campaign for public ownership of rail, 'The Year of Horror'. As part of the activities, we had a 'Ghost

Train' banner made that could be taken to our actions at rail stations, highlighting the negative impact of privatization on the railways. A fun 'gimmick' for sure, but it was intended to help attract local press to the issue of station staff cuts and ticket-office closures. While parts of the union remained sceptical about the overall creative theme (resulting in some learning of my own!) the Ghost Train was a great success in getting local press coverage, including TV, newspapers and online journals, always with a photo. Local community groups and Labour MPs were also keen to be part of the actions. Members learned about gaining local press, working with community groups and MPs – and had a bit of fun along the way.

Maximizing learning opportunities requires planning. However, that planning can be done at an individual level, at workplace or branch level, at staff team level, or at an organizational level. If done at all levels, then we are also maximizing the wider resources of the union for the purposes of education and development.

In my role as Organizing Director for the Transport Salaried Staffs' Association (TSSA) responsible for education, in 2017 I launched a Practical Programme as part of the union's formal education framework. Members who sign up to the programme have a three- to six-month plan of activities they will undertake to apply their learning from previous courses, or to develop skills they need through practical activity, such as recruitment skills. They will be mentored through this by an organizer or fellow workplace representative who has the skills, knowledge and experience to support them. This programme is specifically designed to provide for informal education through pre-planned union activity that also reinforces the idea that education is not simply an event, or classroom-based, but a process that includes the application of their learning on the job. For our organizers, this could be a burden, if they only organize separate individual events for each person or if they don't incorporate education into their organizing. To alleviate this resource issue, activities already planned by organizing staff teams are used as the practical activities. This includes everything from recruitment drives to supporting strikes, from lunchtime education sessions to collective bargaining or disciplinary meetings, depending on the learning needs of the workplace representative involved.

If following the cycle of Issues-Organization-Education-Action, then informal education would be included in the course of organizing around a particular issue. This includes face-to-face workplace surveys, distributing leaflets, sharing stories of how issues affect members, etc. These would be educational opportunities for activists and members alike. Where organizing teams combine their activities with learning opportunities, organizers are able to collectively meet the development needs of individuals across the work in multiple companies, meaning activists could be asked as part of the programme to help recruit in workplaces and companies other than their own. This in itself provides an opportunity to educate members on the connection with other workers in their industry and the importance of building the collective power of the union as a whole. The Practical Programme is still at the pilot stage, but I have high hopes for how it will help develop learning opportunities for our members, as well as embed education into everything we do as a union.

Conclusion

Education is an integral part of organizing and can be included in everything we do as trade unionists. Having a broad approach to the development of workplace representatives and activists through both non-formal class-room-based education and informal education opportunities will allow for the holistic development of skills and knowledge-based education as well as values and principles of unionism. Both are important to the future of the trade union movement if we are to build power in workplaces and industries.

The role of the organizer or mentor is vital in identifying and creating informal opportunities to educate and in helping to guide the thinking and learning from those experiences. Being familiar with a variety of informal methods will ensure an organizer or mentor is able to utilize each opportunity as it arises. Our skills in questioning and influencing through conversations will enable the learning process even further – reclaiming the age-old art of organizing through agitation. If we do not plan these opportunities, however, we leave learning to chance, losing opportunities to educate and not maximizing our use of the time and resources of the unions we strive to build. Whether we are working as individuals or in teams, we have the ability to plan to some degree. Where we are planning for education at all levels, we ultimately maximize our resources and ensure we are placing education at the forefront of everything we do.

10
Getting it right and mixing it up: practical ideas for helping learners to get the best out of the education we provide

Carl Parker and Martin Smith

First thoughts

How many of us have had bad experiences of education or training? It may be from our schooldays, at college or, more recently, in the workplace. Talked at for hours on end, made to endure death by PowerPoint, or set impossible reading lists with no certainty as to why these are just some of the many forms of torture we've probably all been subjected to. Equally frustrating, at the other end of the spectrum, is the teaching that is so 'learner-focused' that it's not clear what the learning outcomes are and whether anything is actually being taught.

As every aspiring trade union educator knows, trade union education aims to avoid passive teaching methods in favour of participatory methods focused on helping our learners be more effective as union organizers and representatives. So we know to avoid, in the main, teaching methods such as lecturing, setting reading, giving demonstrations, etc., and instead to focus on discussion groups, practice by doing (both in the classroom and back at the workplace) and immediate use of learning, such as teaching others.

So far so good, and all part of the accepted wisdom of trade union educators. But, and it's a big but, in our experience, getting the balance right between starting where learners are and teaching to achieve a measurable impact can lead to educators avoiding passive methods almost completely, even when they are most appropriate and effective. It can lead to educators overusing discussion groups to the exclusion of everything else (even when learners will benefit from hearing directly from experienced reps and organizers).

Trade union educators should creatively ensure that there is significant variation in their teaching methods to keep participants engaged and to cover different individual learning styles. They also have to think about how they can, where possible, turn non-participatory methods into active, engaging ways of working that measure the deep learning that is happening and the impact it has on learners' practice.

For example, the right speaker, at the right time, with the right style can be the most memorable part of any course; it's clearly a passive teaching method but it can work. On the other hand, a course that consists of nothing more than a series of small-group tasks and plenary report-backs is a sure-fire way to send everyone to sleep and lose its point for learners.

This chapter is intended to help trade union educators think about the following:

- where typical learners are coming from and what their expectations are;
- how we can help ensure that learners get the most out of their learning experience and use it to change and improve their practice;
- how we can best make discussion groups work (when we use them);
- how we can introduce a significant variety of methods in our course programmes.

What do we know about our learners?

Obviously, a room of a dozen or so learners is going to contain a dozen or so individuals who are all unique. So that's the first thing we know about our learners – they're unique! But we can probably make a number of general assumptions:

- Our learners, being adults, will expect to be treated as adults (Jarvis, 2004). *So let's not fall into the trap of imitating some corporate training scheme that thinks it's acceptable to treat adults like children.*
- They are in a continuing process of growth – not at the beginning of a process (Muller, 2004). *So let's make sure that we don't assume that everyone starts at the same point and be condescending.*
- They bring with them their own unique combinations of experiences and values (Ota et al., 2006). *So let's remember to tap into this experience as an integral part of our training and keep the discussions and problem-solving grounded in their industrial reality.*
- They have their own expectations of the learning process (Freire, 1972a; Giroux, 2012). *So let's be understanding of the adult returning to learning whose last experience was sitting at the back of the classroom bored and ignored; and let's challenge learners to engage in* our *style of learning.*
- They may have competing interests (Glickman et al., 2007). *So let's think about how we can make sure our learning reflects the lives of our learners as mums, dads, carers, social beings, etc.*
- Adults learn best through talking and problem-solving (Freire, 1972a; Jarvis, 2004). *So let's find ways of designing courses that get our learners talking,*

sharing their experiences and jointly solving the real problems they face back at the workplace.

- Most adults have an attention span of 20 minutes (Cornish and Dukette, 2009). *So let's remember to limit more passive learning methods to less than this – and find ways to make passive methods more active.*
- Adults learn through understanding rather than remembering (Bransford et al., 2000). *So let's avoid giving learners the answers and instead encourage them to work towards a deeper understanding of the problems they face themselves before we share ideas and options for solutions with them.*

Much research has been published about individual learning styles, and educators need to be aware of some of the theory around this. Lack of space means that this isn't covered here but aspiring educators should investigate learning style theories such as the VAK (visual, auditory and kinaesthetic) model or David Kolb's learning styles (Flemming, 2001). The work of Paulo Freire has much to offer trade union educators, with its focus on learning through dialogue and situating learning within the real-world conflicts learners face (Freire, 1972b).

Often on trade union courses it is almost impossible to steer a course directly around people's learning styles, but in planning sessions we should ensure that the variety of teaching methods used reflects the potential for the presence of different learning styles; for example, by making sure that all course activities aren't just suited to visual learners.

Aiding retention

We want our learners to retain what they've learned and, at some point in the future, to act or think differently as a consequence of this learning. So, how can we help learners with retention? Much work has been done by educational researchers such as Stephen Brookfield (1995), Dylan William (2011) and John Hattie (2012) on the value of ongoing assessment for embedding learning. Whether the assessment is done by learners themselves or by tutors, assessment of learning during a course can be done through active questioning, quizzes, group discussions, one-to-one sessions with the tutor or through digital platforms such as Socrative. The foundation stone of assessment for learning is often open and transparent learning outcomes shared with learners.

Our experience also shows that essential to retention of learning is relating the topic back to what learners actually do as union representatives in the workplace. This workplace-based assessment can be carried out through recorded coaching and mentoring, and will be enhanced by building networks of learners, and by designing courses so there is a 'recall' course at a later date. It is essential that tutors design courses with learning outcomes and teaching that are geared towards producing the desired impact back in the workplace.

These principles complement Freire's use of fictitious case studies relevant to the industrial situation of each group of learners – this was a means of narrowing learners' focus, so that they identify problems to be solved in their own workplaces. Teaching to secure a measurable impact in the workplace through shared and open learning outcomes towards which learners can assess their progress should become the ultimate goal of trade union education. This means ensuring that learners take meaningful notes during courses and are encouraged to actively engage in the learning process beyond the course. At an intellectual level this could be to read more about a subject, carry out research or identify further development opportunities. At a practical level it means leaving the course with a clear action plan that will delivered back in the workplace. And all the better if the learner can be linked with another union representative or official who can mentor and support them in the delivery of these objectives.

Challenging expectations

When you run a trade union education course all learners will be somewhere on the continuum of having no experience of our style of teaching and our methods to being well versed in what we do and some of the traits that characterize trade union education.

The 'new kid on the block' may well be expecting an experience like the one they had at school, and we have to work hard to help new learners adapt to our participatory and active methods. We know that no-one is fully in the room until they have spoken (Kline, 2009). We should aim to ensure that everyone has spoken in any opening session as a means of getting everyone started and to avoid dominant voices setting the tone. The old lag, on the other hand, may well be expecting a nice gentle start with 'paired introductions' followed by a chance to put his/her feet up in a small-group discussion. We can challenge these unhelpful expectations by the way we start the course and by the variety of methods we deploy throughout. Some examples of how you could have an 'alternative' start to the course are given below. Some of these are just a little different from the usual start and others are intended to shock learners out of any complacency they bring with them. All of them send learners the message that the course they are embarking on is going to be different (and challenging).

Send learners out to do something. Tell them to carry out a survey in the street; or conduct a safety inspection of the training centre; or run a street stall; or take part in a demonstration; or visit a museum; or go for a walk in the area in pairs discussing an issue relevant to the programme.

Introduction bingo. Create a 'bingo' card featuring things that people may have done, and ask learners to find someone who has done what is on the card. They should then find someone else who's done the next item on the card. This gets learners up and about and talking to lots of different people.

Mime, song or action story. Ask the learners to mime a situation (e.g. what a well-organized workplace looks like compared to an unorganized site); or to lead the singing of a song (e.g. 'The Red Flag'); or to do the actions to a story (e.g. Rosa Parks – see the extract under Sample activities, no. 5).

Speed-dating. Arrange the room so that learners can talk in pairs and then, after a short period of time (about a minute), tell one person in each pair to move on to talk to someone else. Keep going until learners have spoken to at least half the group.

Talk, listen actively and present. Put learners into pairs, then ask them to talk to their partner about themselves for two minutes, without interruption or comment, and report back to the whole group. This can be open format or focused on a relevant open question such as 'What do unions need to do to grow?'

Draw a picture, make a collage, etc. Ask learners to embrace their creativity and to introduce themselves or their group on a flip-chart without using words.

Discuss relevant photographs or art work. Ask learners to say what their photograph means to them or to come up with a story about a picture.

Options for variety

You can make sessions interesting and keep learners on their toes by including a variety of methods and techniques. Here, we outline a number of ways in which sessions can be run in order to 'mix it up' and do things differently. Most of the examples given are self-explanatory and there can be many variations on each theme. A number of examples of how these methods have been used in a trade union environment are detailed under 'Sample activities' at the end of this chapter.

Tutor-led discussion. The tutor leads a whole-group discussion, prompting input from the reps on the subject matter and directing the discussion towards real-world problem-solving.

Brainstorming. The tutor leads a session in which ideas/contributions are put forward without stopping to debate or consider them. These can be narrowed down to a couple of issues the group wants to explore, by voting.

Tutor role-play. The tutor adopts a role with an aim – to get learners to respond to a particular situation.

Role-play. A scenario is acted out by learners and observed in order for constructive feedback to be given.

Mini role-play. A scenario is acted out in small groups (e.g. recruiting a union member) and a report given to a plenary session.

Lecture. The tutor talks from the front of the group to impart information.

Slide show. The tutor uses PowerPoint, Prezi, etc., to emphasize the main points of a lecture.

Guest speaker. An outside speaker talks on their specialist subject.

Video-watching. Learners are asked to watch a video and contribute to a discussion (small group or plenary) afterwards. It is important that learners are told what they should be identifying or analysing whilst watching the video.

Video-making. Learners record a short video on their smartphone or on a camera provided for them. If there is sufficient time and resources, learners can be asked to roughly edit their work, which will enable them to develop useful IT skills along the way.

Card sort. A blank flow-chart, list or process is issued to the group together with 'cards' to fill in the blanks.

Sticky notes. A variation on a brainstorm, in which individuals, pairs or groups are asked to write their contributions onto sticky notes and group them on the wall.

Chance cards. Learners choose a card at random with a statement or question for them to respond to.

Pub quiz. Group (rather than individual) quiz.

Electronic quiz or polling. Using an app like Socrative to run a quiz that sends individual answers back to the tutor and collates results.

Out-of-the-classroom activity. Send learners out to run a street stall, gather signatures on a petition, stage a demonstration, etc.

Five-minute paired work. Rather than break into groups, ask learners to work on a problem in pairs without leaving the room.

Wall of news. Provide resources (or encourage learners to download and print their own) to build a visual representation of a subject on the wall.

Magazine quiz. Learners complete a magazine-style quiz to analyse a behaviour or personality trait.

Pin the tail on the donkey. Learners have to work out where they would place information on a map, picture, chart, etc.

Making the most of discussion groups

The advantages of breaking out into discussion groups to undertake a task, followed by a plenary discussion, are well documented. Certain things are known about this:

Everyone takes part. In a group of three or four, everybody can play an active part in a discussion. Those who are quiet or reticent will feel less inhibited about contributing their ideas and opinions – it is also easier for a small group to control especially boisterous or domineering people! Finding solutions to problems themselves is not only more interesting than passively listening to a lecture, it is more realistic and helps learners to gain confidence and improve skills.

There is a better atmosphere. Getting learners to work in small groups is a much less formal way of running a session. People can feel more relaxed and are able to chat to each other freely as a way of working through problems. It also helps trade unionists to get away from the idea that education has to be like school.

Skills are developed. When small groups are preparing reports to be given to the rest of the class they will need to elect someone to chair their discussion and someone else to take notes. These duties can be shared out so that by the end of a course the majority of course members have had a chance to develop the valuable skills of chairing and note-taking.

Work is done collectively. Small groups encourage members to take a co-operative approach to problem-solving. They can listen to and learn from the views and ideas of others in relation to an issue, as they should in the 'real world' back at the workplace. Just as importantly, work can be done at the pace and in the manner that suits each particular group. Small-group work allows for that kind of flexibility.

Such sessions are the most common teaching method in trade union education. Being the most common method used doesn't mean that it is without disadvantages, however. For example:

- it can be difficult for the tutor/trainer to know what is happening;
- groups may not stick to the task;
- the tutor/trainer has limited control over which ideas are put forward in the plenary session;
- there is a possibility of conflict between individuals;
- participants can become confused about what they should be doing.

Making small groups work effectively means minimizing the disadvantages. To do this you need to think about

- how tasks are set;
- how to manage groups during tasks;
- how to handle difficult behaviour from group members;
- how to manage the reporting-back process.

Composition of small groups

Thought needs to be given as to the best way of setting up the small groups. Try to set the groups up so that the advantages of group-working are maximized and the disadvantages minimized.

Some things to consider include balance, control and variation.

Balance

What will help the group work better in terms of a balance of the following?

- Time spent as a rep
- The background of the learners (e.g. industry, ethnicity, experiences as a rep, etc.)
- Gender
- Language.

You may decide in certain circumstances that you don't want balance in the groups. For example, you may want all the experienced learners in the same group so they don't crowd out the inexperienced learners. You need to be sure (and be able to justify) that you are doing this for reasons that will help the dynamics of the whole group and not be divisive.

Control

The allocation of learners into groups can be used as a way of managing them. Placing a strong-willed (and potentially disruptive) participant with equally strong-minded reps can help to rein them in. Also, putting an experienced rep with inexperienced reps may help direct the inexperienced ones, but the tutor needs to be sure that they are being led in the right direction.

Variation

Groups can become stale if they are not changed during a course. Varying the groups also allows for a wider exchange of experiences. Moving learners into different groups can help in dealing with any personality clashes (or sometimes to 'share' a difficult participant around the whole group). The benefits of changing the groups need to be offset against the possibility that learners will feel disorientated by constantly changing groups.

Monitoring small groups

You cannot rely on small groups to function without input from the tutor. It may be difficult to judge when you, as tutor, have to intervene, as on the one hand you need to ensure that everything is going smoothly but on the other hand you want to create an environment in which participants manage their own learning.

However, it is often helpful to look in on a group or listen to a discussion. Groups may be self-conscious about this so it can be a good idea to give

them a little time to settle before you do this. By looking in you can:
- answer any queries about the task;
- check the group's progress on the task – in terms of both speed and content;
- direct the group back on course if they have strayed;
- offer support to learners who may think they are struggling;
- get information that the group may not feed back in the plenary and which it might be useful for you to know about.

These visits should be as unobtrusive as possible and last only as long as is necessary to achieve the above. Visits should be made to all groups so that there is no suggestion of favouritism or victimization.

Using flip-charts
Flip-charts can help group work in the following ways:
- They ensure that the group works together as they have to become focused around the production of the flip-chart content.
- They allow the tutor to assess how the group is getting on with the task, as progress is immediately visible.
- They help ensure that an effective report-back is made as the verbal presentation is backed up by what's written (or drawn) on the flip-chart paper.

Managing report-backs
There are some possible pitfalls when learners report back to the whole group. One obvious danger is that of repetition of the same points if each group has been looking at the same problem/issue. Below are some variations you can introduce to avoid this.

Different problems	If the activity contains more than one question, the group can be asked to report back on just one of the problems. You will need to decide whether the group should be asked to look at all of the problems or just the one on which they are reporting back.
One point from each group	Each group can be asked to make one contribution to the report-back before you move on to another group. If more issues are outstanding after each group has reported you can either repeat the process or open up a 'free for all'.
One point from each rep	Each group carries out the task and arrives at a group consensus. The tutor selects learners at random to give their group's view on a particular point. Care needs to be taken not to put any learners on the spot or under pressure.

General discussion	The small-group work is used to help the learners to prepare themselves for a tutor-led discussion, without any specific report-backs from the groups.
Different media	Groups can be asked to use a variety of different media to report back (for example, they could prepare a leaflet or handout rather than use a flip-chart). You can either ask all groups to use the same method or ask each group to report back in a different way.

Practising (don't call it role-play!)

Some people love the idea of role-play but many don't. You can soften people's reactions to it by referring to it as 'practising' or 'having a go'.

Types of role-play

There are many different ways of running a role-play session to help deliver learning outcomes. Some of these are detailed below.

Role-play observed by the whole group	A scenario is played out by some members of the group with the remainder acting as observers.
Mini role-plays	Scenarios are played out in small groups and observed within each small group – usually followed by a whole-group discussion.
Team role-play	A member of each group or team is nominated to take part in a role-play. The team can stop the role-play to give guidance to their team member or to send in a substitute.
Slo-mo role-play	The tutor controls the role-play and can pause the session to ask observers what should happen next or to suggest that one of the participants tries something different.
Rewind role-play	The tutor can pause the role-play and then ask for it to go back to a previous point for the participants to be guided by the tutor or the group as to what to try doing differently.
Mirror role-play	The role-play rewinds to a previous point and the scenario is played back with another participant taking on the persona of one of the previous participants to highlight body language, presentation style, etc.
Video role-play	The session is videoed, with the feedback being given either privately or by the group.
Tutor role-play	The tutor plays the role of someone who performs badly in a workplace negotiation; for example, a union rep who does something they shouldn't do. This can help to avoid embarrassing learners.

There are some fairly obvious pitfalls in many of the above and the educator needs to beware of how individuals will react to some of the more personally challenging roles they could find themselves playing. Taking care to allocate roles or tasks according to the ability and inclinations of individuals can help with this.

Setting up role-play

Participants need time to prepare for their role-play and need to be given the necessary resources to do so. Role-play can be very effective if 'real-life' documents are used instead of fictional case studies. For instance, if you are setting up a role-play about a disciplinary hearing, you could give the participants a real investigation report and disciplinary letter (anonymized and reproduced with permission). You need to guide the participants as to how to play the roles and to guide the role-play as it goes along (or take on one of the roles yourself). Observers should be guided as to what to look for when they are observing. Role-plays can be pre-prepared or designed by the group during the session (via a quick brainstorm or group activity). Figure 1 gives an example of real-life documentation that could be used in a role-play.

Recruiting at inductions

Observer's checklist

Presentation style	
Representation covered effectively	
Pay bargaining covered effectively	
Legal service covered effectively	
Success stories used	
Clear overall message to join there and then	

Figure 1. Please track a suggestion

Giving feedback

This is where it can all go horribly wrong! Feedback needs to be carefully managed to ensure that it is effective (helps participants spot areas for improvement and confirm what they are doing right) but doesn't leave the person deflated or feeling under attack.

If the group is invited to comment, the tutor needs to guide the feedback to ensure that it is useful for the person receiving it. One way of doing this is 'three stars and a wish' – three things people like followed by one suggested change. This can be written on a sticky note and handed over.

The DESC model (Bower and Bower, 2004) can also be effective. According to this model, feedback is given as follows:

- Describe what you have observed
- Explain the impact this has
- Solution – identify the solution
- Commit to a way forward.

The intention is that feedback is given in a non-judgmental manner and without personal opinion as to whether something was good or bad. Figure 2 gives some ideas for phrases that can be used at each stage.

Giving Feedback – DESC

Description	Describe what you have observed	For me, this is about... I've noticed that... What I just saw was...
Effect	Explain the effect this has	The impact of this can be... What I feel now is... You could see that it made X...
Solution	Identify what you think should happen	Let's think of a solution What can be done about this? I think you need to...
Commitment	Commit to a way forward	To confirm, you're going to try and... So, you'll do... You're going to do X and I'm doing Y

Figure 2. The DESC model

Sample activities

1. Video-watching

Videos can be homemade or obtained from another source. Often, a home-made video with low production values can be much more effective than expensively produced films or training videos off the shelf. Alternatively, finding the right extract from a film can be a way of introducing some variety into your teaching methods. If you are to do this it is important to ensure that the extract isn't too long (we would say 10 minutes max) and that the learners are set a clear task to complete whilst watching the film.

Example 1: A small group of reps from across a logistics network volunteered to be filmed in various simulated recruitment situations – in an induction, talking one to one, and talking to groups in a canteen. We spent an hour developing some very rough scripts around how *not* to recruit new union members and within a couple of hours of filming had enough content to make a 10-minute video. This video has been used dozens of times in various situations, from helping new reps develop their recruiting skills (by asking them to spot the mistakes and report back) through to developing the feedback skills of union officers, who were asked to make notes and then feed back to the rep in the video using the DESC model above.

Example 2: To encourage learners to take notes (both on the course and in their union role), show a short extract from a film (it can be almost any film) and identify different ways for pairs or groups of reps to take notes (mind mapping, linear notes, verbatim notes, key words only, etc.), ensuring that you have a control group who are not allowed to take any notes. Carry on with the session and return a few hours later to run a short quiz based on the film scene that was viewed earlier. This can lead into a discussion as to which method of note-taking was most successful.

2. Making a video
Technology makes it relatively easy to make your own videos. All you need is a half-decent smartphone and an app on a tablet to do some simple editing. It will often be the case that every learner on your course will have a smartphone and, therefore, the means to make a short video. This can make for a different and often entertaining way of taking report-backs during plenary sessions.

Example 1: A short session led by the tutor on why people join trade unions was held, with the group then split into pairs with the request that they devise a 60-second talking-head video on why young people should join their union. All the short videos were emailed to the tutor, who was able to quickly edit them all together to make a six-minute video of the collected ideas of the group.

Example 2: A national negotiating committee was looking at how they would communicate the outcome of their latest pay negotiations. Following a training session on key messages and developing the narrative of the union recommendation, groups of reps were asked to produce a short video to promote the negotiating committee's position. A screening session towards the end of the course gave reps a bit of light relief in what was otherwise a heavy course and also helped cement learning from earlier in the course.

3. Pin the tail on the donkey

This can be particularly useful for challenging learners' thinking or understanding of broader political issues. Learners are asked to decide whereabouts they would pin a number of cards on a map, diagram or other visual aid. The intention is to challenge what learners think they know about a particular situation.

Example: On a course about international trade and the economic effects of trade deals, learners were asked to identify the end location of profit generated in a particular country, by pinning prepared cards onto a map of the world. This then led into a tutor-led discussion about the rise of transnationals and the benefits they gain through trade deals which support their growth.

4. Team role-play – Recruitment

As previously stated, we would rarely refer to an activity as 'role-play'. Instead it would be called 'practising' or 'having a go'. In this activity the group would be split into two smaller groups, with one of the groups having no more than four members. This group of four members is given the brief that they will have to send one of their members into a 'canteen' to talk to a group of employees about joining their union. They will need to think about what resources they will use, how they will break into conversations, and what arguments they will use to persuade people to join. The other group are assigned various personas to adopt (already a member, not interested, keen to join if pay negotiations are mentioned, wants to be left alone to eat their lunch, etc.).

The group of four sends one of their group to the table in the canteen whilst the others observe what they do and say. At any point the tutor or the group can halt the discussion and recommend a course of action. The group can also agree to send a different person to do the talking. This group-managed role-play takes the pressure off individuals and encourages the group to work out how to respond to different situations.

5. Action story – Rosa Parks

This activity is taken from the excellent *Education for Changing Unions* by a collective of Canadian trade union educators (Burke et al., 2004). This can help lower inhibitions in a group whilst introducing a powerful message of inclusion and winning through activism. Learners are asked to stand up and mime the actions of the story whilst the tutor reads and acts out the story. Here is the story:

THE STORY OF ROSA PARKS

It was late one evening in Montgomery, Alabama, when a seamstress named Rosa Parks stood at the bus stop. She looked to her left and saw a bus coming, so she waved her right hand and the bus stopped. Rosa climbed up the three steps of the bus, paid her fare, and proceeded to walk down the aisle. She shaded her eyes and first looked to the left for a seat at the back of the bus. There was no seat. She turned to the right and looked for a seat in the back. There was no seat. She looked straight ahead and still there was no seat in the back of the bus. But right beside her there was a seat. It was vacant. It was also in the white section of the bus.

You see, it was 1955 and there was racial segregation in Alabama.

Rosa had recently completed a course at the Highlander Center, sponsored by a trade union.

Rosa tapped her chin while she decided what to do. She sat down in the seat. She crossed her arms in front of her and sat staring straight ahead. The bus driver told her to move to the back and to give her seat to a white passenger. Rosa just shook her head and refused to move. Passengers started shouting racial slurs. Rosa covered her ears and refused to move. Finally they were approaching her stop, where she would get off the bus. She reached up and rang the bell. She stood up and walked to the front of the bus. She walked down the three steps to the ground. She sat down on the bench at the bus stop and waited. The police came. They made her stand with her hands on the top of her head. They arrested her and jailed her. She sat on a chair in a cold cell.

This brave action sparked the civil rights movement.

Rosa Parks, Dr Martin Luther King, and others called for the Montgomery bus boycott, This resulted in African Americans like Rosa Parks walking great distances back and forth to work each day. For Rosa it was a long walk, so sometimes she walked very slowly. Sometimes she put out her thumb and hitched a ride.

Rosa Parks was fired from her job for her actions. She stood up for rights that day. She stood proud and tall for an end to racism and for dignity and equality. Her actions were the catalyst for a new movement.

Rosa Parks continued the struggle. She marched in demonstrations for freedom. She sat at numerous lunch counters that refused to serve African Americans. She reached for the sky.

Sometimes Rosa felt that being in the movement was like walking in circles. Other times she felt it was like writing new rules on a huge blackboard. Sometimes it was like swimming with sharks. But all the while Rosa was linking with people in an unbreakable chain for freedom.

By sitting in the white section of that bus, Rosa Parks made a better world for all of us.

Let's applaud Rosa Parks!

[Taken from Burke et al., 2004.]

6. Sticky notes
Sticky notes can be very useful, especially when you are trying to move away from small-group work followed by a plenary discussion. Instead of splitting your group into sub-groups you can ask individuals or pairs to write ideas on sticky notes (one per note), to stick them on the wall and to cluster sticky notes with similar content; for example, you can ask learners to write down on sticky notes the reasons people give for joining a trade union.

This doesn't allow for much small-group discussion but does get ideas out into the open in a matter of a few minutes. It also immediately identifies the most prevalent views, because the sticky notes have been clustered. The example above could be followed up, with pairs being asked to consider one of the sticky notes to establish what they would say to a potential member in connection with the idea put forward.

11

Responding to social-movement trade unionism within education

Gawain Little and Lindsey McDowell

Comprehensive education is essential to any successful social movement.
Mobilization alone is insufficient.

Bill Fletcher Jr, keynote address given at the
Justice Works conference for activists, 2015

This chapter explores the radical reform of trade union education provided by the National Union of Teachers (NUT) in the context of a wider programme of renewal involving a shift towards social-movement trade unionism. We start by outlining the context and the process itself, before looking at the core principles and impact of the union's new approach. Within this, we hope there are some lessons for the wider movement. We were both involved in the process we describe, one of us as the union's Training Adviser and the other as a member of the National Executive, and this informs our approach and perspective.

The need for renewal

The past three decades have seen fundamental changes in compulsory education in England. Since the 1988 Education Reform Act, neoliberal ideas have dominated. As Ken Jones observes,

> Conservative legislation sought to drive neoliberal policies into the heart of public policy. An emphasis on cost reduction, privatization and deregulation was accompanied by vigorous measures against the institutional bases of conservatism's opponents, and the promotion of new forms of public management. The outcome of these processes was a form of governance in which market principles were advanced at the same time as central authority was strengthened. (2003, p.107)

This policy direction remained remarkably consistent during the New Labour governments of 1997–2010. In spite of increased funding for education and a somewhat slower pace of fragmentation, the market model remained dominant, with a focus on 'choice' and competition combined with a centralized 'standards' agenda (Docking, 2000). Since the election of the Conservative-led Coalition government in 2010, this process has increased significantly in pace and intensity.

As education historian Brian Simon explained, a key aim of the 1988 Education Reform Act was to put in place 'a subtle set of linked measures... establishing a base which could be further exploited later' (Simon, 1987). What we are now witnessing is the realization of this 1988 project' (Stevenson, 2011).

Key features of these reforms include fragmentation of the education system, liberalization of terms and conditions, and increased emphasis on testing as a critical element of the developing market system and of a centralized accountability regime.

Teacher unions are a specific target of this process of education reform for a number of reasons. Firstly, they present an obstacle to a number of key policies, such as vastly increased private-sector involvement in education. Secondly, teachers' terms and conditions are both a target of neoliberal obsession with smaller government, and seen as a barrier which could deter private contractors from bidding to run state services (see for example Danny Alexander's 2011 statement on public-sector pensions – HM Treasury, 2011). Thirdly, as Howard Stevenson and Justine Mercer point out:

> Teachers are a strategically important group of workers who perform a critical ideological function. If the education system is to be subordinated further to meeting the needs of capital, it is essential that there is greater control over the curriculum, and therefore teachers' work...Attacking the power and influence of teacher unions, as the collective representation of the teaching profession, is therefore both a policy end in itself, and a means to an end. (Stevenson and Mercer, 2015)

In responding to this attack, teacher unions are critically weakened by the fact that their organizational and power structures are based on the very system that is being fragmented by neoliberal reform. According to Carter et al. (2010), this leaves them with three main options.

The first is *rapprochement* – go with the flow in terms of educational and structural change and try to achieve the best they can for members within a shifting context. This means accepting the neoliberal agenda but attempting to ameliorate its worst aspects. Given the importance to the neoliberal project of breaking the collective voice of teachers, this strategy can only be seen as a route to managing decline and a slow death.

The second approach is *resistance*. Teacher unions can explicitly reject neoliberal education reform and resist to the best of their ability, attempting to defend existing structures against government and employer attack. However, this strategy contains two linked weaknesses. Firstly, because it involves a reliance on existing union structures, designed to facilitate national- and local-authority-level bargaining, there is little understanding of how or why union members mobilize collectively to defend their own terms and conditions. Secondly, this reliance on national and local authority structures develops a linked reliance on a small number of 'hero-activists' at national and local level, who carry the weight of the union, and who have what Hahrie Han describes as a 'lone wolf' theory of change and strategy for building power (Han, 2014, pp.8-9). While this approach might have been sustainable when most issues were decided either at national or local authority level, and unions simply had to police the implementation at workplace level, it has proved increasingly fragile and unsustainable as more and more decisions are taken at workplace level.

The third possible strategy is that of *renewal*. The idea behind this is that it combines the rejection of neoliberalism at the heart of the *resistance* strategy with a recognition of the need for renewal of union structures in order to carry out this resistance. Effectively, the fragmentation of industrial relations caused by neoliberal education reform is used to develop a new activist base which is capable of resisting neoliberalism.

However, this is not a given and there is no direct causal link between fragmentation and increased workplace activity. Indeed, it is entirely possible, and undoubtedly one intended consequence of fragmentation, that unions, lacking an activist base at workplace level, simply become excluded from workplace decisions, which are then unilaterally imposed on members. Over time the union will lose membership and influence.

In order for union renewal to take place in response to the decentralization of decision-making, unions need to invest in workplace activism, shifting their culture, resources and strategic orientation to take advantage of the contradictory nature of fragmentation. This is the challenge the NUT has set itself – to develop (or redevelop) a form of social-movement trade unionism.

Our approach to social-movement trade unionism has three key strands. The first is a grassroots organizing approach which is focused on developing industrial and political power in the workplace through the recruitment, training and support of a network of workplace reps and active school groups in the approximately 24,500 workplaces we organize in across England and Wales. The second is a new approach to community unionism which seeks to build joint alliances of teachers, parents and students to oppose neoliberal education reform. This means challenging many preconceived ideas, both about the nature and role of trade unions and about the relationships between teachers, parents and students. Thirdly, there is an explicitly political element to the NUT approach which seeks to define an alternative vision for education around which to mobilize teachers, parents and students. This rests on a fundamental rejection of neoliberalism and opens up questions around the nature of industrial action, taking it beyond 'bread and butter' trade union issues, into battles about the future of our schools and communities.

Reviewing our training programme

It was in this context that a review of the NUT training offer for reps became urgent and essential. A review had begun in 2012 but faltered due to lack of staff capacity. In 2013, the union secured funding to add two new posts to the training team on a temporary basis. The aim was to better support the regional training programme, which consisted of two courses for reps and a course on casework. These courses had been delivered from one national training centre until 2009, and the decision to extend delivery to the regional and Wales offices meant that the union had very quickly gone from training dozens of reps a year to training hundreds of reps a year. Additionally and unsurprisingly, the profile of reps undertaking training had begun to look more like the general membership profile, with greater numbers of women accessing courses nearer home.

On a national orientation tour of courses in the regions and Wales it became clear that a complete overhaul was necessary. Officers were adapting, reworking and in some cases entirely rewriting whole sections of the courses, trying to give reps what they felt they needed to face the rapid and profound changes taking place in education. Whilst efforts had been made at national level to incorporate elements of an organizing approach into the content of the courses, there was no flow in the structure of the learning and little relationship to the wider activities of the union. Fundamentally, the trade union education on offer to reps did not equip them either to make a difference in their workplace or to play a role in the programme of renewal the union was embarking on. It was obvious that the radical changes to the education landscape meant that reps needed something different from their current trade union education and the task would be to rewrite the entire programme.

The review process was comprehensive; in fact it was deeper and lengthier than most people in the union either anticipated or understood. The objective was to rejuvenate the reps' training programme so that it not only addressed the threats posed by the changes to education, but also sought to make the most of the wider opportunities that were being presented. For reps, we could begin to offer a 'greenhouse' learning event, away from their school or college, in which they could reflect on their union group and the dynamics of their workplace, and consider the changing face of public education on a global scale. In this context, giving them the knowledge, skills and understanding associated with learning about the role of the rep might become less of a transaction and more the beginning of a transformation to local leadership.

For the union, the process presented several opportunities. Practically, a wide-ranging review would mean the development of a nationally consistent programme which colleagues in the regions and Wales wouldn't need to spend time rewriting, so that they could focus on delivery and supporting the reps more widely. In addition, investing in the national co-ordination of a regionally delivered programme could increase the capacity of the union to train the significant number of reps it would need in the future.

In the face of the growing attacks on education, and with a commitment not just to resistance but also to renewal, the union employed a growing central team of organizers who were managed from headquarters but deployed in the regions. These organizers work with local branches to build local union capacity. Their focus has principally been on strengthening local lay structures through recruiting and supporting school-based union reps, and rebuilding lay activism in areas where structures have become weakened. As with the education programme, the combination of central direction and regional deployment has been critical in ensuring that the organizing programme is rooted in, and responsive to, the locality, whilst remaining part of a national strategic approach. This contrasts with organizing programmes in a number of other unions (Simms et al, 2012). The NUT's organizing programme is based on John Kelly's application of mobilization theory to industrial relations (see Figure 1 overleaf). This approach proceeds from the perception of and response to injustice (Kelly, 1998) and assumes both a high degree of agency on the part of union activists and a recognition of their political role in challenging injustice and inequality through collective action (Little and Stevenson, 2015). Crucially, it gives an answer to the question of how and why union members mobilize collectively to defend their terms and conditions, and the services they work in.

It was recognized that the review of the education programme offered one way to embed the theory and practice of the union's organizing approach in our workplace structures and ultimately throughout the organization. Crucially, a new programme which was delivered jointly by organizers and regional officers (who had some organizing responsibility but were mostly concerned with individual and collective representation at that time) could contribute to a wider change-management process. The organizing approach and the more traditional approach of the union could be blended together in a way that would make sense both to staff and to the membership. So

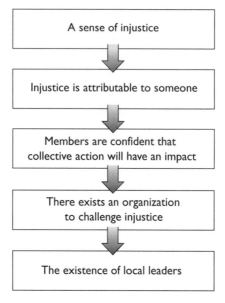

Five **NUT** steps to mobilization
Drawn from Kelly's Mobilization theory

> A sense of injustice

> Injustice is attributable to someone

> Members are confident that collective action will have an impact

> There exists an organization to challenge injustice

> The existence of local leaders

Figure 1

our plan was to use the best of both. The new programme would retain the familiar elements of the existing courses (which the regional officers had been delivering), in which reps learned their rights and responsibilities, the structure of the union, the basics of individual representation and some pointers on recruitment and working with management. Some of the essential skills and tools of organizing, such as listening and clustering, would be added. Most importantly, everything would be reframed into a structure that could help reps to grasp the global context of the experiences of their members, understand the power relationships of the workplace and embrace their role as local leaders, which the organizing approach had brought to the union. This would give the regional teams a learning programme that respected and represented the two fields of expertise and which they could deliver collaboratively.

An example of this is the negotiation session in the first course in the new programme, which many reps refer to positively when asked about the impact of the course. Negotiation, referred to in the course outline as collective representation (see Table 1 on p.195), is given a full half-day on the last of the three days. This allows a critical review of a video and then three rotations of role-play, requiring each participant to play the role of rep, manager and observer. Much of the structure of the session is standard, including the use of scenarios, the problem-information-plan preparation model, and the provision of a checklist of good practice for successful negotiations. Reps perform their roles in pairs, to emphasize that negotiation should be conducted with support from someone in the union group or a rep from another union. The key development in the revised programme is the group preparation for the participants playing the manager in each rotation of the role-play. The tutor working with that group talks about their own experiences of negotiation, particularly including the dirty tricks and sneaky tactics that they have been subjected to. The reps are encouraged to consider how to counter the 'home-ground advantage' that comes with conducting the negotiation in the manager's office or other venue of their choosing, using seating, lighting and other distractions to play power games, making the most of the power associated with their position of authority. The difference in objectives and motivations of the two sides involved in the scenario becomes explicit, something which often in education is obscured by the 'We're all on the side of the children' mantra. Reps begin to understand, in a very concrete sense, the underlying nature of management, seeing line managers as employers' representatives. As Mike Ironside argues,

Management behaviour is primarily driven by the needs of the employer – in a 'free' market their main role is to maximize output and minimize labour costs. The main role of the union rep is to close down managers' freedom to choose how to achieve this.

This nurturing of consciousness is supported by discussions throughout the course on how to build the power and presence of the union side, referring specifically to Kelly's interpretation of mobilization theory in the session that follows. The negotiation session isn't just a role-play but a reflection on industrial relations.

It was agreed that the best way to build the credibility of the new programme, and to make sure the end result was fit for purpose, was to make the development process as inclusive as possible. If staff in a range of union roles felt ownership of the new programme then this would translate into high-quality delivery and a deeper learning experience for the participants. This manifested in two related decisions. Firstly, there would be a review group, which would include the Learning team colleagues tasked with developing the new programme, a regional organizer, several regional officers and a regional secretary. This would be a microcosm of the hundred or so tutors who would deliver the programme when it went live in the regions and Wales. Each member of the group would also be an ambassador for the review process and the new programme amongst their professional peer group within the union. Secondly, the review group would not meet in the union's headquarters in London, where national initiatives are generally conceived before they are disseminated to the regions and Wales, but would meet in a central location elsewhere in the country, to which London-based colleagues would have to travel. It turned out that meetings were held in the office of the Public and Commercial Services Union in Birmingham and it was felt at the time that the choice of venue helped to keep the review process focused on the real world. Given that the work of the review group was mainly to identify the learning outcomes of the new programme, from which the course content and activities would be drawn, this outward-looking perspective was essential. The group considered, at length, what reps in this new fragmented landscape needed to know, do, understand and ultimately be.

The review process was subject to two key forms of scrutiny. The first was by the union's National Executive, which maintained oversight throughout via regular reports to the Training and Professional Development Sub-Committee. The reps' programme was discussed at every meeting, which expanded the pool of expertise involved in the review process and ensured that the work fitted strategically with other union developments and activities.

The second of the checks and balances was the two pilot courses for each stage of the programme. Some participants on these experimental courses were brand-new reps who had been identified by organizers, while others had responded to an email invitation to all reps asking for volunteers to help the union test out its new rep learning programme, and so were much more experienced. Some of the group had also undertaken previous rep training with the union and so were able to compare the courses. The pilot process was necessary not only to test draft materials and activities but also to reinforce the credibility of the new courses with colleagues and the National Executive. Two weeks after the pilots of the first three days' learning, when asked what they had been doing in the meantime, the reps' responses proved that the new course would have immediate impact:

'We managed to get all remaining lesson observations cancelled for this term.'

'I'm meeting the headteacher to raise members' concerns over lunchtime duties and lesson observations.'

'I'm already disputing the directed [working] time calendar.'

'I've been discussing the action short of strike action with all staff in regard to "ideas" our new headteacher has mooted about submitting planning weekly, and we are to have an informal multi-union meeting shortly about it.'

'We've had 50-per-cent improvement in numbers of members taking strike action because of the meeting I held before the action.'

All of these early successes were attributed directly to the knowledge, skills and confidence gained on the courses. Their comments were used in tutor briefings in regional offices and shared with the National Executive, to demonstrate that the focus of the review was to make a tangible difference in workplaces.

Core principles and structure of the new approach

The review of the union's trade union education did not happen in a vacuum. As described above, it was part of a wider process of change, including the development of a broader social-movement approach across the union's work. As the review was taking place, the union was engaging in a wide-ranging Stand Up for Education campaign, which linked the concerns of teachers to neoliberal attacks on the wider system. This provided a clear narrative for the rep training – as well as defending terms and conditions, it was also a fight for the soul of education and the development and articulation of the alternative narrative of education. The first day of the first course includes a discussion on hegemonic theory, exploring the neoliberal 'common sense' that dominates education discussion and the contrary 'good sense' of the union approach (Gramsci, 1971). During the review process, the President of the Chicago Teachers' Union, Karen Lewis, visited the NUT. On the basis of her union's experience of action in 2012, Karen emphasized the need to relate to the public. Although our recent strike over pension cuts had good support amongst the membership, Karen held a mirror up to us. She said that we couldn't win without public support and argued that the public care about teachers and teaching but not particularly about their pensions. Our new approach is embodied in the slogan 'Teachers' working conditions are children's learning conditions' and practical activities in the new training courses emphasize the need for us to be able to articulate our arguments around education to colleagues, parents and the public at large. Reps need to be clear what we are for as well as what we are against.

To reflect this, one of the most fundamental changes we made was to make the training particular to teachers. We felt strongly that the thing that would most motivate teachers to become active in the union was the attack on state education, particularly a workload that is spiralling out of control and a testing regime that is damaging, punitive and nothing to do with high-quality education. Teachers' drive to be active in the union comes from their anger that this is no longer the profession they chose. In terms of Kelly's use of mobilization theory, this is their sense of injustice. Although reps would be undertaking trade union education, we couldn't take for granted that they were trade unionists when they joined the course. We did, however, know that they were teachers, that they would still be teachers when they left the course and that they would go back to organize teachers in their workplace. This meant that it was essential to root the learning, and particularly the opening sessions of the first course, in the reps' lived experience and work outwards from there. The links between the trade union and the attacks on education needed to be explicit.

After much debate within the review group, it was agreed that the NUT reps' training programme would mirror the TUC's stage one course in the sense it would be of 10 days' duration. Whilst the TUC invites members for the same day each week for 10 weeks, it was clear that that model would not be possible for secondary and college teachers because of timetabling. It was agreed that both the initial stage of the NUT course for workplace reps (now called Reps Foundation) and the follow-up stage (now called Reps Advanced) would be extended from two days to three and that four stand-alone one-day courses would complement those to make a 10-day entitlement. Figure 2 shows the structure and overall theme of the days in each of the two stages and the four stand-alone days.

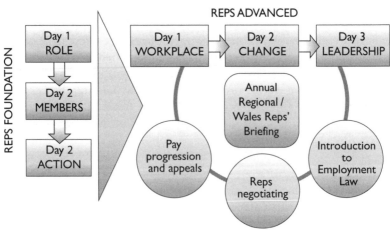

NUT National Training for Workplace Reps 10-day entitlement

Figure 2: NUT national training for workplace reps: new course structure

Three-day courses meant there was time and space to cover all the essentials of standard reps' courses (some of which had been omitted previously and others of which were now covered in more depth) and also to explore the context of the rep role and the union more widely. Additionally, by the third day, the group had established rapport to a much greater degree. This meant that the learning could be much deeper and more challenging by that point in the course. The structure of the Reps Foundation course mirrors the five stages drawn from John Kelly's application of mobilization theory to industrial relations and so the third day not only includes the half-day role-play session on negotiation, but also the culmination of the learning process, at which point reps grasp the importance of intertwining the industrial and educational struggles and realize their power to affect both as local leaders.

The content of the advanced stage of the training built on what was covered in the foundation stage. Table 1 gives an outline of the content at both stages.

	Reps Foundation	Reps Advanced
NUT structures	Knowledge and awareness of Union structures	Participation and influence in Union structures
Role of the rep	Rights, responsibilities and local leadership	Impact in the workplace and upwards/outwards development
Membership development	Identifying non-members and recruiting them to the NUT	Identifying inactive members and encouraging their active participation
Equalities	Specific equalities section, including ethical and legal considerations	Equalities issues throughout, towards an inclusive and representative Union
Individual representation	Where to start with representation and where to find support	Building more complex cases, including ethical and equalities considerations
Collective representation	Negotiation skills – generic, scenario-based	Working with local management – context-specific
Members' meetings	Organizing and leading effective meetings	Workplace democracy including member consultation
Networking	Accessing support including peer support	Providing support through mentoring and clustering
Trade union thinking	Mobilization theory and the need to combine terms and conditions issues with education issues	Trade union philosophies, including social partnerships and social-movement trade unionism
Politics of education	Think Global	Act Local

Table 1: Content of the foundation and advanced courses

Each of the three-day courses was given three principles that would chime throughout the course, underpinning the course and providing extra structure to the learning.

In Reps Foundation these are solidarity (so that reps understand the threats to global education, but also solidarity with others in the room in that the members' issues for one school/college tend to be very similar to those of members in others, because this isn't a problem of one headteacher or one Ofsted grading, but entirely systemic and ideological); collectivism (so that reps recognize that a trade union makes individuals' issues into collective issues and that the strength in a union group is to act together); and trade union presence (as a way to make a difference in the workplace by making the power of the union explicit and tangible, with a consequent impact on the members, on the rep/s and on the employer – we know that less casework is generated in workplaces where there is a strong union presence).

In Reps Advanced the themes are trade union leadership (the reality of being a local leader in the workplace and in the union/movement more widely); democracy (not only how the union works in a democratic sense but also the importance of consulting with members and developing as much active participation in the group as possible); and agency (that reps and members can and do make a difference and that consciousness is power). In both cases these are made explicit in the introductory session and explained in the course materials, and tutors will keep coming back to them throughout the three days. It is clear from evaluation that they resonate with participants.

It was essential that the courses developed, as part of the review took a new approach to learning. The point of the education programme was not simply to train reps to deliver a static function that they could engage in in a transactional way. Historically, the training had implied that the rep would do x, y and z 'for the union' and in return the union would ensure that the rep had the resources necessary. Most commonly this manifested in posters to be put up on the noticeboard and a list of members in the workplace who could be emailed/leafleted.

The increasing fragmentation and pre-privatization of the education system means that the world in which our activists operate is unprecedented and unpredictable. Reps need to be agile, flexible and conscious to deal with whatever might come their way. In addition, we were well aware that the approach we used in activist education would influence the wider development of democracy in the union. 'The more people participate in the process of their own education…the more people participate in the development of their selves. The more people become themselves, the better the democracy' (Freire, 1990).

This understanding is placed at the heart of the new courses. Rather than lecture, the tutors facilitate and there is an emphasis on a participatory learning approach, where tutors and students learn together from their shared and differing experiences. To resist the 'lone wolf' expert approach, there is an emphasis on students learning from each other, using group work and conversation to reflect how reps need to cluster and collaborate in the real world. The courses include a lot of information on the support available to reps, with the intention that no rep should feel isolated. They are encouraged to think on their feet and then research and test so they learn to combine trusting their instincts with accessing support and expertise. Crucially, as well as being reps that act, we need them to be thinking reps who can analyse, plan and lead.

Impact

Speaking to reps who have completed the Reps Foundation course over the past two and a half years demonstrates that it has had a significant impact on their trajectory and their development as union activists. One rep described the course as a 'transformational' event in her life.

> It came at just the right time for me. The combination of the issue at college which led to me becoming the rep and the skills and confidence the course gave me…I started to think, I could do this, negotiating in schools as well, not just my own college.

She went on to talk about how this had led in turn to her taking on the role of Division Secretary and also playing an active role in the local trades council.

Another rep talked about the confidence the course had given them, following which they seconded a motion at Conference and spoke at a fringe meeting alongside the General Secretary of another union. They described speaking at a number of public events since, concluding 'so public speaking is a definite new skill!'

Confidence was a common theme amongst reps when speaking about what they had gained from attending a course. In all cases, this increased confidence led directly into further union activity. When they are asked on the Reps Advanced course about their own successes and those of their union groups, reps are reporting real wins in their workplaces, including winning improvements in pay and other policies, stopping increases in teaching load and attacks on non-contact time, countering oppressive monitoring regimes, and representing members to successful conclusion. In addition, reps we spoke to described supporting other reps (and, in one case, other associations), participating in early career training, attending union conferences, getting involved in trades council activity, organizing marches, protests and public meetings, and taking on other union roles, including as Division Secretaries.

It wasn't just increased confidence that led to greater activity. A big part of it was the political understanding reps had gained on the course. In the words of one rep:

> On the course, there was a real sense that we all had a shared goal. It was about protecting education and about that sense of injustice at what is being done. It is that sense of injustice that makes people want to stand up and fight.

Another rep described the importance of the GERM[1] discussion on the first day:

> Up to that point, I was against academization because it was bringing the market in. But the GERM presentation put it in a global context. Made me realize just how important it was to fight against it at every opportunity.

This was also an important factor in reinforcing reps' identification with the union. As one rep said,

> Some of the issues in the room might be the same, like cuts to TA [teaching assistant] support for children with special educational needs. Others might be different but there were always parallels, like between academization and incorporation [of FE colleges]. The course helped us to draw the links between the issues and reminded us why we were in the NUT, because it is the union that gives us the political context of what is happening.

This making of links was a key theme in reps' description of the courses. The courses had built upon the reps' own understanding of the issues but linked this with the wider context in a way that made them clearer. 'I brought my politics with me but [the course] helped me to make the connections between that and what I do as a rep.'

The change in learning style also featured strongly in feedback from reps. A number referred to the role-play sessions and how 'you've got to think on your feet and keep calm' or how 'the course helped me to think for myself and to make decisions under pressure'. There were also frequent references to the importance of group dynamic, with many reps saying the style of the course meant that they learned as much from the other participants as from the tutors.

This learning also extended beyond the course. A number of reps described staying in touch with colleagues they had trained with, or even building networks with other reps who trained at different points. As one rep put it, 'I can ping someone an email or text somebody that I know. I've got a network of NUT people. I might not have the answer but I might know somebody that does.'

The courses also fundamentally changed how reps viewed the union. Many reps began the course with a transactional view of union membership, some even describing the union as 'insurance' in case something went wrong at work. They all left with a view of the union as a democratic, participatory organization and of member involvement being at the heart of union work. In the words of one rep, 'The union is driven by its members and it's for its members. It is its members.'

This has changed the way these reps engage with their members, and their understanding of collective action:

> I understand the union and collective strength much more. We need to get that understanding out to members. People only see their individual issues. What they don't realize is the collective strength they have, the collective power. The union is about getting them to understand that. If they act together, they have power. That and organization.

That changed understanding continues to influence the approach of these reps as they go on to take up new roles within the union. One rep described how the reps course influences their approach as Division Secretary, a post to which they were elected after completing the course:

> The members *are* the union. When people contact me it tends to be because they have got to the point where they want me to come in and rescue them, either as an individual or as a school group. When I go in, I have to talk about how *we* could do this or *we* could do that. So members get the idea that they *are* the union.

This shows that, in addition to influencing workplace reps themselves, the trade union education on offer to NUT reps is having a wider impact across the union, embedding the values and practices of our organizing approach.

In a very real sense, we are engaged in producing 'organic intellectuals' who can challenge the accepted 'common sense' of neoliberalism (Gramsci, 1971); we are producing the 'local leaders' whose key role involves 'promoting a sense of grievance' through challenging accepted qualities and creating or sustaining 'a high degree of group cohesion' (Kelly, 1998).

Conclusion: Tensions and opportunities

As we have previously remarked, this change did not take place in a vacuum. Many of the reps we spoke to talked about trade union education, and the 'greenhouse' courses they had participated in, as part of a wider package of support that had encouraged them to get active within the union. This included local rep networks, contact with organizers, support from regional and Wales offices and engagement with local lay structures. It was clear that the impact was greatest where most or all of these had been in place. There are a number of things the union can do to support this, for example developing a structured mentoring/buddying programme or organizing regional reps' conferences, but a key part of this will be sharing the good practice that is already taking place in associations across the country and building the opportunities for activist-led informal education initiatives.

This leads on to the question of sustainability. The union can't afford to have a revolving door of reps who resent and then resign the role. The learning is designed to make the role accessible and sustainable. Courses promote job-sharing and the development of democratic rep teams in the workplace. Most reps on the Reps Foundation course make one of their 'quick win' activities after the course to recruit a joint rep or a health and safety rep, or give someone else who is generally supportive of the union a formal role so there is strength in numbers, and they almost all achieve it. But the strain on teachers at the moment is overwhelming and thousands are leaving the profession. We can ensure that reps know that union activity is a way to make a difference, which is what they love about teaching, and that through collective action they can challenge and overcome the pressures.

The emphasis on political context also has an impact on sustainability. Reps who understand that there is an endless struggle for control over work and wages (even when all seems to be peaceful), and that most problems arise from government policy rather than from 'bad' managers, are better equipped to take a longer and more strategic view of events in the workplace. A class perspective opens up an examination of the nature of the links between local and national action, and between industrial and political action. Hard-pressed workplace activists need to know that their union is mobilizing nationally to support them, both in providing resources to assist in their local struggles and in taking political action to address the root causes of their workplace problems. Politically aware union reps are less likely to see leadership sell-outs when things go wrong, and they are more likely to look beyond the workplace towards wider mobilizations of their national union and the labour movement. They are also less likely to attribute individual defeats or setbacks to personal failings or to flaws in the organizing approach, and so have greater resilience in the face of adversity.

At the same time, we need to continue to increase our capacity to train reps. We must not underestimate the scale of the challenge we have set ourselves. Over the past two and a half years, we have trained over 1,500 new reps but that is only the very beginning of the process. There are around 24,500 education workplaces in England and Wales and we don't have 15 or 20 years to train reps for them all. We need to look at how formal training can be complemented by a culture of informal training and support, and explore how a qualitative increase in the number of trained reps becomes a qualitative shift in the learning culture of the union.

The fundamental lesson we draw from all of this is that, whilst the trade union education reps participate in is essential to union renewal, it cannot be separated from the approach of the union more broadly. It needs to be an integral part of an organizing culture across the organization that sees union power as rooted in the membership and prioritizes member engagement and empowerment as the goal of union work.

There will of course be tensions within this process, as in any process of reform or renewal. At times, it may seem easier to stick with traditional ways of working, just as it may seem easier to rely on traditional structures or approaches for negotiation. It may seem that firefighting is the only choice. However, the landscape has changed too dramatically for these options to offer any way forward. The NUT has set a clear strategic direction of renewing itself through the empowerment of grassroots members and the building of strategic alliances with parents and others around an alternative vision of education. Continuing to develop our trade union education, along the lines set out here, and integrating this with a wider programme of radical renewal will be essential to delivering this strategy.

1 The Global Education Reform Movement, or GERM, is a term coined by Finnish educationalist Pasi Sahlberg (2011) to describe neoliberalism in education and the forces that promote it.

12

General Federation of Trade Unions youth festivals: popular education in action

Mike Seal (with Sarah Woolley)

Introduction

'Not a series of speeches, but a genuine engagement with participants to learn from each other and from the amazing experiences of trade unionists throughout the world. Oh, and the barbecue was great and the accommodation and surroundings fantastic.' (Participant comment, 2016)

'I really thought history and trade unions were boring until I went to this event. What an eye-opener, what motivation! I'll definitely get active in my union now.' (Participant comment, 2016)

For four years (with one year off for the General Election) the GFTU has run a youth festival. As can be imagined from the quotations above, these are events quite different from many trade union conferences. This is a conscious difference, due to a recognition within the executive committee of the GFTU that many young people have reported being 'put off' by their experiences at other trade union events. As Sarah puts it:

The EC [Executive Committee] wanted to take things in a new direction. There was a feeling that they wanted to bring more young people into the movement and a suggestion was made for a youth festival. There was a recognition that it needed to be different from a normal conference. If you are coming into the union movement brand new, let alone as a young person – with motions, etc – it can be quite daunting and people ask themselves 'what have I let myself in for?'.

This is an account of how these events came about, their approach, structure and outcomes. It is based on an examination of the minutes of the development of the programme for the festivals, their agendas and outlines of sessions, as well as discussion and interviews with the organizers of the conferences, in particular Sarah Woolley. We are presenting it as an example of popular education in action and, while the organizers have not always been conscious of the principles and ideas behind popular education, they have nevertheless embodied them and this account of the event will hopefully serve as an inspiration to others. We have not arranged the chapter chronologically, looking instead at how the festivals have adhered to the ideas of popular education, but hope that some sense of how the events developed is also conveyed. Finally, we have identified some learning from the conference that goes beyond popular education and brings in other approaches, as well as offering thoughts on how unions organize more generally.

Criticism of traditional banking approaches and undoing previous experiences of education

> There was a recognition that we needed to make things more engaging and not put them off at the first hurdle.

As we noted in the introduction, and Sarah reiterates above, we recognized that traditional approaches to conferences do not work for some. We also recognized that people, including educators, had to unlearn what they expected from education and that learning may have a bad association for many (Freire, 1972b; Shor, 1992). Sarah reiterated this several times in our interview.

> We wanted people to feel the confidence to ask questions and get involved; it's more interactive – people are learning without feeling like they are learning.

The final comment was an interesting one, and I explored it further with Sarah. People sometimes need to learn without realizing they are doing so because of their negative associations with education, which may also involve negative experiences of trade union education.

> Sometimes that's the best way: if you're sent on a training course by your branch and you're not sure if you want to be there but you're given a workbook and told 'here you are', you don't necessarily take things in.

However, the festivals did not shy away from challenge; in fact debate was at the centre of most of the sessions. The session also had a critical edge in not pandering to what people might expect, for as well as having negative associations with education, people can have a consumerist view of it (Joldersma, 1999, Seal, 2017). The sessions were not about entertainment, and were deliberately challenging to consumerist constructions.

> It's easy to pander to what you think young people will respond to but the point is also to challenge them, so instead of doing rap, which they are used to, we might do poetry and allow them to make the connections.

That the sessions helped people make connections seems crucial here and we will return to it when examining conscientization (Freire, 1972b). As Sarah says, part of the challenging seemed directly related to the need to undo some people's experience of schooling (Shor, 1992). This included exposing participants to forms of expression that they might previously have found alienating, but this time encouraging participants to make connections to their lived experiences that previous exposure to literature, in this case poetry, did not do, or was not allowed to do. This in turn might make participants realize how politicized (but under a neutral guise) and deliberately undermining their previous educational experiences had been. Political connections were being made.

> On the Saturday night we had a young woman doing spoken words. Poetry is something that can be out there and you could see the penny drop with everyone at some point or another. Getting people to see that poetry isn't necessarily what you learn at school and that it can be for everyone; this is again part of undoing what people learn in schools.

The events also explicitly challenged the language that unions use. Challenging and deconstructing language is a central component of popular education. There was a deliberate attempt to unpack and deconstruct union language, recognizing that it can make people feel excluded, and involve exercising power, even if inadvertently.

> We started with a jargon buster and one of the house rules – everyone was involved in these so that people bought into the process – was that people did not use jargon and we agreed to challenge each other if there were terms being used that people did not understand. We ended up with 10 sheets [of jargon] – and we've used those as a basis in subsequent years. We all googled them or used each other as a resource 'cause someone often knew. You could see people who were non-members developing confidence and understanding by the end of the conference.

Other conference organizers could bear in mind the need to undo the expectations of participants about what education is, particularly where they have had bad experiences. A jargon buster would be useful in most contexts. So too is the recognition that there are a number of approaches that can engage and challenge people – from poetry to sculpture to theatre – so that it is not just about bringing in the big-name speakers, as we shall explore further.

Knowledge: the co-creation of knowledge and the importance of democracy

The organizers had an instinctive feel for the importance of democracy in learning experiences (Bolton, 2010; Cho, 2010; Freire, 1972). Involving lay people in teaching, as opposed to 'professional educators' was a part of democratizing the experience while also cementing the knowledge of the trainers.

When you're involved and you're participating and you're involved in teaching other people, it kinda works.

Part of the potency of their approach seemed to reside in demystifying the supposed superior knowledge of more seasoned activists, and a recognition that teaching and facilitating can cement one's own knowledge. This can make participants feel closer to the education experience, encourage the sense that this is something that they could engage with and do themselves, in time. Sarah talked about the power of seeing that even the most experienced activist may still have gaps in their knowledge and need to learn.

We had a debate about the EU and had two young speakers – one for and one against – and we all learned something, even those who had been involved in the movement for a long time. We saw that experienced trade unionists did not have a lot of information about the EU and we saw that as a failing of the movement – we all learnt from each other through debate.

Going deeper, the organizers recognized, as does popular education, that knowledge is contextual. This goes beyond students needing to have knowledge contextualized for them. It involves recognizing that in many ways they are experts on that context, and need to be a part of co-creating that knowledge (Batsleer, 2012; Smith, 1994; Ord, 2000). Sarah recognized that this went beyond just the festival and applied to union organizing practice in general.

Whilst I'll go into workplaces and know about employment law, I'm not the best person to know what happens on a day-to-day basis in their workplace. They need to teach me their perspectives on things so that I can say how the law relates to that.

Sarah again showed insight into the nature of knowledge. Not only does it need to be contextualized for people to understand it, but also people need to be involved in its production. Knowledge needs to evolve and respond to new situations, otherwise it stagnates and becomes dogma.

When the economy is changing as much as it is, with zero hours and the gig economy, we have to look at everything differently now – we need to keep up with people.

Zygmunt Bauman talks about a liquid modernity (2000) where the pace of change is so rapid that it is hard to keep track of it. Sarah saw young people, who are increasingly at the forefront of a world that is accelerating in its changeability, as a useful reminder of this. Of course, there are underlying dynamics that move much more slowly. For example, popular education has a class analysis and politics as a foundation and bedrock. For critical educators it is about examining how these foundational ideas manifest in a changing modernity, and in turn how we can effectively respond to this.

> We need a reminder that things change – young people remind us of that. Change. People are wary of change but, when everything is changing around you, you either change with it or die out.

Sarah similarly goes on to say that trade union education, and trade union activity in general, needs to learn and develop in its approach lest it stagnate.

> We need to be more open-minded. We need to learn as much from the students as from the teachers. We've got to get away from the arrogance that we are the teachers and people need to learn from us – whether they are 18 or 108 they still have pockets of knowledge that you might not have.

This was not to say that seasoned organizers could not be learnt from, but the selection of speakers was carefully made so that they would and could relate to young workers' contexts, respect their perspectives and have a sense of humility about their own knowledge. As Sarah describes one speaker:

> He's not an academic: he speaks about his own experience and debunks myths about the media, and he makes it so you don't have to be a politician to be involved. We can't make it scary to do politics – it's important to get people to open their minds.

We will dig down into some of the dynamics of a popular educational approach in the section on conscientization. There is something crucial here about enabling others to make wider connections to their own experiences, as opposed to just learning from the experiences of more seasoned activists. Some of this can be about people opening up, enabling them to see that things are political, and realizing that this is something they can be involved in.

> It's people who live things like economics and politics on a day-to-day basis and make people feel like it's something that could be within them.

The approach to the festival located knowledge in people's experience in terms of context but also in terms of the planning and organization of the event. As Sarah notes about its structure:

We don't proposes and second motions; it's all about learning and workshops. It's about educating people about the trade union movement and how it relates to their lives. We wanted it to be more engaging than informative.

One of the mechanisms they used was to have a speaker give an overarching perspective and then have one of the committee, or another activist, contextualize this knowledge at a local level, showing how they had actually used it.

We have had solicitors from ACAS explaining how that works. I remember explaining that, when I worked in Greggs, they tried to get me to use the chip pans but I knew that I couldn't do that as I was under 18, and people could relate to that. Even if things didn't directly affect people, it meant that they could go back and tell their friends.

Another democratizing technique involved the organizers and planners deliberately spreading themselves out in sessions, and making sure that the participants got to know them personally. The notion that power was to be held by the organizers alone was explicitly challenged.

It was important that the people who planned it were there to welcome everyone. We as a committee dotted ourselves around and spoke to those who were on their own and kinda made sure that no-one was on their own all weekend.

Returning to the jargon buster exercise, the leadership deliberately held each other to account for sticking to avoiding jargon, which, Sarah admitted, could be hard. However, they recognized how important this was, and that this was done publicly to further lessen the perceived power of the event planners. We noted that participants started to follow suit and to challenge both leaders, and each other, in a collegiate fashion (Foley, 2007; Seal, 2017).

We also led by example and challenged each other. It's very hard when you've been involved for a bit – even if you tell yourself not to use abbreviation and jargon, you still end up slipping up; it is very difficult not to do it. We made it into a sport between us to show others that it's fine to challenge.

At a wider level, the whole way that the events were planned tried to be democratic, to bring in new ideas, and to keep a vitality to the events.

Certainly for the 2014 festival, everyone had a voice on the planning committee. We inputted our ideas and then discussed them – one wanted an igloo to do a silent disco, nothing went through without consensus and agreement. Those at the forefront of the first festivals are now taking a back seat and we are now doing things for ourselves.

As she says, an explicit part of this was the intent to develop new leaders;

> We just wanted to keep things regenerating – the whole idea is to identify the leaders of tomorrow. It's a process rather than just an event – people put themselves forward and then join the next committee and it keeps going.

As Sarah implies, the idea was for the planning process to become a cycle of development for people, which in turn becomes a cycle of democracy as power is shared and not allowed to accumulate in any one individual.

> This year we had volunteers coming in, and we'll do the same so there are fresh ideas coming in, but with core people who have done things for a few years – and in turn others in the core will shift and also take a back seat.

A lesser-known part of the Albemarle Report (the document that fore-grounded the development of the modern youth service, which has popular education as a founding idea) talked about the importance of this cycle, and suggested that a leader should not stay in a position for any longer than 10 years, otherwise ideas within an organization, and they themselves, will stagnate. This could be a red herring – some leaders stagnate immediately, while others never do. For critical educators the more important thing is to find ways to maintain one's vitality, and part of this is to be continually humble about one's own knowledge and maintain an empowering approach. Nevertheless, it remains a danger and one that Sarah notes as prevalent within unions. As we shall see in the next section, a leader needs to recognize that our position powerfully determines others, as does our perception of the superiority of our knowledge. This places a responsibility on the educator, and the seasoned activist, to continually explore the limitations of their knowledge, and to actively encourage others to challenge it.

Educators need to give up some of their power – and be seen to do so

Sarah noted that within unions there can be a reluctance to learn.

> Something that I find more now since working in the union full time – people get stuck in their ways or cynical. They'll say 'we've tried everything and nothing ever works', but I don't think that helps. I'll have ideas and they'll look at me and say 'that won't work' and when I ask why they say that they tried it 20 years ago and it didn't. But that were 20 years ago and it might work now…

She equally saw that it happens within trade union education.

> There is a reluctance [to learn] and this includes those who are educators in

the union. You could see it in some of those conferences we've done, people are cynical about new things or things they tried once, and maybe did not even try properly.

There is the question here of why some seasoned activists, and educators, become cynical. One explanation is that they may not have embraced the idea that knowledge, particularly about what constitutes effective activism or organizing, is contextual. While an approach may not have worked before, the context could have changed such that it could be effective now – or at least enough for it to be worth trying again. Sarah identified a different motivation for not wanting to change, one that relates back to the need for some people to move on, or at least find a way to constantly challenge themselves. Her insight is that some seasoned activists become fearful of change, a fear that the good work they have done will be undone, when for a long time they were the ones pushing. Unfortunately, this has consequences, and she noted a dynamic emerging.

There are a lot of charismatic people in the union who perhaps stay a little too long and end up making things in their image. I don't think they always mean it, it's just that they've made it work for so long that they feel that they can't move on, as they fear it would all fall down without them.

It is a wider project to explore why some leaders and activists resist change and become cynical, or need to feel that their knowledge is inherently superior. Sometimes, as Rancière (1992), describes, this can mean holding back our expertise and experience, because allowing others to develop their ideas is more powerful than simply saying to them that 'I am experienced and this is how it will go', even if you are right. While there is an understandable frustration in this, because the wheel might get continually re-invented, it means there are more wheel makers. Also, to complete the analogy, the wheel might turn in unexpected and innovative directions that our expertise had not predicted – perhaps because it will never go over the same ground twice.

Developing generative themes

As we discussed in Chapter 2, the concept of developing generative themes has several components (Seal, 2017). The festivals met several of these criteria. First, they sought to gauge the level of experience of participants, and to find out what might engage them.

We then did a simple quiz, asking yes and no questions to gauge people's experience and understanding of unions. On the Friday night we had Banner Theatre, who were commissioned to do a history of the trade union movement.

I really enjoy them but I'm not classed as a young person any more so it's hard to gauge, but they are well received and people understand them.

Second, the festivals did not shy away from looking at issues of tension and contradictions in the movement. Sarah here is talking about some of the restrictive ways in which unions can concentrate exclusively on shop-floor issues, or on models of organizing that are based on economic structures that are no longer prevalent:

We can't just say 'this is what you need to do in your workplace' because without looking outside it we will never expand. It's not all about factories – I worked across shops and so we had to think wider than just ourselves. The factory negotiation is probably the exception rather than the rule now. It's also looking at other ways people do things – do we do everything right? could we learn from the world? (Definitely). The more perspectives we can have, and the more people are open to other, and wider, perspectives the better we can be.

She saw that change was needed, and we needed to look more broadly into what can inspire changes and new ways of working and educating. One of the criteria for generative themes is that they have wider generative themes within them. Talking about new ways of organizing across new economic situations opens up discussions about the need for new ways of organizing more generally, including new types of democracy, and new educational approaches. This desire to open up discussion is exemplified by the festival's significant emphasis on international work, the third criterion for a generative theme. Generative themes should open up and explore the relevance of wider social issues, and enable people to make those connections. Sarah talked enthusiastically about how an international emphasis in the festivals was achieved and received.

We feel it's important to focus on the international dimension because it's very easy when you come into the union to think, 'well, this is my workplace, this is my branch and that's it'. It kind of blows people's minds to know that most unions are national and there are thousands of members – also that someone on the other side of the world is going through similar things and this is what we can do to help each other. For some, it's like, wow, I didn't realize it was so big!

This shows how generative themes can be developed within the flow of a festival. One session can build on another, enabling people to make connections that they perhaps had not made before, to see that there is a wider social context to unions and, most importantly, that they can be a part of this. In time this could mean that their involvement in their own union deepens, as might their participation in wider aspects of the movement.

Teachable moments: working in the moment

The festivals, both in their planning and their execution, had an organic feel to them, embracing popular education's emphasis on being able to respond in the moment (Seal and Harris, 2016; Smith, 1994). Sarah described several occasions where the organizer made a judgement call about changing things as they went along.

> We were going to have some history snippets but we had kind of been historied out the night before so we had more of a general introduction.

This included being able to respond in the moment, something which is often portrayed as requiring a highly skilled educator if it is to work (Harris, 2014), but which the facilitators seemed to find natural.

> When you saw people starting to look out of the window, you could tell it was going over their heads so we decided to tone it down.

Previous research I have conducted (Seal, 2014) found that the skills of working in the moment as an educator are more about a general disposition to learn and be flexible than something that only the highly experienced can do. The festivals, when they did bring in more seasoned speakers, chose those who had these skills.

> We didn't have lecturers or academics or teachers or anything like that: people came to speak about their experiences in the movement and when they were asked questions by people they could respond and ad lib.

In the aforementioned research, I found that it is often the more seasoned educators who have more educational habits to undo, and that it takes some effort to re-orientate themselves. However, it is worth doing, as it is the main way of revitalizing oneself as an educator. When I say to a student that I will learn as much from them as they will from me, I am being honest, but I am not being selfless here; it is from students that I get new ideas, and refresh others.

Conscientization

The festivals also emphasized consciousness raising, in the popular-education sense of making connections and being released from one's own ways of thinking that re-inscribe existing power structures, starting to see denied knowledges and being able to recognize one's own oppression and one's complicity in re-inforcing it. Sarah here describes the actions of a speaker who was able to help a young woman make those connections for herself:

> I loved the session about alternative ways of being skint. I always remember in one session he asked people what they understood about economics. One young woman said she didn't know anything about it, adding that she just worked in a call centre – but he took her job and broke it down in the simplest terms into economics and she walked away saying that she could now say that she understood economics.

Sarah discussed how the whole ethos of the weekend was about developing this consciousness raising, and enabling people to make connections in their own lives.

> That's the whole purpose of the weekend: to get people to understand things they didn't see the relevance of before.

This seems to again be a dispositional thing. In choosing sessions for a conference, or any educational event, the question is not so much 'is this speaker good or powerful?', or even whether they have the information people need. It is whether the speaker will be able to enable members of the audience to make connections between what is being said and their own lives – will it expand their consciousness of their own situations, enable them to make connections with others and see the relevance of wider social forces?

Beyond popular education

Our discussion also illuminated some points of learning for trade union educators that go beyond popular education. Sarah describes how learning can happen in other ways and places at an event, and that the learning in class may only really make sense and become cemented through more informal mechanisms.

> Trade union courses are very traditional – you have your tutor and you have your workbook – but a lot of the learning is done outside of lessons, in the breaks and in the bar afterwards. We have tried to capture that part.

This approach will have resonance with those who are familiar with the idea of informal education (see infed.org). However, Sarah's final comment above indicates an approach wider than this. Harrison Owen (2008), an American educator and writer on organizations and management, noted that most of the effective learning in conferences happened in the informal spaces outside of, and around, the conferences. He suggested that we should organize conferences based on what happens in these spaces, rather than the formal ones. This was also something that was put into action in the festivals.

We started with icebreakers for people but found that the introduction session, with everyone sitting outside in the garden and chatting, broke the ice before the icebreakers, so now we start like that.

Owen (2008) has developed techniques for running whole conferences on this basis. It is perhaps worth giving a flavour of them. First, the agendas of conferences aren't decided until people arrive. There may be a general theme, and perhaps people are sent papers to stimulate thinking beforehand, but the actual sessions are planned on the day. The principle here is that you can only really know what is going to be effective and appropriate when you know who is in the room. The first hour and a half is dedicated to people volunteering to hold sessions, and explaining what they will be about to others. It you have an idea, you have to take responsibility for starting up debate. It is amazing how quickly the sessions fill up with topics that may never have occurred to the organizers.

After the opening and agenda creation, the individual groups go to work. The attendees organize each session as they go, which may finish earlier or later than the allotted time. Think how often you have been to a session where you either could have finished early, but felt obliged to carry on, or where you have run out of time. Interestingly, participants are free to decide which session they want to attend, and may switch to another one at any time (how often have you gone to a session at a conference only to find it's not what you thought it would be, but felt obliged to stay?). Consequently, a session may have no-one in it. While this may sound negative, it is good for testing out whether those people with a lot to say, who claim that everyone agrees their issues are important, are accurate in their claims.

Open spaces are created where people can come together and do something different, as long as they take responsibility for feeding back what they discuss and agree. Networking can occur before, during, after and in-between the actual face-to-face meetings so that discussions can continue seamlessly. All discussion reports are compiled in a document on site and sent to participants, unedited, shortly after. Sarah and I explored the structuring of trade union conferences in general. Going back to the start of this chapter, there was a recognition that traditional conferences often put new people off, and the festivals were part of a desire to get away from that. A conference could have elements of informality, and open-space technology, interspersed with more traditional sessions and speakers. Sarah discussed her brother's reaction to going to his first conference.

A couple of years ago my brother became a union member and he came to conference – I could see he was totally disengaged. I spoke to him afterwards and he said, 'why were people putting motions across about the things that they did? Why do people get up and say the same things over and over again?'

However, Sarah recognized that conferences are structured as they are for a reason, and are an essential part of a trade union's democratic accountability. What was missing was explaining to people that there is a reason why they are structured like they are and that they have a natural flow to them. This is as much a part of our education as consciousness raising.

> It's a lot of money to put the conference on – to limit motions for education might do more damage than good. We still need the democratic and decision-making structures we have, but people need time and to see why they are important and structured like that. It isn't going to happen by just bringing people along to a conference and expecting them to get it and respond; people need time to see the importance of these things.

Sarah and I thought that if people saw their own worth and potential through events like the festivals, then perhaps they would then be motivated enough to engage in full conferences and see the point in them. Sarah also thought that conferences could learn and change slightly, even in the way they present themselves. Learning from the GFTU education conferences, she describes how her own union is thinking about doing this:

> Something we might also do is to put some thought provokers in there to give people an idea o f what the conference is about. This year we will put down that we have changed things in the light of what people said – it helps give people some sense of ownership.

Sarah also recognized that some of these small changes could be applied to how unions organize in general.

> We need to make sure that we are not excluding anyone – is holding a branch meeting in a pub at seven the best thing to do? It's important to remove barriers – we as a movement put in barriers without thinking about it because that is how we have always done things. That single mum could skype in – we have to adapt to change.

She recognized that it is an attitude change that is needed. At the forefront of organizers' thinking should be whether an approach will exclude others. They should ask if it will help people develop as leaders, rather than simply if it is convenient or what has always been done.

Long-term impact

One striking thing that emerged from my discussions with Sarah was the impact that the festivals have had on people. She was extremely modest, saying that that 'only' 50 per cent have gone on to do something in their union, and 'only' 10 per cent have gone on to develop new initiatives and become heavily involved. This is an extremely high rate of achievement. She noted that for some it had totally turned around their perspective, from a position of relative self-centredness to one of solidarity. She recounts the development of one Musicians' Union member:

> It completely opened his eyes: he moved from someone wanting to sell his music to people to wanting to organize. Others have become members or are now doing things that they would not have done before.

This level of impact is testimony in itself to the relevance of utilizing different approaches to organizing conferences, and shows that there is much to learn from the festivals.

Conclusion

One of the criticisms of popular education is that it is good at describing its intended approach, but lacks examples of it being put into practice. Even many of the examples given in Freire's *Pedagogy of the Oppressed* (1972b) never came to full fruition. The festivals provide such examples. They also offer a challenge to how we should approach big events, and the disposition that an educator needs to develop. Our humility is as important as the wisdom we have from experience, our willingness to learn from others as important as our supposed expertise. We should also seek not to reinforce people's experiences of education, which have often undermined their will to learn as well as their confidence and belief in themselves – but the opposite. We also need to recognize that knowledge, and our organizing principles, have to change with the times and that unless we involve young people and new activists effectively, who may have a better grasp of the pulse of the times, our knowledge and approach will wither. I will finish with another organizer's comment on the festivals.

> Young workers need this event probably more than any other. It's amazing. Music, poetry, workshops, information on rights, a brilliant performance piece on how trade unions have changed the world and incredible stories from guest speakers from overseas, controversial debates and the election of representatives to go on some fantastic events, all blend together to make this one of the most powerful experiences you could imagine.

The only thing I would add is that this kind of event is not just something young people need – it is an approach from which we could all benefit.

13
Popular education in practice: a case study of radical educational praxis in a contemporary UK university

Naomi Canham, Kyna Dixon, Becca Golby, Shannon Gorman, Sophie Imeson, Tom Muskett and Jack Scranage

We are a community of learners (students and staff) who worked together on an elective module, *Critical Psychology in Practice*, offered to students on an undergraduate Psychology degree in the UK. Our module was explicitly designed and delivered using democratic and community-based teaching and learning methods, including critical pedagogy.

This chapter is about our module. In many ways, it did little that was innovative, as it was directly inspired by authentically radical work already undertaken in different cultural contexts. What is more unusual is its setting within a modern UK university as part of a 'mainstream' undergraduate degree programme. In this chapter, we will therefore situate our module historically and politically in relation to the modern UK university. We will describe how critical pedagogy informed the process of teaching and learning on this course. Finally, we will explore some of the complexities associated with its implementation.

The context: the modern UK university

As educational institutions, universities sit at the intersection of a broad range of social and political issues. Much has been written about recent cultural changes in higher education. Such changes have arguably impacted upon how universities are understood and perceived across society, and upon the lived experiences of those who work and/or learn within such institutions. They also have a complex relationship with the kinds of teaching and learning practices that take place within academic settings. It is these practices that we sought to redefine in this module.

To understand how critical pedagogy might inform alternative approaches to university education, it is important to reflect first upon two broader points about mainstream practice. First, we argue that, traditionally, universities often uphold an *elitist and authoritarian* view of teaching, learning and knowledge ownership – a view that is deeply historically rooted. Second, universities have in recent years been reshaped on multiple levels by the prevailing *neoliberal* political culture. Both of these themes will now be discussed in detail.

Elites, authorities, and learning in the university
In the UK, elitism is an issue that is often discussed in relation to university education. For instance, certain universities are sometimes criticized as demonstrating institutional biases (for example, during admissions processes) in favour of already-privileged social groups. This issue has deep historical roots. As Rustin (2016) discusses, the organization and function of universities have always reflected current socio-economic circumstances and, therefore, dominant class structures. Rustin discusses how, centuries ago, the first universities almost exclusively provided 'a site of cultural reproduction and transmission for a predominantly aristocratic social fraction' (p.149). Conversely, during the 1800s, the rapid economic expansion within industrial heartlands elsewhere in the UK led to the foundation of new universities which, while still catering for new forms of social elite, were shaped by the changing economic contexts of their surroundings. As we discuss subsequently, the university as 'inclusive' and 'accessible' is a very modern cultural invention. It is therefore unsurprising that university halls might still be haunted by the elitist ghosts of this past.

While these are important points, from our perspective they are but one way that 'elitism' runs through universities. For instance, another (closely related) form of elitism could be argued to exist through the strongly hierarchical relationships that much teaching and learning in higher education is dependent upon. Within these traditional lecturer-student relationships, there are substantial differences between teachers and learners in relation to their 'rights to know'. For example, lecturers are often positioned as 'experts' who hold a detailed knowledge of a subject which, through their teaching, is transmitted to students (Grasha, 1994). The 'expert' is celebrated in the university, to the point where the majority of UK institutions provide databases of staff details to media organizations in order to rent out expert views on topical matters. Conversely, it has been argued that students/learners are positioned as *not authorised* to know (Cook-Sather, 2002). This is perhaps most powerfully reflected by the lecture – a teaching approach that has dominated Western universities for centuries, but one that reflects 'a conception of education in which teachers who know give knowledge to students who do not, and are therefore supposed to have nothing worth contributing' (Bligh, 1972, p.11). Such a positioning of learners, we argue, is disempowering. In fact, we suggest that mainstream authoritarian teaching practices in modern universities create an oppressive set of educational and social conditions.

The neoliberal university

Over the last five decades in the UK, the number of people attending university has grown significantly. With these greater numbers comes a greater diversity of student in terms of background, heritage and prior experiences of education. For any pro-inclusivity readers, this may appear to be a positive development, particularly given the chequered social history discussed above. However, increased opportunities to attend university have come at a price – literally.

For centuries, university education was understood as providing a broader societal benefit. However, there has been a shift away from this: higher education is now presented as if *benefiting the private individual* (Holmwood, 2011). Accordingly, the higher-education funding burden has also shifted to the individual, resulting in levels of student personal debt that were previously unthinkable. In parallel, universities have increasingly adopted corporate, market-driven principles 'where the demand and supply of student education, academic research and other university activities are balanced through the price mechanism' (Brown, 2015, p.5). These principles assume that such competition-oriented and economically driven management will ultimately drive up educational standards and worker 'efficiency'.

The modern emphasis on individual learner autonomy and responsibility; the corporate governance of education; competition and marketization: all of these speak directly of modern neoliberal values. The resultant changes in culture, values and organizational structure within universities have significantly impacted upon the lived experiences of those who work and learn there. For instance, from a staff perspective, O'Neill (2014) notes a range of consequences including: increasingly high levels of measurement-based management of staff performance; higher workloads and a results-focused culture; and normalization of hyper-performance. To work at a modern university, O'Neill argues, involves submission to an unrelentingly *fast* culture of endless demands on time and, increasingly, a lack of space to reflect upon work or forge meaningful relationships with others (see also Mountz et al, 2015). For students, there may be broadly comparable but superficially different experiences of: juggling precarious and typically exploitative part-time employment with study; attempting to minimize debt by efficiently organizing time, travel and accommodation; being surrounded by messages of 'employability' in the face of stiff competition for training and career opportunities; yet, ultimately being positioned as an 'empowered consumer' of an educational product. Students often report experiencing low teaching contact hours, difficulties contacting overworked staff, and an absence of instructor-learner relationship. Conversely, staff may experience a sense of being overwhelmed by student requests and needs, in a context of many competing role demands.

It is therefore no surprise that space for authentic relationships and dialogue, rather than authority and instruction, may feel impossibly limited within the modern university. But as a group, we feel that we achieved this within our module. We did so by drawing on critical pedagogy principles. These therefore have great relevance to the modern university context.

Critical pedagogy in the modern UK university

Paulo Freire's pedagogic work with illiterate Brazilian sugar-cane farmers may seem a long way from practice in contemporary UK universities. Freire's approaches were developed with communities of learners who were unthinkably socially marginalized, materially deprived and politically disenfranchised. As a group, we acknowledge that our experiences of oppression cannot be compared with these conditions. However, there are still many similarities between some of Freire's most basic criticisms of mainstream education (Freire, 1972b) and the issues addressed earlier in the chapter. Let us provide three simple examples.

First, Freire discussed at length the oppressive impact of hierarchical relationships within the classroom. From a critical pedagogy perspective, circumstances in which teachers are positioned as authority figures result in the replication of deeply problematic oppressor/oppressed dichotomies. Critical thinking is blocked, shared histories are repressed, and subservience to authority figures is fostered (c.f. Shor, 1980). These critiques are directly applicable to practices within the modern university, particularly (but not exclusively) in relation to the didactic lecture. Ironically, so-called 'critical thinking' is valorized in university education. But from a Freirian perspective, it is difficult to resolve the pursuit of critical thought with the arguably oppressive and authoritarian teaching approaches that dominate the sector.

Second, Freire famously provided a critique of the so-called 'banking model' of education. Freire used this metaphor to describe the treatment of learners as if they were empty vessels, devoid of prior or present knowledge, experience or orientation, to be passively filled by the educator. Instead, a critical pedagogy approach would involve an educator *explicitly* orienting to the 'folk culture' of learners as a starting point for an educational relationship, thereby facilitating development of a form of organic intellectualism (Gramsci, 1971; see Romero et al, 2009). Of course, such a process would be made almost impossible by traditional, expert- and authority-based models of teaching within universities, particularly those in which the power relations remain unspoken.

Third, critical pedagogy advocates the raising of critical consciousness (*conscientização*) as a central part of educational praxis. Here, through ongoing dialogue, learner and teacher become mutually aware of their own and one another's social and institutional positioning, and develop a critical awareness of the historically situated constraints and influences on their educational experiences and their lives more broadly. Romero et al (2009) suggest that this process, particularly when mindful of the multiple, intersecting oppressions that each of us may experience, is akin to adding a 'third dimension' of personal and political depth to a learning experience. And, as implied above, in modern higher-education systems there is arguably much to raise mutual consciousness about.

The Critical Psychology in Practice module

We will now move on to consider the module itself, which explicitly tried to address the issues discussed above. It is an optional third-year undergraduate course titled *Critical Psychology in Practice*, delivered as part of the undergraduate Psychology programme run at Leeds Beckett University, UK. Leeds Beckett is a relatively new university which was previously a polytechnic (an old UK term for an Institute of Technology), receiving a diverse student cohort often drawn from relatively local communities. There is a relatively high proportion of Black and Minority Ethnic students, and students who are the first within their families to attend university.

All students in the cohort had already undertaken a compulsory theoretical Critical Psychology module in the first semester of their third year. This module presented a range of philosophical and theoretical perspectives which sought to challenge and/or deconstruct 'mainstream' approaches to the subject. For instance, students studied a range of emancipatory perspectives on subjects such as gender, race, sexuality, disability and mental health, were introduced to philosophical frameworks such as post-modernism, and began to apply theoretical perspectives from feminism, post-colonialism, queer theories and critical disability studies. Students were encouraged to look past academic psychology's beneficent claims of 'science', and instead reflect on its history, philosophical roots and unintended, arguably oppressive consequences.

Critical Psychology in Practice followed this module and aimed to provide students with an opportunity to focus on opportunities for the application of critical and radical thinking. Students explored how contemporary approaches to education, healthcare, social care and social policy could be rethought through critical theories. Critical pedagogy itself was a topic of one week's sessions; other topics included social justice-oriented psychological approaches, frameworks for deconstructing institutional biases in services and professional practices, and user movements that have sought to democratize services and the relationships within them. Throughout the course, there was a critical focus on the tendency of Western academic psychology work to overlook cultural contexts other than those associated with core capitalist countries, and an explicit attempt to balance this bias with often overlooked psychological work from liberation groups.

Given the module content, there was a clear educational (in addition to humanistic) benefit in designing the course using critical pedagogy approaches: in doing so, students would personally experience topics from the course as 'users' themselves. We will now provide an overview of some of the approaches that were deployed in this module, interspersed with our personal insights about their use.

A democratic curriculum

While topic areas for each week were assigned in advance, much of the course was developed reactively, based upon the outcomes of the prior session. For the first three-hour teaching session, the instructor began by outlining some key arguments that have been made about the neoliberal university. Then, in a structure that was replicated across several weeks of the course, students were invited to discuss, first in small groups and then in larger groups, the extent to which they felt these arguments could be applied to make sense of their own experiences.

There was some hesitancy within the group at first, and initial discussion-based sessions had to be facilitated and supported. However, even at this stage, the group began to reach consensus on previously unspoken aspects of their learning experiences that they found challenging: the quantity of content sometimes presented in lectures; the limited opportunity to interact with the material or the staff delivering it; assessments requiring memorization of large amounts of content; and assessment regimes that appeared inflexible to individual circumstances. During discussions, the instructor sought to provide multiple perspectives on group experiences (including contributing comparable experiences), and encouraged the students to analyse these challenges socio-politically.

These discussions enabled the group to begin to reflect upon the power relations within the classroom and broader university, and to identify 'between-the-cracks' sites for resistance (see Britt and Rudolph, 2013). For instance, one of the two module assessments was a portfolio of group and individual work, comprising a poster, a written reflection, and a viva. This portfolio reported a piece of group work where students were required to develop a 'critical' approach to practice within health, social care or education. Typically in universities, most aspects of module design (including assessments) are specified months before courses run. However, within the quality assurance system at Leeds Beckett University, there is no requirement for *weightings* of portfolio components to be specified in advance. Therefore, the group discussed how this presented an opportunity to agree democratically what percentage of overall marks would be constituted by each of the three portfolio components.

From a learner perspective, some hesitancy emerged around whether this empowerment would serve any function other than to allow some students to take 'the easy route'. From an instructor perspective, there were powerful feelings of anxiety about handing over control even of such a relatively small aspect of the module. But what actually happened was the opposite: over the course, the group experienced a change whereby there developed a collective will to achieve something through the assessment projects that meant more than a mark. Portfolio percentages were agreed based on the group's perception of the work required for each component. Furthermore, the group democratically elected to base *all* of their work on developing critical practices within the university. Hence, the final assessment event at which posters were marked was transformed into a piece of collective praxis, to which other staff and students were invited.

Slowness

Very early in the course, the group discussed whether to adopt a *slow* approach to learning and study on this module (c.f. O'Neill, 2014) in which space for discussion, dialogue and contemplation took priority over content density. Although there was some hesitancy at first, the group opted for this. Single guided readings were provided as opposed to multiple chapters of textbook reading, didactic instruction was kept to a minimum, and activities were designed to provide space for dialogue. Drawing on the constructive alignment approach to curriculum design (Biggs, 1996), sessions were driven by pursuit of learning outcomes rather than prior stipulation of finite content and material. Later in the course, some seminar sessions were left completely unplanned. This at first generated much anxiety from an instructor perspective, but ultimately provided important contemplative space for student-led learning.

From a learner perspective, the pace of the module was unique: in attending to slowness, the learning environment was transformed. Students reported no longer dreading attending lectures, or staring down at their phones during seminars. Instead, removing the pressure to learn appeared to provide a more genuine opportunity to process content, with some students reporting that they found themselves more actively discussing the module topic with friends and family and spending spare time spontaneously reading related materials.

Authorized knowing: 'conscientização' and challenging authority

Our module utilized a number of activities and session designs that aimed to facilitate mutual dialogue between group members. Mindful that students are typically not 'authorized' knowers, many activities began with the group exploring and sharing everyday experiences. Learning therefore began within the cultures and constraints experienced by the students themselves, rather than reflecting a single (privileged) world view: indeed, the instructor's role became one of facilitating students to understand and situate their own struggles using theoretical perspectives from the module.

Practically, many activities on the module were directly inspired by the work of Ira Shor (e.g. 1980) in the US community-college system. Although working in a different historical and geopolitical context from that of this module, Shor drew explicitly on Freirian principles to develop an educational praxis based upon empirical examination and then analysis of everyday experiences. Examples of Shor-influenced activities on this module included group members sharing their most difficult or painful educational experiences, and exploring times in which their mental health and wellbeing might have been impacted upon by the demands of precarious employment in a neoliberal economy. In an attempt to reverse classroom hierarchies, the instructor would frequently sit with the rest of the class while learners spoke (if they wished) from the front of the room. From an instructor perspective, such activities were genuinely transformative in enabling a deeper, connected insight into the lived experiences of this generation of university learners; from a learner perspective, the rethinking of everyday experience by using theory scaffolded their learning of the course material while transforming the nature of future experiences. As one learner remarked:

> Observing the teaching methods on this module and seeing how sometimes classes work on just trial and error from our responses, breaks down power structures, showing the tutor may make mistakes but our opinions are welcomed. The ability to have open dialogue in seminars and voice your opinion without fear of judgement is unique. What is most comforting is to find that most people feel exactly the same way you do or are able to help you with your situation.

223

During all activities, the instructor contributed personal stories and made disclosures comparable to those of the learners. However, the very real social and institutional power held as a function of the tutor position was never denied. In order to resist this ever-present classroom power dynamic, from early in the course the group was supported to *challenge* theory and teaching by using insights from their lived experiences. This principle (of valuing experience before theory) is central to some Latin American psychological approaches such as Liberation Psychology, where it is described as *realismo-critico* ('critical realism': see Martín-Baró, 1994) and is intended to combat oppressive and authoritarian top-down interpretations of human behaviour and experience. By the end of the course, even didactic parts of teaching sessions became transformed into dialogue, in a way that could be appropriately challenging towards the instructor. From some learners' perspectives, this rejection of traditional educational hierarchies felt uncomfortable at first, but ultimately appeared to lead to the attainment of both deeper learning of content and higher levels of critical consciousness. As one learner describes:

> Within both lectures and seminars I was surprised by the breakdown of the power imbalance which usually occurs within education with our tutor asking our opinions about the topics being studied, and the encouragement we received to share and even critique and question the theories and ideas. Initially this shocked me and at first I thought 'but I don't have any opinions about this' (which is incredibly ridiculous considering one topic was about university and education, an experience I am a part of) because I have gone through my university career being told that I am not allowed an opinion which doesn't come with a reference after it. During lectures on other modules students are told that we can't speak over the lecturer unless we have questions about understanding the content, yet in this class we could have entire discussions amongst students ourselves and our tutor about how valid or relevant certain theories are. At first this method of teaching was incredibly overwhelming because, as I had first mentioned, I didn't think I knew enough or had as strong an opinion about certain things as other people to be able to join in. Maybe my opinion would even be wrong because I hadn't read about it somewhere else first, but the more I talked the more I realized that by enabling discussions about the content, not just one to one, student to teacher, but also amongst students ourselves, the more confident I felt in understanding the content within different contexts.

Developing a community of learners: unheard voices, authentic care and humanistic capital

As noted above, mainstream academic psychology is frequently criticized for excluding the voices of the oppressed and marginalized (see Fox et al, 2009). Much of this module sought to challenge this status quo by exploring approaches to psychology that resist the dominance of the discipline by individualistic, White, male, cis-gendered and heteronormative interests. As a community of learners, the differences between us reflected this otherwise-overlooked diversity, and therefore it felt crucial to offer an authentically caring space within our curriculum for unheard voices to be listened to.

To do so, influence was taken from the work of Augustine Romero and colleagues with Mexican American (*Chicana/o*) young people in US high schools. As a population, Chicana/o people experience significant structural and institutional oppression through the education system, as is reflected by the very low graduation rates for such young people. In this context, Romero et al (2009) have drawn upon a combination of critical pedagogy and critical race theory to develop the so-called *critical compassionate intellectualism* (CCI) model of education, initially delivered through a controversial high-school course entitled *Raza Studies*. This course, reflecting many Freirian concepts, seeks to situate Chicana/o learners within the context of their own cultural oppression, raising consciousness about broader structures that impact upon learning experiences and 'individual academic success'.

While developed in a different cultural context, many aspects of the CCI approach had relevance for our module. To provide an illustration, one week's topic was post-colonialism. In our seminar session, we modelled mainstream psychology as *metaphorically* colonizing the experiences of diverse groups through its homogeneity and (mis)representation of these. Prior to the seminar, the instructor and a small sub-group of volunteering learners each wrote an account of either themselves or someone they knew that described a real situation that they considered to be misrepresented by mainstream psychology. For instance, one learner contributed an account of a Black family member who they felt was misunderstood and discriminated against by White mental-health services; another wrote a passionate account of experiences of drug use within their family and its intersections with exploitative modes of precarious employment. These accounts were then read out by the instructor and sensitively and compassionately discussed by the group using post-colonial (and other) theories. Learners were positioned so that they could remain anonymous or alternatively 'own' these experiences. The instructor then also contributed their own account non-anonymously, to model the 'humanizing' of a psychological topic. This was a powerful session which many students reported finding cathartic and transformative.

An indirect consequence of such compassionate and dialogic activities was their impact on the group's relationships and, ultimately, the building of a community. From a learner's perspective, the collective needs and preferences of the group frequently became more important than pursuit of individual marks and success, and when the opposite did reoccur (which it frequently did) this became legitimate grounds for shared personal reflection. The consensus was that learners felt valued in class, and experienced a sense of freedom of self-expression. The relationship between instructor and learners also became transformed. As one learner remarked:

> This sense of community extended to our tutor, who, although of course representing an authority figure, rejected the practices of other tutors in his engagement with us. As a result, the developed relationship between them and the group was levelled: though he may have directed and focused the activity during seminars, I never felt that he overpowered any of our voices. I for one found this incredibly refreshing, as it made me feel able and more willing to contribute to the class. I wasn't worried that my answer would be wrong and I felt valued as a participant. At the same time, I feel like his approach granted him more respect within a student-tutor relationship, as his views were equally respected by us, rather than just accepted without challenge.

The instructor experienced reciprocal feelings of respect and care towards the group. A comparable experience was reported by Romero et al (2009): highlighting the importance of facilitating a loving, authentically caring relationship in the classroom, they note that 'if students see their teachers as human beings, they are more likely to invest humanistic capital in that teacher. And, once this humanistic capital has been gained by the teacher, the relationship between teacher and student can become a reciprocating, authentic relationship' (p.223). In our experience, the authenticity of this relationship extended beyond the classroom to tutor relationships, dissertation supervision, and even into projects such as the co-writing of this chapter.

Reflective conclusion: opportunities and barriers

Above, we have provided an overview of an undergraduate module based upon critical pedagogy principles. The educational philosophies underpinning this course explicitly challenged *status quo* assumptions about university teaching, and sought to develop learners' critical consciousness of broader cultures pervading higher education. We were able to carve a 'slow' space in which dialogic, learner-first and authentically caring educational relationships developed. Based on student feedback, the experiences of learners were overwhelmingly positive.

Earlier in the chapter, we argued that university education is currently characterized by authoritarianism on one hand, and neoliberal values on the other. What we did not explore are the inherent contradictions between these

positions. Expert models of teaching are, in many ways, politically conservative – they valorize institutional hierarchies, protect power relationships,
and uphold traditions of (arguably) elitist and oppressive social practices.
Conversely, neoliberal ideologies promote the sovereignty of the individual,
free marketeering, consumer choice, and liberal notions of equality. In an
era where there has been a revolution in how people communicate and use
information, authoritarian teaching practices may increasingly jar with
students' organic experiences of more democratic and collective interactions
with 'knowledge'. Moreover, neoliberal practices of educational governance
may similarly be unsustainable in terms of finances, human resources and
their poor fit with educational philosophies (Rustin, 2016). Therefore, the
frameworks adopted on this module may represent both a timely viable
alternative to traditional teaching approaches, and a legitimate mode of
resistance against neoliberalism. In saying this, this module did still generate
several challenges, and we conclude by reflecting on some of these.

Purely practically, there were workload-related complexities associated
with this module. The new forms of authentic instructor-learner relationship that arose from this course are to be celebrated. However, current
approaches to planning workload for university staff typically assume
an absence of such relationships, and therefore a relative lack of teacher-
student contact outside the classroom. Unsurprisingly, therefore, the
instructor experienced significant time demands when running this
module. This work was crucial to ensure that the module ran with integrity,
but impacted upon the instructor's other role commitments. Similarly, all
students on the module simultaneously undertook courses taught by other
instructors using more conventional methods, and some reported experiencing a lack of engagement, having become disillusioned with traditional
university teaching methods. This complex and difficult issue may well have
negatively impacted upon educational outcomes in these other modules.

Finally, it remains impossible to shield the module from the prevailing
culture in which it is situated. The forces of neoliberalism are omnipresent.
For example, on the strength of learner feedback, our module received a
university-level 'Module of the Year' award (the very process of which,
ironically, provides a canonical example of a neoliberal management
practice!). This has led to cross-institutional interest in some of the methods
described above. However, as with all radical praxis (e.g. Portwood-Stacer,
2013, p.47), there is risk that approaches from this module may be superficially
appropriated (or even commodified or 'branded') without appreciation of
the underpinning theoretical frameworks that we believe enabled such a
transformative experience for us all. *Critical Psychology In Practice* t-shirts,
mugs and stationery sets, anyone?!

14

The Northern College: social-purpose mission and pedagogy

Jill Westerman

The Northern College, based in Barnsley, is one of the four English residential adult-education colleges. Like Ruskin College it has a long history of trade union and working-class education.

The College was established in 1978 as a place of learning for adults who had missed out on educational opportunities in their earlier lives. It emerged from the powerful labour movement in South Yorkshire and since its inception the college has sought to provide a wide variety of courses, from those aimed at people taking their first steps back into learning, often from disadvantaged communities, through to courses for people studying at university level, as well as programmes of study for activists and workers across the trade union, community and voluntary and public sectors.

When I introduce myself as the principal of the Northern College one of the first questions I am often asked is 'why residential education?' In some ways this is unsurprising, as residential education is relatively rare in the world of adult learning. But I do wonder if the heads of public schools or those running executive leadership training are asked the same question: going to public school usually involves boarding or residence; executive leadership training or strategy events are often residential and, although this is changing, studying at university still usually means a period of residence away from home.

Why is residence employed as part of the educational experience in these contexts? It is because residence extends learning beyond the formal or classroom situation. It gives individuals the opportunity to mix at leisure with their peers, discussing or reflecting on what has been learned; to learn a wider range of things from each other in different environments; to compare experiences and to set the learning within a group, community and social context.

What these other forms of residential education all have in common is that they are largely used by an elite and not available to the majority.

The adult residential colleges extend these opportunities for intense and enhanced learning to working-class people, who may have been excluded from previous opportunities, or live in an environment which makes learning difficult. For trade unionists the colleges offer the chance to live and work alongside their peers, learning from each other's experience of trade union representation and activism. This opportunity not only means more intense and deeper learning, but also the separation from the normal routines and pressures of everyday life often results in rapid and profound shifts in perception and understanding which go significantly beyond the more obvious outcomes of a course of study.

The opportunities offered by the residential colleges go some small way towards offsetting the structural educational inequality that pervades our entire system. I've been at the college for over 23 years, starting as a part-time tutor, and one thing I've learned in that time is that working-class people are anything but stupid. However, if you just landed on earth and looked at the statistics for educational achievement you might believe that they were. For example, just 28 per cent of white British boys eligible for free school meals achieve five A*-C GCSEs, compared with a rate of 59 per cent for other children. Most will never catch up in terms of educational attainment (Parliament, House of Commons, 2014).

The government Social Mobility report (Parliament, House of Commons, 2016) says: 'From the early years through to universities, there is an entrenched and unbroken correlation between social class and educational success.' Even in our own world of adult education, social class remains a key predictor of participation, with 54-per-cent participation by social classes AB compared with 26 per cent for unskilled workers or those on limited incomes (NIACE, 2015).

Given these statistics, we shouldn't need to have to make a case for working-class adult education, but unless we do it is overlooked again and again in the setting of public policy and educational funding priorities. Yet all those of us who work in this area know the difference that adult education makes to individuals. I would like to illustrate this by bringing in the voice of a student – Dan, who was an Access to HE student at Northern College in the mid-1990s.

After leaving school at the age of 16 with no qualifications (school was just a place I went to get a free meal...nothing more and nothing less) I embarked in my parents' and brothers' footsteps to a life of benefit dependency. It was difficult being born into a broken and fractured family...It is clear that my time at Northern College changed me more than any other. It made me realize that I wasn't as thick or stupid as people thought I was...the seed of self-betterment through the application of learning was planted and over the following years it slowly grew.

He goes on to say how he gained a degree, became a librarian and had a successful career but was then made redundant. So he returned to education, did a postgraduate degree and is now working as a university lecturer.

But he says:

> However, what I have achieved are just mere footnotes to the things that are truly dear to me. Firstly my son has just completed his first year of university. Whilst most of my mum's other grandchildren spend their days selling drugs, sniffing gas and/or resigned to a life on benefits, my son is the first one to go to university. This is ultimately down to the college and the foundation it gave me.

This, in a nutshell, presents many of the positive arguments for lifelong learning and residential adult education, including the lasting intergenerational benefits – not only Dan's life was turned around, but that of his son John too. And this has many knock-on impacts on the communities in which they live. One example: 97 per cent of students said they felt motivated to do more for others after attending a Northern College course.

The mission of the Northern College is: 'To provide outstanding adult residential and community education for the empowerment and transformation of individuals and communities.'

Education, and in particular lifelong learning, is central to both individual and community growth, and to future community, economic and social wellbeing. Our social-purpose mission also highlights the college's commitment to supporting activists who work to transform and empower individuals and communities. Everything we do comes from that values base. We want to transform the world through education, and trade union education plays a large part in that aspiration.

The focus on both individuals **and** communities is important. In 1978, the beginnings of the college were within a society and a region with a strong and cohesive sense of self-identity: an identity focused on community and the individual within the community. The political upheavals that began the following year, and reached a sort of culmination in the collapse of the miners' strike in 1985, brought a profound and significant shift in those values of community and cohesion. The idea of the individual actor became the predominant discourse alongside a challenge to the notion of any sort of collective social endeavour – 'there is no such thing as society'.

Inevitably, education did not escape the effects of this deep cultural shift.

The focus moved to the individual, to vocational skills rather than adult education, to a system which prioritized exam and employment outputs as pre-eminent beyond other more personal or social outcomes. Tom Schuller (2004) has written about the benefits of education as the development of different types of capital. Different sorts of educational capital have been prioritized at different points in our system: Schuller talks about human capital (qualifications, skills, knowledge); social capital (the networks which contribute to our civic life and the way in which we share common goals); and identity capital (the individual's self-concept, life goals, enjoyment). I would add another: economic capital, or the ability of the individual to contribute to the economic success of the nation, carrying with it a focus on *Homo economicus* (economic man), and portraying humans as narrowly self-interested agents.

Of course these different types of capital are not mutually exclusive; one of the joys of education is the multiplicity of benefits it brings, some of which are unforeseen and unexpected. Nonetheless, over the last 30 years I can see how these different benefits have been foregrounded within FE and Skills, with consequent shifts in public funding from one area to another.

During this time the social-purpose mission of the Northern College has remained consistent and is predicated on the importance of community and on the importance of the group within learning. It has not always been easy to maintain this focus as education policies (and funding levels) have shifted over recent years, but the importance of our mission is evident on a day-to-day level within the college.

The value of the collective is fundamental to trade unionism, and also to trade union education. Equally, the Northern College, since its beginnings, has had strong links with groups within the communities it serves. Outreach workers will make contact with a group of tenants, or parents, or a group supporting those in recovery from addiction or mental illness, and design a bespoke course to suit their particular needs. The group attends together and learns together, supported by a social-purpose pedagogy which challenges the focus of mainstream Western life on the individual rather than the community.

There are signs that there are some shifts in political discourse which may, in time, lead to an altered hegemony, wherein the value of a cohesive society becomes a central focus. David Cameron's Big Society initiative did not achieve this outcome. On the day I am drafting this contribution, Theresa May (2017) has written an article in the *Telegraph* in which she says:

> Overcoming these divisions and bringing our country together is the central challenge of our time. This means building the shared society. A society

that doesn't just value our individual rights but focuses rather more on the responsibilities we have to one another; a society that respects the bonds of family, community, citizenship and strong institutions that we share as a union of people and nations; a society with a commitment to fairness at its heart...this government will seize the opportunity to build the shared society by embracing genuine and wide-ranging social reform.

Big Society has become the Shared Society. I hope it is a more successful initiative.

Yeats said: 'Education is not the filling of a pail, but the lighting of a fire.' Our aim at the Northern College is to light fires wherever we can and resist the notion of education as the filling of an empty vessel, what Paolo Freire (1972b) calls the 'banking' concept of education, where knowledge is considered to be concentrated in the teacher and then deposited into students. The banking notion fits a world view within which *homo economicus* purchases education as a type of product, an instrumental process which results in direct economic benefit. The current national focus on skills rather than education can be seen as dangerously close to this model.

The process of education is as important as the content. Within the Northern College, and indeed most adult and trade union education, the pedagogical approach is one of participation, where the individual is part of a learning community that has a vast range of experience to share. Learning becomes a joint and dynamic process within which students and tutors are challenged, even disturbed, by the views and knowledge of others and where old assumptions change and shift as new thinking and understandings emerge.

This pedagogical approach is not easy. Stephen Brookfield (2005) has written about the ways in which hegemony and ideology influence our expectations of education and in particular the relationships and distribution of power and authority between tutors and students. But it is vital if those previously excluded by reasons of class, ethnicity or background, are to flourish. As Tait Coles (2014) wrote about schools:

> Teachers can't ignore the contexts, culture, histories and meanings that students bring to their school. Working-class students and other minority groups need an education that prepares them with the knowledge of identifying the problems and conflicts in their life and the skills to act on that knowledge so they can improve their current situations.

Critical pedagogy is the only way to achieve this. The philosophy was first described by Paulo Freire and has since been developed by the likes of

Henry Giroux, Peter McLaren and Roger Simon. Critical pedagogy isn't a prescriptive set of practices – it's a continuous moral project that enables young people to develop a social awareness of freedom. This pedagogy connects classroom learning with the experiences, histories and resources that every student brings to their school. It allows students to understand that with knowledge comes power – the power that can enable young people to do something differently in their moment in time and take positive and constructive action.

The 'continuous moral project' is equally vital for adult learners. Exposing, discussing and understanding the ways in which both individuals and communities are influenced by differences of class, ethnicity, power and prior experiences of education are an essential part of developing a critical understanding not just of the world around us, but of our potential to be heard, to have influence and impact on our world.

Within the Northern College, teacher educators have focused on this pedagogy within the development of a 'social purpose' model of teacher education. We have trained many union tutors, supporting them to identify and overcome barriers to learning with workers who have often had very poor experiences of education previously. Tutors have become confident educators, working to empower employees across a diverse range of organizations.

The nature of our pedagogy encourages a focus on 'reflexive' practice, where educators are encouraged to go beyond simple changes to teaching and learning, to examining their own identities as practitioners. Moving from being a trade union representative to a teacher requires a vital shift in thinking, and individuals often go through a process of 'unlearning' previous tutoring habits and re-imagining themselves in a teacher role. On our courses tutors gain confidence in using new teaching techniques; taking advantage of technology and the latest thinking in pedagogy, while considering how to balance their representative duties with the facilitation of open, reflective spaces which may at times challenge existing union practice. In the process many union tutors have gained a new love of teaching and learning, going on to become fully qualified teachers by progressing from the Level 3 Award in Education to our Cert Ed/PGCE programme.

Speaking of the 'love of teaching' and the 'love of learning' gives an inkling of the emotional power of education and the changes it can bring. One student talked of it as 'like having stardust sprinkled on me': the individual benefits can be immense. But the stakes are higher than any individual benefit. Interviewed in the *New York Times*, Henry Giroux says:

I begin with the assumption that education is fundamental to democracy.

No democratic society can survive without a formative culture, which includes but is not limited to schools capable of producing citizens who are critical, self-reflective, knowledgeable and willing to make moral judgments and act in a socially inclusive and responsible way. This is contrary to forms of education that reduce learning to an instrumental logic that too often and too easily can be perverted to violent ends. (Evans and Giroux, 2016)

And there is another quotation, this time from a politician, that is a more chilling illustration of the necessity of education as a means of sustaining democracy:

There was no point in seeking to convert the intellectuals. For intellectuals would never be converted and would anyway always yield to the stronger, and this will always be 'the man in the street'. Arguments must therefore be crude, clear and forcible, and appeal to emotions and instincts, not the intellect. Truth was unimportant and entirely subordinate to tactics and psychology.

This has recently been doing the rounds on social media with some people thinking it was said by Donald Trump. In fact it was Josef Goebbels on the rise of the Nazi party in Germany. Goebbels also said: 'A lie once told remains a lie, but a lie told a thousand times becomes the truth.'

In our 'post-truth' world of sophisticated media manipulation, with fake news on social media and where people are looking for simple answers to complex situations, adult education has a huge role to play in supporting people to develop a critical engagement with the world around them, to be able to see through manipulative and simplistic media messages and form their own political opinions.

In this context trade union education becomes increasingly valuable. Of course it is important that workplace representatives are well trained and able to represent the interests of their members. But, in common with the mission of the Northern College, trade union education has a wider social purpose: to empower people to understand the complex interaction of forces that lead to inequalities, prejudice and the abuse of power as these relate both to the individual and their communities, and to develop a critical examination of the world we live in supported by a group of peers learning together. This in turn will create stronger and more influential unions, working towards a vision of a fairer society and closer communities.

Section Four

Learning from the world

Introduction to Section Four

Doug Nicholls

As part of its regular international study visits, the Executive of the GFTU visits trade union centres overseas and always takes a close look at their education programmes.

We have considered the powerful Freirean-influenced education programmes in Brazil, the Scandinavian approaches, the progressive education approach taken by colleagues in the United States which led to the still highly relevant publication *Teaching for Change, Popular Education and the Labor Movement*, (Delp, L., et al, 2002). We have considered how the extreme pressures on the Australian and New Zealand/Aetearoa trade union movements were relieved by a new approach to organizing and educating workers. Through our associations with the Global Labour Institute and the International Federation of Workers Education Associations we have become aware of the extension of popular-education methods in many countries.

In his chapter on the great Cuban educationalist Julio Mella, GFTU Education Officer John Callow provides a useful reminder of the rootedness of the passion for a transformed education system in movements of social transformation. Just as we saw Cuba's university sector transformed, so we have experienced more recently the transformation of Venezuelan universities into institutions of people's power and knowledge. Trade unionists of course have been very much at the heart of these transformations.

Over the last three years we have turned particularly to a dialogue with the Latin American organization ESNA. For a British audience, this may be best described as a combination of a trade unionists' Workers' Education Association, with the Labour Research Department, the Institute of Employment Rights and the International Centre for Trade Union Rights.

ESNA, supported by Cuba and all of the countries committed to overturning the neoliberal and militaristic regimes in Latin America, full squarely adopts the 'learning for social action' approach. Speakers from ESNA have enlightened GFTU audiences with an analysis of their method, which is touched on briefly in Julio Gambina's chapter, kindly translated for us by the GMB's International Officer Bert Shouwenberg.

There is a growing international movement designed to release the modern university from the neoliberal market, which has replaced the Enlightenment passion of enquiry, research and speculative educational debate with filthy lucre, making education a commodity to be chopped up, price tagged and sold to the highest bidder. Trade union education is indeed part of the wider social purpose of reclaiming all knowledge, science and art for our purpose.

As the pioneers who formed the modern British trade union movement at the end of the nineteenth century said:

> We want to see the necessary economic knowledge imparted in our labour organizations, so that labour in the future shall not be made the shuttlecock of political parties. Our trade unions shall be centres of enlightenment and not merely the meeting place for paying contributions and receiving donations...our ideal is a co-operative commonwealth. (Tom Mann and Ben Tillett, *The New Trade Unionism*, 1890)

15

A comet in the night: Julio Antonio Mella and the genesis of popular education in Cuba

John Callow

Summer shadows lengthening over Mella's laurel tree at the University of Havana; Modotti's photograph reworked in plaster, paint and chiselled stone in squares and public buildings; movie theatres, streets and schools renamed in his honour: all of these attest to the continuing presence of Julio Antonio Mella (1903-29) within the consciousness, and conscience, of the modern Cuban state. Eternally young, on account of his tragic early death, his role in founding the first Communist Party of Cuba accorded him a central place within the pantheon of the revolution's heroes after 1959, while his contemporaries – university friends, party comrades, lovers, and liberal political commentators, alike – seem to have been somewhat in awe of the dynamism of both his physicality and his intellect. He was, as one of his student comrades later recalled, 'young, beautiful and insolent, like a Homeric hero' (Thomas, 1971, p.566). And it is this image of Mella as Achilles 'with a razor mind' – gifted and brave, fallible and ultimately doomed – that has been largely accepted by posterity.[1]

In the space of a public career that lasted almost six years to the day (from his leadership of the first insurgency on the university campus at Havana, in January 1923, to his death at the hands of a dictator's hired gunmen, on a street corner in Mexico City, in January 1929) he established himself as both a national figure within Cuba and as an international, and internationalist, force within the world Communist movement.[2] His plans to land men and munitions, from Mexico, as the catalyst for a revolution in Cuba appear eerily prescient of those of Fidel Castro and his comrades as they went aboard the *Granma* a full generation later; while his specific appeal to youth, as the catalyst for progress, optimism and revolutionary change, would seem to have found both their echoes and their amplification in the Parisian student revolts of 1968, and in the counter-cultural politics, Situationalism, and calls for educational autonomy championed by Daniel Cohn-Bendit and Rudi Dutschke. Moreover, his recovery of the 'radical' elements within the thought of José Martí and his subsequent development and practice of Martí's educational ideals helped to forge an inclusive and liberating pedagogy within Cuba that remains central to the educational theories and policies of that state through to the present day. Restless, rebellious, charismatic, difficult and questioning: Mella was unafraid of power and sought to harness its latent potentialities among both the privileged and the dispossessed – the artist and the artisan, the peasant and the worker, the new immigrant and the indigenous peoples of Latin America.

Within this context, he is emblematic not just of the trajectory of the Cuban Revolution but of several themes within the Left that were once commonplace (Hatzky 2004, pp.17-22). Among these are: a sense of operating in the mainstream of a culture that has its roots firmly and unequivocally in the European Enlightenment; an acceptance of the benefits of industrial and technological advance; and a willingness to countenance direct action and a recourse to armed struggle in order to achieve a thoroughgoing transformation of society. Crucial to these beliefs were the sense that the internationalist Socialist movement was swimming with 'the tide of history' in an upward curve of social and economic progress; and that an unwavering commitment to universal education – conducted by and for the great mass of the people – would (and should) form the cornerstone of any progressive political project. Knowledge meant power for the working class, and equality of educational opportunities would inevitably result, it was argued, in a more egalitarian and meritocratic society. Moreover, the struggle for control of the curriculum, and for access to higher and further education for the many, as opposed to the few, were viewed not just in – quite literally – academic terms but as a vital part of the wider battle to secure revolutionary social change. Political consciousness did not suddenly form, through individual inspiration or personal experience, but as the result of the praxis of collective action shaped by lifelong learning. A total, immersive politics demanded not just a total art but also a total education, through which to forge the Socialist woman or man of the future.

If today the European Left finds some, or perhaps all, of these assumptions uncomfortable or questionable – not least in the light of the collapse of European Communism in 1989 or the capitulation of Western social democracy before neoliberalism in the 1990s – then it might be argued that this tells us more about a current existential crisis and retreat from the hard considerations of power, than about the efficacy and appeal of Mella's project and message during his lifetime. Perhaps more importantly, it remains a worthwhile exercise to understand, and possibly recapture, the sense of sheer empowerment and possibility that the radical Left offered to those otherwise rendered hopeless and marginalized – politically, educationally and economically – across the Southern hemisphere, by the effects of neocolonialism and empire over the course of the nineteenth and early twentieth centuries.

Indeed, in the 'Post-Fordist' age when education is increasing viewed as a marketized commodity, as opposed to an inalienable right and as a means to self-realization, the 'business' of competencies, metrics, selection and intensive testing may appear all the more tawdry when set alongside the vision of those like Mella, who sought to build – from nothing – a grassroots pedagogy that linked the avant garde to the masses, to remove the barriers of privilege and financial constraint to educational provision, and to celebrate learning, creativity and talent for their own sakes, stripped of mystification and the teleology of the dollar sign and the 'free market'. As a consequence, he may appear to be a far more radical figure and to have surmounted far greater obstacles in the course of his all-too-brief career when his achievements are viewed from our contemporary perspective, rather than by the standards and expectations of the hopeful, modernist 1920s.

Mella himself stood at the intersection of empires, social classes and ethnicities. The illegitimate son of a Black, Dominican dressmaker (Nicanor Mella) and a British heiress of Irish heritage (Cecilia McPartland), he was originally known as Nicanor McPartland before adopting his father's surname – and the Christian names 'Julio Antonio' – as a *nom de guerre* at the start of his adult, political career in Cuba. Though born in Havana, his mother's protracted ill-health saw him despatched to join his father in New Orleans when he was just a few months old. He did not return to settle for any length of time in Cuba until he was seven years old, dividing his time between the households of his mother and his father's new wife (Contrera, 1987, p.13). He was educated, initially, by private tutors, and then by priests in a succession of private, Roman Catholic colleges, from which he managed to be expelled on account of his anti-clericalism and anti-authoritarian behaviour. His character appears, from childhood onwards, as being just as fiery and unconventional as his upbringing was, otherwise, comfortable, privileged and even patrician (Dumpierre, 1965; Guanche 2009; Hatzky, 2004; Ortiz, 1999; Thomas, 1971).

Life in the multicultural crucible that was New Orleans in the early 1900s ensured that he knew English, French and a smattering of Latin, alongside Spanish, and allowed him to experience North America for himself. But it was Mella's return to Cuba and his enrolment in a state school that led to his imagination being fired by an encounter with Salvador Diaz Miron, a teacher who told him from first-hand experience about the Mexican Revolution of Zapata and Villa, and explained its social and political dimensions. If background and temperament had served to make Mella a rebel, then contact with Miron (who had been both poet and politician) provided him with a positive role model, a cause, and a reason to fight that went beyond mere opposition to established order.

Yet impressive exam results and a more liberal educational regime did not naturally translate into a smoother progress through the system, and Mella switched institutions and course programmes with alacrity before finally arriving in the Department of Law, Philosophy and Letters of the University of Havana in September 1921 (Dumpierre,1965; Thomas, 1971). By that time, the establishment of a workers' and peasants' state in the USSR and the example of the Argentine students' movement, which had toppled a dictatorship in March 1918, seemed to offer further blueprints for radical action. In a land where illiteracy was the norm, rather than the exception, and where 68 per cent of the population received no schooling at all, the University of Havana represented not only a bastion of privilege but also an arm of the corporatist state, where the awarding of professorial chairs acted as a form of political patronage – distributed by President Zayas to allies and family members – rather than as recognition of academic ability and achievement (Cabrera & Almodobar, 1975; Ortiz, 1999).

Few of the faculty published and some did not even lecture at all, while diplomas were often rewarded on scant merit for fictive courses according to favour or ability to pay. However, it was the inadequacy of the curriculum and paucity of teaching resources (particularly as regarded laboratory apparatus) that provoked Mella's ire, rather than just the corruption and venality that appeared to be endemic within the system. To begin with, resistance was located around the university's sports clubs, which offered a rudimentary organization (with access to funds and a democratic structure) and a space where non-aristocratic students, often orientated to the sciences and more vocational courses, and far more focused upon the need to achieve high grades and find a profession after graduating, could congregate and debate. Consequently, Mella, who had initially made his impact on the campus as a star of the rowing team – triumphing at successive regattas – found himself with both a stage and a ready audience, concerned at poor teaching standards, high fees and rising living costs, amid a savage trade depression and mounting economic crisis (Contrera, 1987; Whitney, 2001).

Yet from the first, the demands of the students reflected not only a core set of immediate practical concerns – aiming at the reform of antiquated syllabuses, the equipping of a medical school, and the holding of professors to account through a bolstered administration – they also sought under Mella's inspiration a wider, and far more radical (and radicalizing) commitment to the autonomy of the university as an institution free of government inter-ference, and with the academic freedom to research, teach and debate outside the channels and messages hitherto prescribed by the state (Guanche, 2009, pp.27-28). Mella made his own position clear in an editorial for the newly founded student newspaper, *Alma Mater*, on 4 February 1923. Education possessed a social function, as well as a strictly empirical purpose in terms of equipping individuals with the requisite insights and skills for their professional development. The true function of a university, he wrote, was not to become a 'factory' for the awarding of titles and diplomas, nor a simple 'trade school' where the means to making a living were taught. Rather, 'the modern university must influence social life in a direct way, should signal the path of progress, must lead through action that progress between individuals, [and] must by means of their teachers, communicate the mysteries of science and the experience of human knowledge' (Guanche, 2009, p.30). Moreover, it was the student body, itself, as constituted in the new Students' Federation, that would act as the conscience – and regulator – of the academy, and as the catalyst for change. It understood, far more clearly than the authorities and tenured, often absentee, professors, 'the true work of the university' and aimed to mount 'a successful campaign to ensure that the new University of Havana fulfils its mission to the wider society in which we live' (Guanche, 2009, pp.30-31). If academia had abrogated its responsibility towards the students in favour of a cosy accommodation with the state, then – Mella proposed – the students themselves should fill the vacuum, taking over and managing the development of the curriculum.

His critique of the established order was sharpened by the decision of the university to award an honorary doctorate to the US ambassador, Enoch Crowder, who had transcended the conventional role of the diplomat to become the voice of North American commercial and political interests in Cuba, and (as the 'Special Representative of the President' from 1921-23) was the real power in the land. Bright, erudite and ruthless, this former military man understood – just as surely as Mella – the need to guide the educational curriculum, not least through his commissioning of an allegedly 'impartial' history of Cuba that emphasized the benevolence and rationality of US policy in shaping the polity of a state which was otherwise incapable of being governed by a people who were cast as irrational, childish and often savage. Charles E. Chapman's *A History of the Cuban Republic*, published in 1927, would prove enormously influential, shaping attitudes towards Cuba across campuses in the Western hemisphere, and becoming the standard text for Cuban students until the advent of the Revolution, more than a generation later (Castaneda et al, 1975; Cabrera and Almodobar, 1975; Miller, 1999; Dumpierre, 1965).

It was this neocolonial vision of Cuba as being both economically and intellectually dependent upon the US that Julio Mella was to repeatedly challenge in the pages of the student press. The fullest expression of his views was to be found in his 1928 magazine article, *Where is Cuba Headed?*, written during his exile in Mexico, subsequently published in pamphlet form and destined to become the key text for the reform movement that was finally to sweep the dictator General Gerardo Machado from power five years later. If Cuba did not act swiftly, warned Mella, then it was 'headed toward becoming a formal colony of the United States (like Puerto Rico and the Philippines), toward the destruction of everything on which a nation is based', as the result of Machado's aping of Mussolini's populism, his curtailing of the last vestiges of parliamentary democracy, and the "Sweet" Economic Situation', as far as the US was concerned, that saw the Cuban economy shackled to its purchasing power and almost entirely dependent upon the sugar crop (Mella, 2003, pp.265-269). Reliance upon monoculture had been tacitly accepted until the crash in world sugar prices in the early 1920s that saw a marked downturn in living standards, a rise in poverty, and a widening gulf between the 'haves' and the 'have-nots'; all of which threw the subjection of the nation to foreign capital into stark relief.

The crux of Mella's critique was that the chronic failure to realize the potential of indigenous agriculture, industry and mineral resources, in the wake of independence, was the direct result of US imperialism. His account of the Sixth Pan-American Congress, held in Havana in 1928 (and accompanied by the occupation of the university by troops in an attempt to forestall protests against the arrival of US President Calvin Coolidge), emphasized (in variance to the Comintern line) that North American imperialism was neither based on military conquest (like the Roman empire) nor upon the projection of industrial and financial power (like the British empire) but upon the 'absolute economic domination [of client states] with political guarantees when they appear to be necessary' (Miller, 1999, p.202). This subtle but crucial distinction was extended to the restrictive and restricted nature of the tertiary-education sector on the island.

The malaise of Cuban education – elitist, regimented and limited, both in terms of access and focus – was, therefore, not to be treated in isolation but as a core element in a national reform movement that aimed to transform every aspect of national life by force, if necessary, as well as through argument. The students were at the forefront of this current, but – under Mella's direction – they did not act alone but as part of a wider confluence of interests that embraced the intellectuals and artists of the avant garde, who coalesced around the *Minoristas* (the 'Minority' group); organized labour (primarily in the form of the railway workers', typographers', weavers', tobacco and dock workers' unions); and the reconstituted 'Veterans' movement that had grown out of the revolutionary struggle of the previous generation with Spain. Mella himself was the link between each of these potential power bases. The *Minoristas* had been founded in 1923, with a manifesto that embraced modernism, and a guiding belief in progress and national renewal. In particular, they were quick to denounce government corruption and encroaching US domination of Cuban trade, industry and cultural life. Among their number were the poets Nicolás Guillén and Rubén Martínez Villena, and the essayist Juan Marinello, all of whom would later join the Cuban Communist Party and become major artists and social commentators in their own right. At the same time, Mella had become known to industrial workers and the peasantry as the protégé of the trade union leader, Alfredo Lopez, who had turned the movement outwards: away from the small, traditional crafts-based unions and towards mass general unions (or *sindicatos*) organized around single industries or factories. Lopez was to play an important role in wresting the ideological orientation of the Cuban labour movement away from anarchism, which had been dominant through Spanish influence since the 1880s, and towards socialism. This process was accelerated by the internal crisis of Cuban anarchism, in the late 1920s, as the result of collaboration with the government, infiltration by police agents, and the deportation of many leading activists; which led many union members to demand a more organized and efficient fighting political body. However, Lopez's own political trajectory – from syndicalism to Marxism – and his presence at the head of the CNOC (the *Confederacion National Obera Cubana*), the general union founded in 1925 along the lines of the Spanish CNT, were equally important. The first works by Lenin had arrived in Cuba via the rucksacks of leftwing merchant seamen docking at Havana from Europe in 1918, and they quickly spread through the cities and the university campus. However, they would reach the countryside, and penetrate the factories, largely as the result of the efforts of Mella and his friend, the poet José Zacarías Tallet, who constantly toured the provinces, speaking on Marxism to groups of workers and peasants, with Lopez's blessing and organizational backing. If Mella is remembered in Cuba today for his legendary rendezvous with the crew of an embargoed Soviet freighter (the *Vatslav Vorovski*), when he spent 'four hours under the Red Flag'; then it was the long – and far less dramatic – process of speaking, explaining and persuading about the merits of socialism to these small and clandestine groups of his fellow countrymen that actually resulted in the planting of that banner upon Cuban soil (Thomas, 1971, p.566).

A number of independent communist groups (often with a cellular structure and a mere handful of members) had already sprung up, some born out of the ashes of earlier socialist parties, some based around Jewish-Polish immigrant communities, and with one establishing a foothold within the union of house painters. Mella joined one of the first groups based in

Havana, in 1924, and was instrumental in the creation of the first unitary Communist Party in August 1925, quickly overcoming the 'workerist' opposition to the idea of an intellectual in its leadership. He 'dazzled' not only his critics but all those who came into contact with him, recalled the veteran party member, Justo González, writing in 1963 (Thomas, 1971, p.576). Indeed, such was his reach that it was his legacy – and authority – that would be consistently appealed to by Blas Roca (the leader of the pre-revolutionary party from 1933-61) and evoked by Fidel Castro at the opening session of the first congress of the re-forged party in 1975. Thus, it was his portrait that would dominate the stage at the 5th party congress in October 1997, rather than those of José Miguel Pérez or José Peña Vilaboa, the first two general secretaries, as the totemic 'founder' of Cuban Communism; and his writings which were republished as the key documents that signalled the establishment of Marxist thought and praxis upon the island (Batlle, 2005; Castaneda et al, 1975; Ortiz, 1999).

In an age when 'student politics' is often used as a derogatory or dismissive term, to denote superficiality or naiveté, it is worth recalling the risks that Mella and his student comrades ran in embarking on a path of activism. Mella would find himself expelled from the university, in September 1925, and placed at the head of General Machado's 'death list', while some 200 students would be killed during the military crackdown on the Havana campus in 1928-31 (Beals, 1933, p.289). Forcible deportations, used to break the anarchist movement, were extended to the trade unions and political organizations, with José Miguel Pérez finding himself arrested, after less than two weeks in charge of the fledgling Communist Party, effectively 'sandbagged' and sent back to Spain. He would perish, at the hands of a Nationalist terror gang, a decade later during the Spanish Civil War. The wave of strikes, supported by the student movement, that convulsed Cuba in the autumn of 1925 were broken through the use of paramilitary force. Enrique Varona, the general secretary of the railway workers' union, was murdered in the street, while Mella's friend and mentor, Alfredo Lopez, was thrown to the sharks by Machado's secret police in a technique – prefiguring that of Pinochet's death squads in the 1970s – that became a favourite in order to make opponents of the regime 'disappear' without leaving a trace. In such a context, Mella was engaging upon a course of action that necessitated considerable nerve, bravery and selflessness. It took one sort of courage to shoulder a way through the police lines during a demonstration outside the presidential palace, but quite another to elude the secret police and the assassin's bullet (Thomas, 1971, p.566). As a consequence, the contemporary renunciation of physical force by the Left and disdain for those who, in the past, advocated armed resistance, appears misplaced or even ahistorical when seeking to evaluate the career of those like Mella, who understood the seizure of power in terms of the French, Mexican and Russian revolutionary experiences. It was for good reason that Diego Rivera chose to paint him in his mural 'Insurrection' that graced the walls of the Mexican Ministry of Education, standing alongside Tina Modotti, handing out rifles to the multitudes (Marnham, 1999, pp.224-225). Mella never had the slightest doubt that you could not have a revolution without a revolution.

It was this awareness that led him to ally the students with the Veterans' movement. Dissatisfied with their treatment at the hands of successive regimes since independence was won by arms in 1898, and angered by arrears in pensions and the failure to realize promised land reform, the Veterans – often Afro-Cubans – felt that they had sacrificed most during the revolutionary war but gained the least, following the withdrawal of Spanish power. While the students were largely dismissive of the older generation that had gained Cuban independence only to amass great private fortunes, to swap a colonial master (Spain) for a neocolonial one (the US), and to systematically exclude the vast majority of the people from political and economic power, Mella recognized a legitimate channel for progressive, nationalist protest and a reservoir of support and knowledge. As a result, he joined the Supreme Council of the Veterans' and Patriots' Association, alongside Manuel Sanguily, a close comrade of José Martí, and Carlos Garcia Velez, the son of a hero of the wars of independence (Whitney, 2001, pp.29-30). The language employed in the Veterans' manifestoes – evoking 'rectification', 'regeneration' and 'honest' governance – neatly dovetailed with that of the student movement (Whitney, 2001, p.32). Mella, therefore, attempted to conjoin the Veterans' movement with other interest groups – most notably the trade unions and women's groups – in his ambitious plan to break the educational monopoly in Cuba.

Initially, the students met with great success. They forcibly occupied the campus buildings and plazas, unfurled a vast Cuban flag over the steps of the university and demanded the removal of corrupt professors and the clients of the regime. It was said (and later recorded by Hugh Thomas) that as soon as Mella began to speak under the shadow of the great laurel tree that grew in the university courtyard the lecture halls would empty, leaving the professors to hector rows of empty chairs (Thomas, 1971, p.566). With a boycott of classes running into its second month, and the university effectively paralysed, President Zayas agreed to meet with a delegation of 15 students. For a moment, the youngsters seemed overawed by the opulence of the palace, the dress uniforms of the guards and the aura of authority that surrounded the President. Then Mella pushed his way forward – in an encounter that would provide fertile and dramatic material for novelists –

and began to lecture Zayas on the lack of formaldehyde in the biology labs, the atrophied curriculum and the uninterest of the professors who knew nothing and only cared about their pay cheques (Poniatowska, 1992, p.7). Caught off guard, Zayas promised that he would convene a meeting with the Minister of Education and the President of the University. It was a major climbdown and a propaganda triumph for the student movement (now convened as a formal body, the Federation of University Students or FEU), which propelled Mella onto the national stage, as he declared the university to be now 'free' or 'liberated' from state interference (Ortiz, 1999, p.29).

Concessions came quickly. Zayas issued a presidential decree promising a modicum of reform, including the creation of a tripartite university administration that brought together professors, students and 'distinguished' alumni, and aimed at the 'normalization' of life on campus (Ortiz, 1999, pp.79-85). Yet the appointment of a new – socially and politically conservative – rector, Jose Antolin del Cueto, who attempted to close the university down (as the prelude to a purge of activists) resulted in further walkouts and the hosting of rival elections by the student body which, sensationally (and very publicly) returned Mella himself to office. Maintaining the tempo of the campaign, Mella now stressed the autonomous role of the student body in forging educational policy, and convened a 'First National Congress' of Cuban students in October 1923. With their own newspapers, administration and *de facto* parliament, the students not only pressed for the dismissal of 'corrupt' or 'incompetent' teachers but also widened their demands to encompass a criticism of the Platt Amendment and the nation's economic dependence upon the US. More radically still, Mella proposed – and saw adopted – a plan to break the elite monopoly of education through the founding of a 'José Martí Popular University', which would combine a literacy campaign among the masses with free, universal education delivered by – and for – a combination of progressive academics, trade unionists and students. In this manner, the student federation aimed to supplant the state and to present, on the one hand, a strategy aimed at raising basic educational standards (which saw teams of activists spreading out of the urban centres into the countryside) with, on the other, a highly ambitious programme of higher education that envisaged the growth of the curriculum to encompass practical skills, such as child rearing and sexual health, alongside lectures on political economy, socialism, historical studies and medicine. At the university's inaugural meeting, in the newly requisitioned amphitheatre of the Havana campus, the stress was upon combating 'dogmatism', philosophical 'idealism' and all manner of 'anti-scientific' thought (Dumpierre, 1965, p.49).

Key to this process was Mella's reclamation of José Martí's ideas and contention that his educational programme could not be separated from his social policies. The legacy of José Martí had been claimed by successive regimes since independence, and each had – to a greater or lesser extent – recast him in its own image, emphasizing the liberal and nationalist currents in his writings. What Mella did, over the course of a series of articles and through the founding of a free university named in his honour, was to strip away the accretions and distortions that had tarnished his memory and to present him afresh to the Cuban people as an anti-imperialist, an heir to both the Enlightenment and the French Revolution, and as a social revolutionary rather than a reformer (Mella, 1978, pp.11-18). In particular, Mella sought to chart Martí's relationship with the nascent working-class movement of change unions and socialist societies, and to outline the subsequent careers of many of his closest comrades who founded the first recognizably socialist political parties on the island. If the North Americans had been suddenly presented with a vision of George Washington with all the attributes and social ideas of Daniel Shays, it would have been no less radical and challenging than for Cubans, in the 1920s, when viewing Martí through Mella's eyes. Nowhere was this clearer than in the educational sphere, for Mella was keen to emphasize that, for his hero as for himself, social liberation was replicated, amplified and made truly possible through the liberation of the mind. Learning was not 'value free' but rather socially conditioned and conditioning. The curriculum might, therefore, be constricted to the recitation and regurgitation of 'facts' by rote, as it was under the rule of Zayas and Machado, or it might be open and emancipatory, as it was envisaged by Martí and Mella. That such interpretations are the norm in Cuba's contemporary educational system should not obscure either the originality of Mella's approach in the 1920s, or his success in influencing the developing pedagogy of the revolution after 1959. Indeed, both the literacy brigades that spearheaded the *alfabetización* campaign of 1961 – who succeeded in eradicating illiteracy in rural areas – and the celebration of Martí as a proto-socialist figure find their genesis within his student writings (Martí, 1979, p.32).

Work and study – practice and theory – went hand in hand, as Mella's youthful band of teachers (many of whom were feminist activists from the newly formed 'Women's Club of Cuba') were supplemented by leading members of the tobacco workers' union, in an attempt to break 'the monopoly of culture' of the elites and to equate levels of political consciousness, or revolutionary activism, with the attainment of learning among the working class and peasantry (Castaneda et al, 1975; Contrera, 1987; Dumpierre, 1965). This then was education by and for the working people, conducted at breakneck speed by an extremely heterogeneous and highly dedicated network of political activists (Dumpierre, 1965, pp.49-55). Mella and his comrades had already wrested control of the university campus away from the academic and political authorities; now, they aimed to go one better and seize control of the entire educational system. Though one might question the dualism of their approach to pedagogical problems (with clear 'right' and 'wrong' answers apparent to most questions), and the assumption that higher educational standards inevitably result in collective, socialist progress as opposed to individual, private gain, their ambitions were not quite so unrealizable and wild-eyed as they may at first appear. Cuba lacked a developed educational system, and had (unlike much of the rest of Latin America) escaped the domination of both non-tertiary and tertiary sectors by the religious orders. The patchwork, and extremely patchy, system that existed relied primarily upon the profit motive and was largely non-existent outside the urban centres. As a consequence, it was not unreasonable to think that the trade unions – in alliance with a stratum of progressive intellectuals – might hope to fill this void (Contrera, 1987). After all, they possessed the constituency, the vision and the sheer political will necessary to effect such a rapid extension of provision and such a radical overhaul of the curriculum. The abuses of the current system were so stark and the skills shortage – in terms of scientists, doctors and technological specialists – so acute that Zayas' supporters, within both the media and urban middle classes, had few cogent counter-arguments to make. Instead, they sought to offer more concessions, including the dismissal of more than 100 corrupt, unqualified or absentee professors from the campus and the promise that, henceforth, the post of rector would be elective on a two-year cycle. The student movement had reached its zenith, with most of its original demands met and the FEU, under Mella's direction, widening its remit to call for the creation of a Latin American Students' League that would organize around Simón Bolívar's vision of a united continent.

However, the youthful, restless nature of the student body was its weakness as well as its strength. University life is transitory, with undergraduates committed to three- or at most five-year courses. As a consequence, the memories and experiences of the 'class of 1923' could not be expected automatically to inform the politics of those who arrived on campus at the close of the decade. The student body would renew itself but the FEU could, and should, not have been expected to remain constant, in terms of both personnel and programmes. Viewed in this light, Mella's founding of the José Martí Popular University was extremely prescient, in that it attempted to institutionalize the gains of 1923 and to dissolve the artificial barriers between workers and intellectuals on a permanent basis. The students had become, in effect, the social conscience of Cuba and the watchdog of abuses perpetrated by the state. This, however, necessitated that – as the perceptive US reporter Carlton Beals put it – before General Machado, Cuba's new hard man, 'could consolidate his power, he had to destroy Cuba's educational system' as exemplified by the control of the FEU over the Havana campus, and the José Martí University's trail-blazing curriculum (Beals, 1933, p.281).

Unsurprisingly, Mella was one of the dictatorship's primary targets. He was summarily expelled from the university in September 1925, and charged with an array of treason and terrorism offences against the state in the November of that year (mostly arising from his work with the trade unions and membership of the fledgling Communist Party). His response, in the first instance, was to take to the podium at the university lecture theatre in order to denounce Machado, before the faculty, as a 'tropical Mussolini'; in the second, it was to go on hunger strike – which would have probably killed, or at least crippled, a less physically robust individual – and which succeeded in garnering considerable public support and in speeding his release (Beals, 1933, pp.281-282). Thereafter, Mella was, quite literally, a 'marked man', to be targeted by Machado's death squads and, after eluding several attacks, he managed to escape to Mexico in February 1926. His flight effectively terminated his involvement with the FEU and curtailed the work of the José Martí University, while Machado quartered his soldiers in the Havana campus, imposing martial law and shutting the university entirely in 1927-28 and again from 1930-33. At the same time, all schools (high, commercial and industrial) were placed under military supervision, and some even under direct control of the army. Large numbers of students were expelled and, against a background of intimidation and beatings, an elderly philosophy professor (Enrique José Varona) was roughed up by police who broke into his home in order to break up a student gathering, while the rector – who was by no means a militant – resigned in protest. Two lecturers (Dr. Ramón Grau San Martin and Dr. Guillermo Portela) who refused to continue teaching while surrounded by soldiers, were seized and imprisoned on the Isle of Pines, in cells close to the one newly vacated by Mella. 'Today,' wrote Carlton Beals, 'the students no longer sing their way up and down the hill; the gardens are overrun with weeds. Armed soldiers guard the various entrances, lifting gun and bayonet against everyone who approaches too close...the main patio has been converted into an encampment of [army] tents'. The FEU was outlawed and went underground, as the 'University Student Directorate', and spawned a myriad of clandestine groups. At the height of the clampdown, Mella met his end, amid encroaching night and gunshots, leaving a sense of promise unfulfilled and much that was undone.

'What ifs' – though not necessarily within the remit of the professional historian – cannot but help spring to mind. Mella's politics were caught in the moment, frozen in time, just as surely as his image was captured in the blink of the shutter of Tina Modotti's camera; starting, assertive and alluring, yet incapable of departure, further exposition and full realization. Would a living Mella have effected a successful socialist revolution in Cuba a generation earlier than Castro and Guevara? Could such an unbridled spirit have been contained for long within the encroaching ideological conformity of the Comintern, not least when he had already been accused, in Mexico, of Trotskyist 'errors' and sympathies? Or would maturity have led him to measure and compromise? (On this count, it is worth remembering that he quickly recanted and sought to reach an accommodation with the leadership of the Mexican Communist Party that preserved both his party card and his power base.) Whatever the case, and with the answers unknowable, closed off to us by death, his legacy can perhaps be best registered in the continuing life of the Havana primary school that bears his name. There, amid the crumbling frescos of an old colonial mansion (owned before the revolution by an Anglo-Cuban family, in an echo of Mella's own ancestry), a working man mends the children's shoes for free, his wages subsidized by the state, the flat roof and corner turrets serve as a playground and a series of 'dens'; while scientific textbooks sit alongside those on modern languages and heavily illustrated guides to geography and recent history. It is a place of light, laughter and learning; for the many rather than the few, where there are no longer tuition fees to pay and class sizes average 15 and are restricted to a maximum of 25. Mella's posthumous triumph lies in the establishment of universal healthcare, in the 10 per cent of Cuba's annual budget spent upon education, and in the eradication of illiteracy in a land where more than 60 per cent of school leavers go on to some form of tertiary education, including study at 15 universities. Far more than a figurehead, Mella's ideas continue to inform and to guide, not least in the radical pedagogy that teaches – in stark contrast to the emphasis on testing that currently dominates government policy in much of the world – that co-operation as opposed to competition is not only expected between pupils, but is considered the key to academic success and the creation of a healthy civil society. Viewed from this perspective, Julio Mella appears not so much as the 'rebellious angel' or the 'young forerunner' of the revolution, as his biographers have chosen to style him, but as a comet: Nicolas Guillen's fiery, red arrow that scribed a shining arc into the darkest of night skies, illuminating all that lay in its path and charting a unique course through the heavens.

1 C. Beals, *The Crime of Cuba,* (J.B. Lippincott Company, Philadelphia & London, 1933), pp.265-266; P. Marnham, *Dreaming with his Eyes Open. A Life of Diego Rivera* (Bloomsbury, London, 1998 rpt. 1999), p.225; and N. Contrera (ed.), *Julio Antonio Mella. El Joven Precursor* (Editoria Politica, Havana, 1987), passim. His good looks and athleticism, as opposed to his political career, have often dominated accounts of his life. Thus, two academics teaching on North American campuses recently styled him – in somewhat patronizing, racial terms – as a 'light-skinned mulatto Adonis'; see: D. Cluster & R. Hernandez, *The History of Havana* (Palgrave Macmillan, Houndmills, Basingstoke, 2006, rpt. 2008, p.163.

2 In this manner, Mella's image appeared on the cover of a German digest of radical art and popular culture, shortly before its suppression by the Nazis. He was styled by Willi Munzenberg as *the* 'South American Workers' Leader', whose death was commemorated annually across the continent as 'Mella's day'. See: *A-J-Z,* number 3 (January 1932), p.1.

16

Learning from Latin America: experiences of training in ESNA

Julio Gambina

E SNA (*Encuentro Sindical Nuestra América* = Union Meeting of Our America) is a transnational trade union, education and research body supported by the trade union movement across Latin America. The inaugural meeting of ESNA was held in Quito, Ecuador, in 2008 with the support of the World Federation of Trade Unions (WFTU) to address a pressing need, identified by trade unions throughout 'Our America', to develop a common plan of action to tackle social injustice. ESNA works with a range of social and educational organizations, including universities, and is committed to developing progressive, political educational opportunities for trade unionists.

The ESNA training policy is deployed in different ways on a regional basis:

a. as integrated initiatives in various member organizations;
b. as pedagogic initiatives that integrate the participation of delegations from various countries in activities organized by one of the training centres belonging to member entities;
c. as national activities of the member centres or institutes of ESNA.

What follows are some considerations derived from concrete experiences in planning, execution and evaluation that I had while a member of the ESNA programme.

Initiatives

In this case the courses for training the trainers stand out, carried out for example in Brazil, Cuba or Uruguay, with technical assistance on each occasion from the training centres belonging to ESNA-affiliated trade unions in the host country.[1]

The activities were undertaken based on a concept of 'teaching-learning' like that which emerged from the tradition of popular education established by the Brazilian pedagogue Paulo Freire, author of *Pedagogy of the Oppressed* and *Pedagogy of Hope*; texts and proposals for education that revolutionized the social practices of the popular movement well beyond the educational process.

Why emphasize popular education? This is out of a conviction that self-learning is important – as is awareness of the social practices that affect those involved in work. The intention is to go beyond the practical reality of employment to think about transformation and emancipation from work.

In the ESNA training programme we started by recognizing the new realities of capitalist exploitation and workers' responses in their daily lives, which required participative investigative action carried out by the subjects themselves. The investigation was, therefore, not conducted from outside the working class but from within. Ultimately, the pedagogy utilized cannot come from professional knowledge outside the process of exploitation but rather from the local or popular knowledge of those involved, who are themselves affected by the process of contemporary capitalist production. In every case, professional knowledge supports the development of self-learning by the subjects involved.

The first 'training the trainers' activity took place in Cuba at the school of the Cuban Workers Federation (CTC). The participants in the activity were taken from those of us who were part of the training teams of the unions affiliated to ESNA, which meant that there were teachers, researchers, planners and organizers of pedagogic initiatives from many nations.

It was evident from the outset that the different protagonists were working according to a range of conceptual frameworks. One concept emanated from the Cuban participants, drawing from a process of anti-capitalist social construction since the 1959 revolution which was very different from the day-to-day conditions of workers in capitalist countries. The perceived realities were very different if one looked at countries with a neoliberal orientation and open economies such as Mexico, Peru or Colombia, rather than other countries where there were everyday criticisms of the hegemonic discourse, as in Argentina, Brazil or Uruguay.

The general agreement was processed on the basis of ESNA principles, a class-conscious project setting out a social practice that was anti-capitalist, anti-colonialist, anti-imperialist and pro-socialist. These are definitions that manifested themselves in different ways depending on the national context, the degree of regional articulation of these processes and the integration and dynamics of the global situation.

Discussing the state of global capitalism became a central theme of the pedagogic debate in training the trainers, as it needed to accept the diversity of national circumstances contained in the various national and regional projects of social transformation dealt with by ESNA.

This is an important issue because of the need to realize workers' unity everywhere in contemporary capitalist development, which has brought an increase in direct exploitation, precariousness of employment and the expansion of outsourcing, especially by large transnational companies, not to mention different forms of restricting the workers' rights won through struggle over the years.

A relevant statistic is the growth of labour vulnerability, calculated by the ILO as affecting 42 per cent of workers – 1,400 million people out of an estimated total of 3,400 million workers.[2]

The different forms of vulnerability include unemployment, sub-employment, outsourcing and various forms of labour and wage precariousness. These suggest that the labour movement needs to adapt the traditional union model, which is associated more with the history that unfolded between the nineteenth and twentieth centuries. That traditional model is very distinct from the realities of the twenty-first century. Current realities have prompted debate about a new union model, sustained in trade union democracy and liberty, that engages with the variety of situations that workers confront on a daily basis, be they in regular or irregular work, employed or unemployed, active or passive.

Discussing the contemporary era based on the variety of perspectives in ESNA is the first step towards coming up with educational approaches that will fit all the different circumstances. This involves discussing the capitalist offensive against workers, the threat to the environment and the planet, and the productive model and pattern of consumption that affects society as a whole.

Local activities with regional participation

A general review of activities at the national level, though involving both local participation and invitees such as teachers or participants from other countries, indicated that these took place in three ESNA regions: the North, which included Mexico, the US and Canada; Central America and the Caribbean; and South America.

For the North, the pedagogic activities were carried out in various cities of Mexico with the participation of US residents and also representatives from Central America and the Caribbean.

One of the specific problems of Mexican trade unionism is the corruption and bureaucratization of traditional trade unionism – at this time ESNA's pedagogic activity aimed to strengthen the articulation and training of class-conscious organizations.

In this setting the constitution of the new trade union federation of Mexico, which organized the fifth ESNA in Mexico City in 2012, stands out. It was preceded by different training activities that included hundreds of workers from that country.

The objective of those activities was raising awareness to consolidate the national project of the new federation and of the continent in development with ESNA, paying attention to the existence of millions of Mexican emigrants in the US with close family and union connections to their country of origin. Some of them were active participants in the training initiatives in Mexico.

The content of this training was affected by local factors in the context of the global crisis, made worse by the nature of the frontier and the dependence of the Mexican economy on that of the US, the epicentre of the global crisis unleashed in 2008. The need for a new union model always constituted one of the training themes, so discussion of the principles and direction of the new central federation of Mexico and of ESNA sparked participants' interest in the activity.

As a teaching participant in these activities, I ratified the validity of the teaching-learning method; the contributions made by the participants permitted a deeper analysis of the forms of exploitation, exclusion and marginalization to which the capitalist order condemns millions of people.

In the Caribbean and Central America zone, activities in Nicaragua, Cuba and Panama stand out. The diversity of the situations presented derived from investigative and participative action based on popular-education techniques. I have already mentioned the difference of the civilizing project in Cuba and its specifics but at the same time there are regional themes that enabled workers in the Caribbean and Central America to contribute to a debate about the subordinate role of the region in the global system.

This involved discussing the dependent character of economies based on primary production for export, and the general underdevelopment of the economy and society, all of which inevitably affects the strategy of the labour movement. There was particular discussion of Nicaragua and Panama and the strategy of the big transnationals who take advantage of legislation and, sometimes, official policy to restrict labour rights and drive down wages to make export products competitive.

In the South, activities were carried out in Venezuela, Colombia, Peru, Paraguay, Brazil, Uruguay and Argentina. Each of these presented a great variety of local problems, supplemented by the participation of invitees from neighbouring countries who added to the worries of the local participants. What all these cases have in common is the participative methodology that promotes conscious subjectivity so as to present an alternative, popular project with content that is anti-capitalist, anti-colonial, anti-imperialist and pro-socialist.

It is interesting that in all cases there was participation from young people and women who had been discriminated against in wage terms by the bosses – especially in the case of the women. Thus, in the development of the activities, two topics appeared that represented a challenge for ESNA and for the workers' movement. Patriarchy goes beyond the capitalist order. The patriarchal order comes from a long time ago and is reproduced at every level of contemporary society, including within socialism. The struggle against patriarchy is part of the process of teaching-learning and at the same time the object is to eradicate it from daily social practice, including the process of training.

Discrimination against young people also needs to be combated at the same time as young people's active participation in training is promoted – as teachers and/or researchers just as much as participants.

Activities of each national or local centre

I will concentrate here on an initiative undertaken in Argentina that involved me being in charge of the Institute of Studies and Training belonging to the CTA-A (*Central de Trabajadores de la Argentina*).

In the summer of 2017, in the city of Montecarlo, 1,160 kilometres north of Buenos Aires, we were able to attend an educational activity organized in conjunction with the Institute and the Peasant Liberation Movement (MCL).

The educational event was rooted in the experience of ex-*yerba mate* workers, the *tareferos* who, prevented from continuing to work in the *yerba mate* companies and having been excluded from the labour market, had become 'landless' peasant farmers. It was of especial interest to the teaching group to be able to hear the experiences of workers who had reconverted to being peasants, especially those who were 'landless', and how they had managed to obtain land on which to produce crops, as much as to understand their daily lives of survival and production.

It is interesting to describe the classroom in which the educational activity was carried out during two intense weeks. The school was located in a rural area in the hills of Misiones province, five kilometres outside the city of the same name, in a peasant settlement – a leafy area by the river that constituted the border between Argentina and Paraguay. The opposite bank could easily be made out just by looking across, and you could shorten the crossing distance in a canoe or by swimming, though this was not to be advised because of the strong current and nature's aquatic hazards.

The classroom was in the open air, the school area surrounded by big trees that prevented the sun's rays from entering directly, tempering the heat that approached 40 degrees. The classroom was organized with a big table in the centre, with austere hand-crafted benches in a circle around it, that also served to offer food to the participants in the activity.

In that classroom, more than 60 participants carried out the educational tasks over two weeks, an agenda that included reading texts, group debates, and presentations on different subjects, including classes in which the participating peasants described their experiences. In this they explained the transformation from workers to peasants, the occupation of unused territory and the fight to keep it in the face of demands by their former owners who up until then had not worked it and, on seeing the clearances and the productive process, initiated a legal and political campaign for its appropriation.

The police and judiciary of the complicit repressive state did not hesitate and the protagonists explained the dissuasive mechanisms used against the initiatives to seize land and commence production, something the peasants supposed to be a clear anti-capitalist measure against private property and a real agrarian reform in the traditional sense of appropriating the land for those that work it.

Amidst the elements of the training, there emerged an analysis of the situation globally, regionally and locally, especially aimed at coming up with a theoretical summary of their own daily social practice in production, in self-sufficiency and in the collective distribution of the surplus through marketing to the neighbouring population. This last point provoked an interesting debate on 'de-commercializing' for their own consumption and commercial distribution of the surplus under hegemonic market rules.

Even so, educational elements on the study of costs were offered as the collective aimed to sell some food produce a little under the market price in the nearby town. In the same vein, with some technical assistance, the event covered some theoretical and practical elements related to forming co-operatives and outlining types of self-management that can be applied to the development of collective action.

The experience was viewed very favourably by the participants and the teaching team who lived with them in the encampment under the same conditions as the collective. There was a co-existence in the study and the daily activity that enabled us to relate the experience to many similar situations in the continent and the wider world.

I mention this training activity because of the challenge it represents: the different forms of vulnerability and the marginalization in the labour market that arise from the exploitation of the workforce require diverse but integrated responses within the labour movement as well as in popular educational material for social liberation.

By way of summary

In the short time in which the ESNA training, research and technical assistance programme has been rolled out, many activities have taken place, generally through our own resources and effort, though during the last year we have received financial assistance from sectors of the British trade union movement. International co-operation could do a great deal to help the deployment of bigger training activities and other functions relative to the ESNA programme.

There is a long way to go. Nevertheless, the anticipatory imagination of the training programme initiators today and the pedagogic activities that they produce can contribute to the growth and improvement of ESNA and its affiliated organizations. Without doubt, it is part of a labour-movement strategy to confront the capitalist offensive against workers, nature and society.

There is no doubt that the dominant classes have the initiative – they have a strong training strategy seated in the formal teaching process, associated with the multimedia operations of the communications transnationals and the production of a notion of common sense that favours profit, capitalist accumulation and global domination.

Against this strategic collection of operations of the capitalist system, the labour movement faces the challenge of generating a reply through newly integrated offensives. Educational initiatives will constitute a key part of any popular strategy aimed at revolutionary transformation of the local, regional and global reality.

1 The ESNA training programme was approved at the end of 2010 in Caracas, on the occasion of the third ESNA. The training activities started in 2011.

2 ILO report on perspectives of work in 2017

About the authors

Ozan Nadir Alakavuklar works as a senior lecturer at Massey University School of Management. His research interests are based on social movements and alternative forms of organizing. He is a member of the editorial collective, *Ephemera*.

John Callow is the Head of Education at the GFTU, having previously worked for the Amicus and GMB trade unions. He was, for eight years, the Director of Archives at the Marx Memorial Library, and is a visiting tutor at the University of Suffolk. He holds a doctorate from Lancaster University and has written widely on the Labour and trade union movement. *His books include GMB@Work: the Story behind the Union, 1889-2013* (2013) and *Phoenix Rising: James Connolly & the Re-Conquest of Ireland* (2016). He also contributed a chapter, on the radical politics of the East End of London, to *What would Keir Hardie say? Exploring Hardie's vision and its continuing relevance to 21st Century Politics* (2015).

Dr John Fisher was born in Hull and attended the University of Southampton, where he first became involved in trade union education. In the 1970s he was appointed Lecturer in Adult Education at the University of Surrey, where he developed a wide-ranging programme of TU education in partnership with the TUC and a number of unions, especially with the national office and London and South-East Region of the T&G (now Unite). In 1995 he was appointed Director of Research and Education for the T&G, and oversaw a programme which at that time had over 10,000 TU students per year. Just before retiring, in 2005, he wrote *Bread on the Waters*, a detailed account of T&G education from 1922 to 2000. John Fisher believes that TU education is at the core of trade unions' organizing mission and brings out the best in trade unions, and that trade union tutors are unsung heroes and heroines of the movement.

Julio Gambina holds a PhD in Social Sciences from the University of Buenos Aires (UBA) and is a professor at the National University of Rosario (UNR). He is the President of the Foundation for Social and Political Research (FISyP) and is Director of the Center for Studies and Training of the Argentine Judicial Federation (CEFJA) and member of the Board of Directors of the Institute of Studies and Training of the Central Argentine Workers CTA). He serves as president, with Camille Chalmers, of the SEPLA – Society of Political Economy and Critical Thinking in Latin America, for the period 2016-2018. He acts as a postgraduate professor in various aspects related to his specialty in the national universities of Buenos Aires, Cordoba, Mar del Plata, San Luis, Río Cuarto, Patagonia and in the Latin American countries of Chile, Brazil, Colombia and Paraguay. He is a visiting Professor in Distance Courses for UNASUR and is the Argentine representative in the Central of Workers of Argentina and in the Union Meeting Our America (ESNA). He was a consultant in the Plurinational State of Bolivia in 2012 and 2013.

Joel Lazarus, having worked as a stockbroker for five years, undertook postgraduate study at SOAS and the University of Oxford. He completed his DPhil at St Anthony's College, Oxford, UK in 2011. Since then, he has taught and researched at various universities and has been involved in radical democratic pedagogical initiatives in universities and communities. After 11 years in Oxford, Joel moved to Bristol in July 2017.

Gawain Little teaches maths at a primary school in Oxford, UK, and is a member of the NUT's National Executive Committee. He is Chair of the NUT Professional Unity Committee, an officer of Unify – the campaign for one education union, and a member of the editorial board of Education for Tomorrow. He edited the book *Global education 'reform' building resistance and solidarity* for Manifesto Press and is a regular blogger and contributor to the *Morning Star*.

Sophie Imeson, Becca Golby, Shannon Gorman, Jack Scranage, Naomi Canham and **Kyna Dixon** are third-year psychology students at Leeds Beckett University, all of whom have a particular interest in critical and political perspectives on experiences of learning and teaching.

Lindsey McDowell is the Training Adviser for the National Union of Teachers. She designs and delivers learning programmes for union reps, members, officers, secretaries and staff, working across England and in Wales. Her emphasis is on democratic and facilitated learning and building sustainable relationships that enable learners to support and develop each other beyond the training room. Lindsey believes passionately in the transformative power of trade union education and is the mother of two incredible young women.

Michael McGrath began working life as an electrician in construction and shipbuilding, before attending the University of Edinburgh as a mature student. A member of the Communist Party from the age of 16, he has been a shop steward, convenor and trade union official. After taking an Honours Degree in History and teaching qualification, he wrote a PhD in literature and philosophy, focusing the work of the Scottish socialist writer and author of *A Scots Quair*, Lewis Grassic Gibbon. He has worked in adult, higher and trade union education. He is a continuing student of Marx, Gramsci and Bourdieu.

Tom Muskett is a Senior Lecturer in Critical Psychology at Leeds Beckett University. Tom has a background in clinical practice as a speech and language therapist, where he became interested in social, critical and deconstructive accounts of disability and education. This has led Tom to develop a particular interest in the application of community-oriented theories and liberation frameworks in modern Higher Education, in order to develop socially-just and inclusive pedagogies.

Doug Nicholls became active in the community and youth workers' union in 1976. He was elected as the union's general secretary in 1987, a position he was re-elected to until 2012. In that year he was elected General Secretary of the General Federation of Trade Unions. From 1984 to 1994 he was secretary of Coventry trade union council. In the 1984/85 miners' strike he was secretary of the Coventry miners' support committee. He is currently chair of the campaigning organization chooseyouth and vice chair of Ruskin College's board of governors. Doug has written very widely on trade unionism, history, literature and youth work and his last book *Youth Work for Youth Workers* (Polity Press, 2013) advocated a revival of emancipatory popular education practice through lifelong learning. For over twenty years Doug was involved in the validation of university proposals for youth, community and play work training courses and a member of the staff side of the joint negotiating committee for youth and community workers.

Carl Parker is currently GMB's National Education Officer, where he has developed the training programme for new tutors. His first involvement in trade union education was as a lay tutor with NUCPS in the mid-1990s, followed by several years in Usdaw's education department. Carl was instrumental in the introduction of Usdaw's Organizing Academy in 2003 and managed the Academy until leaving Usdaw in 2013. The Academy is a six-month secondment programme for lay representatives and has been central to the union's growth and leadership development. Carl has also developed courses for, and taught on, the GFTU programme for reps, officers and TU managers. His particular area of interest within trade union education is to ensure that learners have a varied experience on training courses and that learners are able to put into practice what has been learnt.

Jane Parker is Professor of Employment Relations and HRM at the School of Management at Massey University. She is co-editor in chief of *Labour and Industry: A journal of the social and economic relations of work*; an Associate Fellow of the Industrial Relations Research Unit at Warwick University; and Co-Director of Massey's People, Organization, Work and Employment Research (MPOWER) Group. Jane's research interests include trade union strategy and organizing; employee consultation and engagement; diversity and inclusion at work; and comparative employment relations.

Nadine Rae is the Organizing Director for Equalities, Education and Projects at the UK Transport Salaried Staffs' Association (TSSA). Nadine started in 2000 as an organizer in New Zealand, organizing casino workers for the former Service & Food Workers Union (now part of E tū). She then worked for Uni Global Union and supported organizing in a number of global contexts, including India, Switzerland, South Africa, Chile. She now lives in Derby, United Kingdom, where she continues to build union organization and power through her role at TSSA. In all her roles, she has kept a focus on activist education and development as being a crucial part of organizing powerful unions.

Mike Seal is Head of Criminology and Youth and Community Work and

Reader in Critical Pedagogy at Newman University Birmingham. He has worked in the youth work, community development, homelessness and drugs sectors for 25 years. He has written six previous books including *Philosophy and Youth Work* with Simon Frost and *Responding to Youth Violence through Youth Work* with Pete Harris, as well as over 30 academic and professional publications. He has conducted over 25 pieces of major research, specializing in participatory research, involving those being researched as researchers. He has done this with prisoners, people on probation, ex-rough sleepers, drug users, ex-gang members and the local community. He is a committed trade unionist, having been an activist in Unison and UCU.

Dave Spooner is the co-director of the Global Labour Institute in Manchester, supporting national and international trade union organizations with education and research. GLI specialises in international organization and political education. Dave has a background in international workers' education, having previously worked for the Workers' Educational Association, the International Federation of Workers Education Associations, the Transport & General Workers' Union (now Unite the Union), and international labour movement NGOs.

Alan Smith manages and leads one of the largest youth and community work programmes in the UK at Leeds Beckett University. He is Vice Chair of the National Youth Agency Education and Training Standards Committee and is Co-Chair of the Joint Education and Training Standards Committee for England, Scotland, Wales and All-Ireland. He has been involved in the professional education of youth and community workers for more than 21 years, and has been at the forefront of policy and practice developments for most of that time. He has held key roles within the Community and Youth Work Training Agencies Group (TAG) – the professional association for lecturers in youth and community work. In 2015, Alan was awarded a National Teaching Fellowship by the Higher Education Academy for the transformational nature of his teaching and the impact it has had on countless students, and those they go on to work with.

Christine Smith is a member of the Community and Youth Studies teaching team at Plymouth Marjon University. Prior to this she worked in the voluntary, community and statutory sectors. Christine has extensive experience as a youth and community practitioner, including community education, community development, outreach work and guidance. Christine has been a Senior Youth Officer with responsibility for staff development, training and quality assurance and a Principal Youth Officer for a Local Authority Youth Service. She is currently a Trustee on the Board of the Plymouth Citizens Advice Bureau with a specific interest in Social Policy and Equalities.

Martin Smith is Head of Community Organizing and Workplace Engagement for the Labour Party. After several years' activism in anti-racist and trade union campaigns he started as a full-time Community and Workplace

Organizer with Battersea and Wandsworth TUC in 1995. On secondment to the TUC organizing department in 1998, Martin helped to write, develop and deliver the training programme for the first years of the TUC Organizing Academy and co-authored the three day 'Winning the Organized Workplace' programme for union reps with colleagues from South Thames College. Moving to the GMB in 1999, Martin successfully implemented the GMB@Work programme of organizational change, membership growth and new training programmes for long-standing GMB reps, becoming Head of Organizing within GMB in 2005. Between 2005 and 2016 GMB grew by 15 per cent overall, largely as a result of increased and better-focused activism among lay members.

Jo Trelfa draws on 22 years' work in higher education in informal education and social sciences as well as 12 years as youth worker and community worker with individuals, groups, communities and organizations in the UK, Western Asia, and, projects in South America and the Caribbean. Her PhD focus is reflective practice and professional identity formation within a frame of social justice, the anchor to her working practices and values and on which she is published, offers knowledge exchange, and presents at conferences.

Jill Westerman is Principal of the Northern College, one of the four English adult residential colleges which has a long history of involvement in the labour and trade union movements. It provides educational opportunities for adults with few or no qualifications as well as trade union studies courses. It is recognized as outstanding in all areas by Ofsted. Jill has worked in adult education for 30 years, and was previously employed as a community worker in public housing and in a women's refuge. She has published research on aspects of leadership in education and has been chair of the Further Education Trust for Leadership. Jill was awarded a CBE in 2010 for services to adult learning.

Sarah Woolley is a full-time official with the Bakers, Food and Allied Workers Union (and also the youngest one they've ever had). She became a member at 16 when she started working for Bakers Oven, which later became Greggs. Shortly after the transfer over to Greggs she became a shop steward and later sat on the executive council as the female representative. She also sits on the GFTU executive council and has helped with organizing the Youth Festival for the last 2-3 years, which she considers has opened her eyes to the next generation of young members' issues and will help her to encourage engagement in the union movement going forward.

Acknowledgements

[Chapters 1 and 3] John Fisher would like to acknowledge all those who supported, organized and delivered top-quality trade union education rain or shine, and especially Pete Batten, Barry Camfield, Les Ford, Pat Hayes, Diana Holland, Chris Russell and Adrian Weir.

[Chapter 6] Mike McGrath would like to thank many for their friendship and support but, in the present context, principally comrades Iain Reekie, Unite National Tutor and Jim Mowatt, Unite Director of Education.

[Chapter 9] Nadine would like to acknowledge first and foremost the strong trade union women who have inspired her, supported her and developed her understanding of organizing and trade unionism. This includes Louise Chinnery, who ran the first-ever training Nadine had as an organizer, introducing her to skills that she still uses today; Darien Fenton, who helped her understand what it means to truly organize and empower people; Christy Hoffman from whom she learned so much about what it takes to win and Adriana Rosenzvaig, whose insights always surprised and inspired her. She also would like to acknowledge Audrey and Toni, two activists she had the pleasure of working with who had a vision beyond her own and changed people's lives as a result. Lastly, Paul Goulter, who threw her in the deep end believing she could swim, and she did.

[Chapter 10] Carl and Martin would like to thank Mike Seal for his support in putting together this article especially his patient observations and interventions. They would also like to acknowledge the work of James Rees (former Head of Education at Usdaw) and Peter Jarvis (former Deputy Head of Education at Usdaw) in developing many of the ideas put forward in this article.

[Chapter 11] Gawain and Lindsey would like to thank the following people for their contribution to the process described in this chapter: the reps' training writing team – Steve Bartholomew, Jon Hegerty, Lindsey McDowell; the reps' review group – Kit Armstrong (Regional Secretary, Midlands), Noel Hulse (Regional Officer, North West), Darren O'Grady (then Regional Officer, London), Jessica Pearce (Regional Officer, South West), Elvira Shepherd (then Training team), Vin Wynne (Senior Organizer, Northern); members of the NUT National Executive Training and Professional Development Sub-Committee; and all of the reps who have participated in the training and changed it in their own way. They would also like to acknowledge the support of Kevin Courtney, Howard Stevenson, Mike Ironside and Jon Hegerty in writing the chapter itself.

[Chapter 12] Sarah Woolley would like to thank Doug Nicholls for instigating the meeting with Mike Seal that led to the chapter and the organizing committee for the GFTU youth festival.

References

Aliakbari, M. and Faraji, E. (2011). *Basic Principles of Critical Pedagogy*, paper presented at 2nd International Conference on Humanities, Historical and Social Sciences, *IPEDR* Vol 17.

Alinsky, S. (1971). *Rules for Radicals*. Chicago: Random House.

Anderson, P. (1978). 'The Limits and Possibilities of Trade Union Action', in Clarke, T. and Clements, L., *Trade Unions Under Capitalism*. Hemel Hempstead: Harvester Press.

Aristotle (1976). *The Nicomachean Ethics*. Harmondsworth: Penguin.

Arendt, H. (1958). *The Human Condition*, Chicago. University of Chicago Press.

Atkins, J. (1981). *Neither Crumbs nor Condescension*. Aberdeen: Aberdeen People's Press.

Baccaro, L., Hamann, K. and Turner, L. (2003). 'The politics of labour movement revitalization: The need for a revitalized perspective', *European Journal of Industrial Relations*, Vol 9, No 1: 119–133.

Barratt-Brown, M. (1968). *What has really changed in the educational needs of workers?* London: Routledge.

Ball, S. (2013). 'Education, justice and democracy: the struggle over ignorance and opportunity' [Online] http://robertowencentre.academicblogs.co.uk/education-justice-and-democracy-the-struggle-over-ignorance-and-opportunity/ (accessed 1 June 2017).

Banks, S. (ed.) (2010). *Ethical Issues in Youth Work* (2nd ed.). Abingdon: Routledge.

Barry, M. and Wailes, N. (2004). 'Contrasting Systems? 100 Years of Arbitration in Australia and New Zealand', *Journal of Industrial Relations*, Vol 46 No 4: 430–447.

Batlle, L. (2005). *Blas Roca – Continuador de la obra de Balino y Mella*. Havana: Editorial de Ciencias Sociales.

Batsleer, J. (2012). *What is Youth Work?* London: Learning Matters.

Batsleer, J. (2008). *Informal Learning in Youth Work*. London: Sage Publications.

Bauman, Z. (2000). *Liquid Modernity*. Cambridge: Polity.

Beals, C. (1933). *The Crime of Cuba*. Philadelphia and London: J.B. Lippincott Company.

Bean, R. (1994). *Comparative Industrial Relations: An Introduction to Cross-national Perspectives*. London: Croom Helm.

Beck, D. (2016). 'Re-seeing and re-naming the world: Community development and prefigurative democratic work', *Radical Community Work Journal*, Vol 2, No 1 [Online].

Behrens, M., Hurd, R. and Waddington, J. (2004). 'How does restructuring contribute to union revitalization?' in Frege, C. and Kelly, J. (eds) *Varieties of Unionism: Strategies for Revitalization in a Globalising Economy*. New York: Oxford University Press.

Benjamin, W. (1998) [1934]. *Understanding Brecht*. London: Verso.

Bennion, A., Scesa, A. and Williams, R. (2011). 'The Benefits of Part-Time Undergraduate Study and UK Higher Education Policy: A Literature Review', *Higher Education Quarterly*, Vol 65 No 2, April: 145–163.

Bentham, J. (1995) [1787]. *Panopticon Writings*. London: Verso.

Beynon, H. (1975). *Working for Ford*. Wakefield: E.P. Publishing.

Biggs, J. (1996). 'Enhancing teaching through constructive alignment', *Higher Education*, Vol 32, No. 3: pp. 347–364.

Bligh, D.A. (1972). *What's the Use of Lectures?* San Francisco: Jossey-Bass.

Blumenfeld, S. (2016). 'The Global Financial Crisis, the Great Recession, Trade Unions and Collective Bargaining in New Zealand'. Paper presented at the 2016 Labour, Employment and Work Conference, Wellington, 28–29 November.

Boltanski, L. and Chiapello, E. (2007). *The New Spirit of Capitalism*. London: Verso.

Briskin, L. (2007). 'Cross-Constituency Organizing in Canadian Unions: A Vehicle for Union Renewal'. Paper presented at the 8th European Congress of the International Industrial Relations Association, Manchester, 3–6 September.

Bolton, G. (2010). *Reflective Practice, Writing and Professional Development* (3rd edition), California; SAGE Publications.

Booton, F. (1985). *Studies in Social Education: Vol 1, 1860-1890*. Hove: Benfield.

Bourdieu, P. (1990). *In Other Words: Essays Towards a Reflexive Sociology*. Stanford: Stanford University Press.

- (1998). 'The Essence of Neo-Liberalism: Utopia of Endless Exploitation' (translated by Jeremy J. Shapiro), *Le Monde Diplomatique*. Available at: http://mondediplo.com/1998/12/08bourdieu.

- (2010). *Distinction: A Social Critique of the Judgement of Taste*, (2nd edition). Abingdon, Oxon: Routledge.

Bower, G. and Bower, S. (2004). *Asserting Yourself.* Boston: De Capo Press.

Braverman, H. (1989). *Labour and Monopoly Capital: The Degradation of Work in the 20th Century*, 25th Anniversary Edition. New York: Monthly Review Press.

Bradford, S. (2007/2008). 'Practices, Policies and Professionals: Emerging discourses of expertise in English Youth Work, 1939–1951', *Youth and Policy*, Nos. 97 and 98: 13–28.

Braidotti, R. (2013). *The Posthuman*. City: John Wiley and Sons.

Bransford, J.D., Brown, A.L. and Cocking, R.R. (2000). *How People Learn: Brain, Mind, Experience, and School*. Washington, DC: National Academy Press.

Brito, I., Lima, A. and Auerbach, E. (2004). 'The logic of nonstandard teaching: A course in Cape Verdean language, culture, and history', in Norton B. and Toohey K. (eds), *Critical Pedagogies and Language Learning*. Cambridge: Cambridge University Press.

Britt, C. and Rudolph, S. (2013). '"All our hands would tell about the community": re-imagining (im)possible teacher/student subjectivities in the early years of primary school', *International Journal of Critical Pedagogy*, Vol 4, No 2: 35–52.

Brookes, G. (2009). 'Trade Unions and New Zealand's Economic Crisis'. Links: International Journal of Socialist Renewal. May. Available at: http://links.org. au/node/1111 (4 February 2017).

Brookfield, S. (1995). *Becoming a Critically Reflective Teacher*. San Francisco: Jossey-Bass.

- (2005). *The Power of Critical Theory for Adult Learning and Teaching*. Maidenhead: Open University Press.

Brown, G. (1977). *Sabotage: A Study in Industrial Conflict*. Nottingham: Bertrand Russell Peace Foundation Ltd.

- (1980). 'Independence and Incorporation: The Labour College Movement and the Workers' Education Association Before the Second World War', in Thompson, J.L. (ed.) *Adult Education for a Change*. London: Hutchinson.

Brown, R. (2015). 'The Marketisation of Higher Education: Issues and ironies', *New Vistas*, Vol 1, No 1: 4–.

Burke, B., Geronimo, J., Martin, D., Thomas, B. and Wall, C. (2004). *Education for Changing Unions*. City, Ontario: Between the Lines Publishing.

Cabrera, O. and Almodobar, C. (1975) (eds.). *Las Luchas Estudiantiles Universitarias, 1923-1934*, Havana: Editorial de Ciencias Sociales.

CACC (2017). *Climate Refugees – The Climate Crisis and Population Displacement: Building a Trade Union and Civil Society Response Conference*, London, 11 February. Retrieved on 12 February 2017 from: http://www.campaigncc.org/ nationalconference

Caffentzis, G., and Federici, S. (2014). 'Commons against and beyond capitalism', *Community Development Journal*, 49(1), 92-105.

Caldwell, P. (1981). 'State Funding of Trade Union Education', *Trade Union Studies Journal*, No. 3, p4-34.

Cameron, D. (2009). 'The Big Society': Hugo Young Memorial Lecture, 10 November. Retrieved on 4 February 2017 from: http://www.conservatives. com/News/Speeches/2009/11/David_Cameron_The_Big_Society.aspx

Canovan, M. (1992). *Hannah Arendt: A Reinterpretation of Her Political Thought*. Cambridge: Cambridge University Press.

Capizzi, E. (1999). *Learning That Works*. Niace/TUC, London.

Carr, W. and Kemmis, S. (1989). *Becoming Critical: Education, Knowledge and Action Research*. Lewes: Falmer.

Carter, B., Stevenson, H. and Passy, R. (2010). *Industrial Relations in Education: Transforming the School Workforce*. London: Routledge.

Castaneda, E., Duchesne, C., Cabrera, O., Alonso, G. and Vignier, E. (1975) (eds.). *J.A. Mella, Documentos y Articulos*. Havana: Editorial de Ciencias Sociales.

Cherrington, R. (2012). *Not Just Beer and Bingo: a Social History of Working Men's Clubs*. London: Author House.

Cho, S. (2010). 'Politics of Critical Pedagogy and New Social Movements',

Educational Philosophy and Theory, 42(3).

Chowdry, H., Dearden, L., Goodman, A. and Jin, W. (2012). 'The Distributional Impact of the 2012-13 Higher Education Funding Reforms in England' in *Fiscal Studies*, 33 (2), pp. 211-236.

Clarke, T. (2014). *Another Angry Voice: Economics, philosophy and other stuff from an independent Yorkshire blogger*, [Online] Available at: http://anotherangryvoice.blogspot.co.uk/2014/03/ubi-left-libertarianism-nonagression.html

Clawson, D. (2008). 'Neo-liberalism guarantees social movement unionism', *Employee Responsibilities and Rights Journal*, 20(3), 207-212.

Clegg, H. A. and Adams, R. (1959). *Trade Union Education with Special Reference to the Pilot Areas: A Report For The Workers' Educational Association*. London: WEA.

Coates, K. And Topham, T. (1970). *Workers' Control*. London: Panther.

Cohen, M. (1990a). 'The Labour College Movement Between the Wars: National And North-West Developments', in Simon, B. (ed.), *The Search for Enlightenment: The Working Class And Adult Education in the Twentieth Century*. London: Lawrence and Wishart.

- (1990b). 'Revolutionary Education Revived: The Communist Challenge To The Labour Colleges', in Simon, B. (ed.), *The Search for Enlightenment: The Working Class And Adult Education in the Twentieth Century*, London: Lawrence and Wishart.

Cole, G.D.H. (1925). 'Thinking For Yourself', *TGWU Record*, 25 January.

Coles, T. (2014). 'Critical pedagogy: schools must equip students to challenge the status quo', *The Guardian*, 25 February 2014.

Cook-Sather, A. (2002). 'Authorizing students' perspectives: Toward trust, dialogue, and change in education', *Educational Researcher*, 31(4), 3-14.

Coombs, P. Prosser, H. and Ahmed, M. (1974). *Attacking Rural Poverty: How non-formal education can help*. Baltimore: John Hopkins University Press.

Contrera, N. (ed.) (1987). *Julio Antonio Mella: El Joven Precursor*. Havana: Editoria Politica.

Corfield, A, (1969). *Epoch In Workers' Education*. London: Workers' Education Association.

Cornick, E. (2011). *Industrial Democracy: A Forward Step in the Advance towards a Socialist Society?* [Online] Available at: http://redflag.org.uk/frontline/sept11/industrialdemocracy.html

Cornish, Fl., Haaken, J., Moskovitz, L., and Jackson, S., (2016). 'Rethinking prefigurative politics: introduction to the special thematic section', *Journal of Social and Political Psychology*, 4(1), pp. 114-127.

Cornish, D. and Dukette, D. (2009). *The Essential 20: Twenty Components of an Excellent Health Care Team*. Pittsburgh, PA: RoseDog Books.

Craik, W.W. (1964). *Central Labour College*. London: Lawrence and Wishart.

Crosby, M. (2003). http://www.actu.org.au/organising/news/1054172545_875.html (accessed 3 April 2017).

CTU (2007). *Te Huarahi Mo Nga Kaimahi: The CTU vision for the workplace of the future.* October. Wellington: CTU.

- (2013). *Under Pressure: A detailed report into Insecure Work in New Zealand.* October. Retrieved on 7 February 2017 from: http://www.union.org.nz/ wp-content/uploads/2016/12/CTU-Under-Pressure-Detailed-Report-2.pdf

- (2016a). *The New Zealand Council of Trade Unions – Te Kauae Kaimahi: Trade Union Directory 2016.* Retrieved on 4 February 2017 from: http://www.union. org.nz/wp-content/uploads/2002/06/NZCTU-Trade-Union-Directory-2016. pdf

- (2016b). New Zealand Emissions Trading Scheme Review 2015/16. Submission on Priority Issues, 19 February 2016', https://www.union.org. nz/wp-content/uploads/2016/11/160219-New-Zealand-Emissions-Trading-Scheme-Review-2015-16.pdf

Cunniah, D. (2007). *The role of trade unions in workers' education: The key to trade union capacity building.* [Online] http://actrav-courses.itcilo.org/en/a3-58346/ a3-58346-resources/background-paper-ilo-we-symposium.pdf (Accessed: 13 May 2017).

Daniel, W.W. and Millward, N. (1990). *Workplace Industrial Relations in Britain.* London: Policy Studies Institute.

Davies, B. (1967). *The Social Education of the Adolescent.* London: University of London Press.

- (1999a). *From Voluntaryism to Welfare State: A History of the Youth Service in England, Volume 1, 1939-1979.* Leicester: Youth Work Press.

- (1999b). *From Thatcherism to New Labour: A History of the Youth Service in England. Volume 2, 1979-1999.* Leicester: Youth Work Press.

- (2008). *The New Labour Years: A History of the Youth Service in England, Volume 3, 1997-2007.* Leicester: National Youth Agency.

Davies, R. (2012). 'Youth work, 'protest' and a common language: towards a framework for reasoned debate', paper delivered at the annual conference of the association of lecturers in youth and community work 2012, Lake District.

Degener, S. (2001). 'Making sense of critical pedagogy in adult literacy education', *Review of Adult Learning and Literacy* 2(2), pp. 23-45.

Deleuze, Gilles and Felix Guattari (1987). *A Thousand Plateaus: Capitalism and Schizophrenia* (trans. Brian Massumi). Minneapolis: University of Minnesota Press.

Department for Business, Energy and Industrial Strategy (2016).*Trade Union Membership 2016 Statistical Bulletin* [Online] www.gov.uk/government/ statistics/trade-union-statistics-2016 (Accessed 1 June 2017).

Department for Business, Innovation and Skills (2016). *Trade Union Membership 2015: Statistical Bulletin,* BIS/16/271. Retrieved on 3 February 2017 from: https://www.gov.uk/government/uploads/system/uploads/attachment_ data/file/525938/Trade_Union_Membership_2015_-_Statistical_Bulletin.pdf

Department for Education and Employment (1998). *The Learning Age: A*

Renaissance for a New Britain. London: HMSO.

Department for Education (2010). *Positive for Youth: a new approach to cross-government policy for young people aged 13 to 19. London: HMSO.*

Department of Education and Science (1969). *Youth and Community Work in the 70s. Proposals by the Youth Service Development Council (The 'Fairbairn-Milson Report'). London: HMSO.*

(1982). Experience and Participation. Review Group on the Youth Service in England ('The Thompson Report'). London: HMSO.

Department of Employment and Productivity (1968). *Report Of The Royal Commission On Trade Unions And Employers' Associations 1965-68* (The Donovan Commission). London: HMSO.

Dibben, P. (2004). 'Social Movement Unionism' in Harcourt, M. and Wood, G.(eds), *Trade Unions and Democracy: Strategies and Perspectives*. Manchester: Manchester University Press, pp. 280-302.

Docking, J. (ed) (2000). *New Labour's Policies for Schools*. London: Fulton.

Donkin, R. (2010).*The History of Work*. London: Palgrave Macmillan.

Dorling, D. (2011). *Injustice. Why Social Inequality Persists*. Bristol: Policy Press.

Douglas, J. and McGhee, P. (2016). *Trade Unions and the Climate Change Fight*. Briefing paper, AUT, 5 July. Retrieved on 6 February 2017 from: http://briefingpapers.co.nz/2016/07/trade-unions-and-the-climate-change-fight

Dumpierre, E. (1965). *Mella. Esbozo Biografico,* Instituto de Historia, Academia de Ciencias de Cuba, Havana.

Edwards, B. (2016). 'The future of the unions', *New Zealand Herald*, 22 October. Retrieved on 18 March 2017 from: http://www.nzherald.co.nz/nz/news/article.cfm?c_id=1andobjectid=11731947

Edwards, C (1983). 'Student-Centred Learning and Trade Union Education: a Preliminary Examination, *The Industrial Tutor,* Vol. 3, No. 8.

Estlund, C. (2013). 'Individual employee rights at work', in C. Frege and J. Kelly (eds). *Comparative Employment Relations in the Global Economy*. Abingdon: Routledge, pp. 29–48.

Evans, B. and Giroux, H.A. (2016). 'The Violence of Forgetting', *New York Times,* 20 June 2016.

Fairbrother, P. (2008). 'Social movement unionism or trade unions as social movements', *Employee Responsibilities and Rights Journal*, 20(3), pp. 213-220.

(2015). 'Rethinking trade unionism: union renewal as transition', *The Economic and Labour Relations Review*, 26(4), pp. 561-576.

Fieldhouse, R. et al. (1996). *A History of Modern British Adult Education*. Leicester: Niace.

Fisher, J. (2005). *Bread On the Waters: A History Of TGWU Education 1922-2000*. London: Lawrence and Wishart.

Flanders, A. (1970). *Management and Unions: The Theory and Reform of Industrial Relations*, London: Faber.

Flemming, N. (2001). *Teaching and Learning Styles: Vark Strategies*. London: Neil Flemming Publishing.

Fletcher, B. (2015). 'Building People Power: What Clues Can History Offer?', keynote address at Justice Works 2015 (accessed at https://youtube/ Bv3Ndv2zfqk 12/3/16).

Fletcher, B. and Gapasin, F. (2008). *Solidarity Divided: The Crisis in Organized Labor and a New Path toward Social Justice, a new direction for labor by two of its leading activist intellectuals.* Oakland, CA: University of California Press.

Foley, P. (2007). *A Case for and of critical pedagogy: Meeting the challenge of liberatory education at Gallaudet University.* Paper Presented at the American Communication Association's annual conference. Taos: New Mexico, 2007.

Fordham, P. (1993). 'Informal, non-formal and formal education programmes' in YMCA George Williams College ICE301 *Lifelong learning, Unit 1 Approaching lifelong learning.* London: YMCA George Williams College.

Forth, J. and Bryson, A. (2015). Trade Union Membership and Influence, 2014. London: National Institute of Economic and Social Research, September. Retrieved on 3 February 2017 from: http://www.niesr.ac.uk/sites/default/ files/publications/Forth%20and%20Bryson%20%282015%29%20Trade%20 Union%20Membership%20and%20Influence%201999-2014.pdf

Foster, B., Murrie, J. and Laird, I. (2009). It takes two to tango: evidence of a decline in institutional industrial relations in New Zealand. *Employee Relations, 31*(5): 503-514.

Foucault, M. (1991). *Discipline and Punish: The Birth of the Prison,* London: Penguin.

(2006). *The History of Madness,* London: Penguin.

Fox, D., Prilleltensky, I. and Austin, S. (2009). 'Critical psychology for social justice: concerns and dilemmas' in D. Fox, I. Prilleltensky and S. Austin (Eds.). *Critical Psychology: An Introduction* (2nd Edition). London: Sage (pp. 3-20).

Freedland, C. (2012) *Plutocrats – The Rise of New Global Super-Rich and the Fall of Everyone Else.* New York: Penguin.

Frege, C., Turner, L. and Heery, E. (2004). *The New Solidarity? Trade Union Coalition Building in Five Countries.* ILR Collection, Cornell University. Retrieved on 4 February 2017 from: http://digitalcommons.ilr.cornell.edu/ cgi/viewcontent.cgi?article=2026andcontext=articles

Freire, P. (1972a). *Cultural Action for Freedom.* London: Penguin.

- (1972b). *Pedagogy of the Oppressed,* London: Penguin.

- (1985). *The Politics of Education: Culture, Power and Liberation.* London: Bergin and Garvey Publishers.

(1990). 'Educational Practice' in M. Horton and P. Freire *We Make the Road by Walking: Conversations on Education and Social Change.* Philadelphia: Temple University Press.

Fyrth, J. (1980). 'Industrial Studies in an Industrial Society', in Coker, E. and Stuttard, G. (eds.), *Industrial Studies 3.* London, Arrow.

Gardner, M. (1995). 'Labor Movements and Industrial Restructuring: Australia, New Zealand and the United States', in Wever, K. and Turner, L. (eds). *The*

Comparative Political Economy of Industrial Relations. Industrial Relations Research Association (IRRA) Series. University of Wisconsin, Madison, WI: IIRA, pp. 33-70.

GFTU (2017) GFTU Education programme at https://user-tkb9xx.cld.bz/GFTU-Education-in-Action-2017-2018, accessed 31 May 2017

- (2015) *Future of Trade Union Education,* GFTU, Quorn

Giroux, H. (2012). On Critical Pedagogy. New York: Continuum Press.

- (1985) *Introduction. In Freire, P. (1985) The Politics of Education. Culture Power and Liberation (1st ed.). London: Bergin and Garvey: 11-25.*

Glickman, C., Gordon, S., and Ross-Gordon, J. (2007). Supervision and instructional leadership: a development approach. New York: Pearson.

Goldman, G. (1995). *Dons and Workers: Oxford And Adult Education Since 1850.* Oxford: Clarendon.

Gowan, D. (1983). 'Student-Centred Approaches Revisited', *Trade Union Studies Journal,* No. 7, p54-62.

Gramsci, A. (1971). *Selections from the Prison Notebooks.* London: Lawrence and Wishart.

- (1919). Masthead, *Ordine Nuovo.*

Grant, A. (1980). 'Trade Union Education, A TUC Perspective', *The Industrial Tutor,* Vol 5, No 1.

Grasha, A. F. (1994). 'A matter of style: The teacher as expert, formal authority, personal model, facilitator, and delegator', *College Teaching, 42*(4), 142-149.

Gravell, C. (1984). 'Trade Union Education: Will State Funding lead to State Control?' *Trade Union Studies Journal,* No. 8.

Greer, I., Greenwood, I and Stuart, M. (2007). 'Community unionism and the neoliberal state in British steel regions'. Paper presented at the 8th European Congress of the International Industrial Relations Association (IIRA), Manchester, 3-6 September.

Griggs, C, (1983). *The TUC and The Struggle For Education 1868-1925.* Lewes: Falmer Press.

Guanche, J.C. (ed.) (2009). *Julio Antonio Mella.* Cuauhtemoc, Mexico: Ocean Press and Ocean Sur.

Guardian (1978). 'Education for the Labour Movement: UK Experience Past and Present'. Quoted by McIlroy, 1.9.1978, *op. cit.*

Guillen, N. (1987). 'Mella', in Contrera, N. (ed.) *Julio Antonio Mella: El Joven Precursor,* Havana: Editoria Politica.

Gumbrell-McCormick, R. and Hyman, R. (2013). *Trade unions in Western Europe: Hard times, hard choices.* Oxford: Oxford University Press.

Hall, R. and Winn, J. (2017). *Mass Intellectuality and Democratic Leadership in Higher Education.* London: Bloomsbury Academic.

Hamann, K. and Kelly, J. (2003). 'The domestic sources of difference in labour market policies', *British Journal of Industrial Relations, 41*(4), pp. 639-663.

Hampton, P. (2015). *Workers and Trade Unions for Climate Solidarity: Tackling climate change in a neo-liberal world.* Abingdon, Oxon: Routledge.

Han, H. (2014). *How Organisations Develop Activists: Civil Associations and Leadership in the 21st Century*. Oxford: OUP.

Hansome, M (1931). *World Workers' Educational Movements – Their Social Significance*. Columbia: Columbia University Press.

Harrison Rob, (2014). [Online] Available at: *People Over Capital: The Co-operative Alternative to Capitalism*. http://www.goodreads.com/book/show/18528095-people-over-capital

Hattie, J.A.C. (2012). *Visible Learning for Teachers. Maximizing Impact on Achievement*. Oxford: Routledge.

Hatzky, C (2004). *Julio Antonio Mella (1903-1929): Eine Biografie*. Frankfurt am Main: Vervuert Verlag.

Heery, E. and Adler, L. (2004). 'Organising the Unorganised'. In Frege C. and Kelly J. (eds). *Varieties of Unionism: Strategies for Union Revitalization in a Globalizing Economy*. Oxford: Oxford University Press, pp.45–69.

Heery, E. and Kelly, J. (2004). Professional, participative and managerial unionism: an interpretation of change in trade unions. *Work, Employment and Society*, *8*, 1-21.

Holland, J. (2012). 'Community Democracy', *Red Pepper*, 4 September at: http://www.redpepper.org.uk/community-organising-a-new-part-of-the-union/ (accessed 11 January 2017).

Holly, D. (1976) . 'Politics of Learning', *Radical Education*, Vol. 7:6.

Holmwood, John (2011). 'The history of higher education reform and the Coalition's betrayal'. *Open Democracy*. Available online at: http://www.opendemocracy.net/ourkingdom/john-holmwood/history-of-higher-education-reform-and-coalitions-betrayal

HM Treasury (2011). Statement by the Chief Secretary to the Treasury, Rt Hon Danny Alexander MP, on Public Sector Pensions. London: HM Treasury.

HMSO (1918). *Interim Report of the Committee on Adult Education Industrial and Social Conditions in Relation to Adult Education*. London: Department of Employment
- (1973). *Adult Education: a Plan for Development*. London: Dept. of Education and Science.
- (1967). *Royal Commission on Trade Unions and Employers' Associations*. Cmnd. 3623, para 712.

Hoare, A. and Johnstone, R. (2010). 'Widening participation through admissions policy – a British case study of school and university performance', *Studies in Higher Education*, 36 (1), pp. 21-41.

Holford, J. (1994). *Union Education in Britain: A TUC Activity*. Nottingham: Department Of Adult Education, University Of Nottingham.

Holgate, J. (2009). 'Contested terrain: London's living wage campaign and the tension between community and union organising', in McBride J. and Greenwood I. (eds.), *The Complexity of Community Unionism: a Comparative Analysis of Concepts and Contexts*. Basingstoke: Palgrave Macmillan, pp. 49-74.
- (2015). 'Community organising in the UK: a "new" approach for trade unions? *Economic and Industrial Democracy*, *36*(3), pp. 431-455.

Holly, D. (1976). 'Politics of Learning', *Radical Education 7,* Winter, 1976, pp. 6-17.

Hopkins, P. (1985). *Workers Education: an International Perspective.* Milton Keynes, Open University Press.

Hurd, R., Milkman, R. and Turner, L. (2003). *Reviving the American Labor Movement: Institutions and Mobilization.* ILR School, Cornell University. Retrieved on 7 February 2017 from: http://digitalcommons.ilr.cornell.edu/articles/760/

Hyde Park (2017). Speakers Corner at https://www.royalparks.org.uk/parks/hyde-park/things-to-see-and-do/speakers-corner, accessed 31 May 2017.

Hyman, R. (1999). *An emerging agenda for trade unions?* Discussion paper DP98/1999, International Institute for Labour Studies, Geneva.

ILO (1999). *Report of the Director-General: Decent Work, 3.* Geneva: ILO.

- (2007). *The Role of Trade Unions in Workers' Education, the Key to Capacity Building.* Geneva: International Workers Symposium.

- (2017). *ILO at Nobel laureates' summit: Employment is key to peace.* Press release, 3 February. Retrieved on 5 February 2017 from: http://www.ilo.org/global/about-the-ilo/newsroom/news/WCMS_543589/lang--en/index.htm

Industrial Relations Centre (1998). *Unions and Union Membership in New Zealand: Annual Review 1998.* Wellington: Industrial Relations Centre, Victoria University of Wellington.

Jarvis. P. (2004). *Adult Education and Lifelong Learning: Theory and Practice,* 3rd ed. London: Falmer Press.

Jeffs, T. and Spence, J. (2008). 'Farewell to all that? The uncertain future of youth and community work education', *Youth and Policy Double issue: Youth Work Training,* 97/98, Autumn 2007/Winter 2008, pp. 135-166.

Joldersma, C. (1999). 'The tension between justice and freedom in Paulo Freire's epistemology', *Journal of Educational Thought.* 35(2): pp. 129-148.

Jones, J. (1986). *Union Man.* London: Collins.

- (1984) 'A Liverpool Socialist Education', *History Workshop Journal,* Issue 18, Autumn 1984, pp 92-101.

Jones, K. (2003). *Education in Britain: 1944 to the Present.* London: Polity Press.

Jones, O. (2012). *Chavs: The Demonization of the Working Class.* London: Verso.

- (2014). *The Establishment: And how they get away with it.* London: Penguin.

James, P. and Karmowska, J. (2012). 'Unions and Migrant Workers: Strategic Challenges in Britain', *Transfer: European Review of Labour and Research,* 18(2): pp. 201-212.

Jess, C. (2016). *What is the future(s) of New Zealand trade unions?* Paper presented at the 2016 Labour, Employment and Work Conference, Wellington, 28-29 November.

Joldersma, C. (1999). 'The tension between justice and freedom in Paulo Freire's epistemology' in *Journal of Educational Thought.* 35(2): pp. 129-148.

Kelly, H. (2015). Helen Kelly's CTU Conference Address: Media Release. 13 October. Retrieved on 2 February 2017 from: http://www.union.org.nz/news2015helen-kellys-ctu-conference-address/

Kelly, J. (2015). 'Trade union membership and power in comparative perspective'. *Economic and Labour Relations Review*, 26(4), pp. 526-544.

(1998). *Rethinking Industrial Relations: Mobilisation, Collectivisation and Long Waves*. London: Routledge.

Kessing-Styles, L. (2003). 'The relationship between critical pedagogy and assessment in teacher education' in *Radical Pedagogy*, 5(1).

Kincheloe, J.L. (2005). *Critical Pedagogy Primer*. New York: Peter Lang Publishing.

Kingdon, J. (1995). *Agendas, Alternatives, and Public Policies*, London: HarperCollins College Publishers.

Kirton, G. (2006). *The Making of Women Trade Unionists*. Aldershot: Ashgate.

Kline. N. (2009). *More Time to Think*. London: Fisher King.

Linbaugh, P. (2006). *The London Hanged: Crime and Civil Society in the Eighteenth Century*, London: Verso.

Little, G. and Stevenson, H. (2015). 'From Resistance to Renewal: The Emergence of Social Movement Unionism in England' in Little, G. (ed.) *Global Education 'Reform': Building Resistance and Solidarity*. London: Manifesto Press.

Liveright, A. A. (1951). *Union Leadership Training: A Handbook of Tools And Techniques*. New York: Harper.

Luce, S. (2004). *Fighting for a Living Wage*. London: ILR Press.

Lucio, M. and Perrett, R. (2009). 'Meanings and dilemmas in community unionism: trade union community initiatives and black and minority ethnic groups in the UK', *Work, Employment and Society*, 23(4), pp. 693-710.

LWMANZ. (not dated). *About*. Retrieved on 10 February 2017 from: http://www.livingwage.org.nz/about

Lyddon, D. (not dated). *The Union Makes Us Strong: TUC History Online – Part 5: 1980-2000*. Retrieved on 5 February 2017 from: http://www.unionhistory.info/timeline/1960_2000_5.php

Mace, J. and Yarnit, M. (1987). *Time Off To Learn*. London: Methuen.

Malling, J. (1955). 'Report on Work with Trade Unionists in the Extra-Mural Area of the University of Leeds', *Trade Union Education* (WEA), No. 1, January 1955.

Mandeville, B. (1732). *The Fable of the Bees*, quoted by Linbaugh (2006)

Mao Zedong (1937). *On Practice: On the Relation Between Knowledge and Practice, Between Knowing and Doing*, Beijing: Communist Party of China, Philosophical Papers.

Marnham, P. (1999). *Dreaming with his Eyes Open: A Life of Diego Rivera*. London: Bloomsbury.

Marti, J. (1979). *On Education*, ed. and intro. P.S. Foner, New York and London: Monthly Review Press.

Martín-Baró, I., Aron, A., and Corne, S. (1994). *Writings for a liberation psychology*. Harvard: Harvard University Press.

Martinez Lucio, M. and Stuart, M. (2002). 'Assessing partnership: the prospects for, and challenges of, modernization', *Employee Relations*, 24(3), pp. 252-261.

Martinez Lucio, M. and Perrett, R. (2009). 'The Diversity and Politics of Trade Unions' Responses to Minority Ethnic and Migrant Workers: The Context of the UK', *Economic and Industrial Democracy*, 30(3): pp. 324–347.

Mason, P. (2015). *PostCapitalism: A Guide to Our Future.* London: Penguin.

May, T. (2017). 'I'm determined to build the shared society for everyone', *The Telegraph*, 7 January 2017.

McAlevey, J. F. (2016). *No Shortcuts: Organizing for Power in the New Gilded Age.* Oxford: Oxford University Press.

McAlpine, K. and Roberts, S. (2017). 'The Future of Trade Unions in Australia'. Paper presented at the 2017 Association of Industrial Relations Academics of Australia and New Zealand (AIRAANZ), Canberra, 7-10 February.

McGrath, M. and Reekie, I. (2014). *Unite Education Theory and Practice – Beyond Functionalism*, Unite, London.

McIlroy, J. (1979). 'Student-Centred Learning and Trade Union Education: a Preliminary Examination', *Labor Studies Journal*, Vol. 2, No. 1.

- (1980). 'Education for the Labour Movement: UK Experience Past and Present', *Labor Studies Journal*, Vol. 4, No. 3, Winter.

- (1986) 'Goodbye Mr Chips?', *The Industrial Tutor*, Vol. 4, No. 2, pp. 3-23.

- (1990). 'The Triumph of Technical Training?' in Simon, B. (ed.), *The Search for Enlightenment: The Working Class and Adult Education in the Twentieth Century.* London: Lawrence and Wishart.

McIlroy, J. (1996). 'Independent Working-Class Education', in Fieldhouse, R. et al., *A History of Modern British Adult Education.* Leicester: NIACE, pp. 264-289.

McIlroy, J. and Spencer, B. (1985). 'Methods and Policies in Trade Union Education; a Rejoinder', *The Industrial Tutor*, Vol. 3, No. 10, pp. 49-58.

Mella, J.A. (2003). 'Where is Cuba Headed', in Chomsky, A., Carr B., and Smorkaloff, P.M. (eds.), *The Cuba Reader. History, Culture, Politics.* Durham and London: Duke University Press.

(1978). 'Glosas al Pensamiento de Jose Marti', in Rosello, H. (ed.) *Siete Enfoques Marxistas sobre Jose Marti.* Havana: Editoria Politica.

Michels, R. (1949). *Political Parties: A Sociological Study of the Oligarchical Tendencies of Modern Democracy.* Illinois: The Free Press.

Millar, J.P.M. (1925). *TGWU Record.*

- (1979). *The Labour College Movement.* London: NCLC Publishing Society Limited.

Miller, C. (1983). 'Student-Centred Learning in Trade Union Education; Some Further Considerations', *Trade Union Studies Journal*, No. 8.

Miller, D. and Stirling, J. (1992). 'Evaluating Trade Union Education', *The Industrial Tutor*, Vol. 5, No. 5, Spring, pp. 15-26.

Miller, N. (1999). *In the Shadow of the State: Intellectuals and the Quest for National Identity in Twentieth-Century Spanish America.* London: Verso.

Ministry of Education (1945). *The Purpose and Content of the Youth Service. A Report of the Youth Advisory Council appointed by the Minister of Education in 1943.*

- (1960). *The Youth Service in England and Wales* (The Albemarle Report), London: HMSO.

Ministry of Education, Ontario, Canada (2013). *Know thy impact: Teaching learning and Leading*. An interview with John Hattie. Ontario.Ministry of Education. Retrieved from: http://www.edu.gov.on.ca/eng/policyfunding/leadership/spring2013.pdf (5 July 2017).

Mitchell, G. (2000). *Responsible Body: The Story of 50 Years of Adult Education in the University of Sheffield*. Sheffield: University of Sheffield.

Moody, K. (1997). *Workers in a Lean World*. London: Verso.

Morris, W. (1908). *News from Nowhere*, London: Longman.

Mountz, A., Bonds, A., Mansfield, B., Loyd, J., Hyndman, J., Walton-Roberts, M. and Curran, W. (2015). 'For slow scholarship: A feminist politics of resistance through collective action in the neoliberal university', *ACME: An International Journal for Critical Geographies*, 14(4), pp. 1235-1259.

Muller, J. (2004). *How Adults Learn*, Online Journal of the International Child and Youth Care Network, Issue 60, (3) pp. 323-333.

Nesbit, T. (1991). 'Labor Education', *Adult Learning*, 2(6), pp. 14-32.

Nesbit, T. and S Henderson, S. (1983). 'Methods and Politics in Trade Union Education', *Trade Union Studies Journal*, No. 8. TUC (1968) *Training Shop Stewards*. London: TUC.

Newman, A. and Jess, C. (2015). 'Renewing New Zealand Unions: The Service and Food Workers' Union and Living Wage Aotearoa'. Paper presented at the Labour, Employment and Work Conference, 27-28 November 2014.

Newman, A., Tunoho, M. and Brown, E. (2013). 'The living wage campaign: Collaboration in practice'. Paper presented to the Public Health Association Conference, New Plymouth, NZ, 17-19 September.

Newman, C. (1993). *The Third Contract*. Sydney: Stewart Victor Publishing.

Newman, M. (1993 and 2007). *The Third Contract: Theory and practice in trade union training*. London: Stewart Victor Publishing.

NIACE (2015). Adult Participation in Learning Survey. Available at: http://learningandwork.org.uk/sites/niace_en/files/resources/2015%20Adult%20Participation%20in%20Learning%20-%20Headline%20Findings.pdf?redirectedfrom=niace

Nicholls, D. (2008). 'The Sleeping Giant Awakes', http://www.cywu.org.uk/index.php?id=8andtype_id=18andcategory_id=20andarticle_id=91 accessed 31.5.17

- (2015). 'Future of Trade Union Education'. [Online] http://www.gftu.org.uk/wp-content/uploads/2015/07/Future-of-trade-union-education.pdf (Accessed 1 May 2017).

- (2016) 'Youth Work and Youth Services: Our Shared Future'. [Online] https://indefenceofyouthwork.com/2016/04/04/youth-work-and-youth-services-our-shared-future-doug-nicholls-ponders/ (Accessed 1 May 2017)

- (2017a) Blog comment, https://www.morningstaronline.co.uk/a-131d-TUC-Congress-2015-Trade-union-education-for-social-change-join-the-discussion#.WX4c1dPytsM.

- (2017b) 'Reviving Trade Union and Popular Education', https://

indefenceofyouthwork.com/2017/02/23/doug-nicholls-on-reviving-trade-union-and-popular-education/ (accessed 10 April 2017)

Nowak, P. (2015). 'The past and future of trade unionism', *Employee Relations*, 37(6), pp. 683-691.

NZ Companies Office (2016). *Union membership return report 2016*. Retrieved on 3 February 2017 from: http://www.societies.govt.nz/cms/registered-unions/annual-return-membership-reports/2016

NZ Ministry for Business, Innovation and Employment (MBIE) (2016a). *Amendments to the Employment Relations Act 2000 (March 2015)*. Retrieved on 5 February 2017 from: http://www.mbie.govt.nz/info-services/employment-skills/legislation-reviews/amendments-to-the-employment-relations-act-2000

- (2016b). *Employment Standards Legislation Bill*. Retrieved on 18 March 2017 from: http://www.mbie.govt.nz/info-services/employment-skills/legislation-reviews/employment-standards-legislation-bill

NZ Ministry for the Environment. (2007). *United Nations Framework for the Convention on Climate Change (UNFCCC)*. Retrieved on 7 February 2017 from: http://www.mfe.govt.nz/more/international-environmental-agreements/multilateral-environmental-agreements/united-nations

Obach, B. (2004). *Labor and the Environmental Movement: The Quest for Common Ground*. Cambridge, MA: MIT Press.

Ohara, M., Saft, S. and Crookes, G. (2000) *Teacher Exploration of Feminist Critical Pedagogy in Beginning Japanese as a Foreign Language Class*. Paper presented at the University of Hawai'i, Manoa, 2000.

O'Neill, M. (2014). 'The slow university: Work, time and well-being', *Forum Qualitative Sozialforschung/Forum: Qualitative Social Research*, 15(3).

Ord, J. (2000). *Youth Work Curriculum*, Lyme Regis: Russell House.

Ortiz, J. (1999). *Julio Antonio Mella: L'Ange Rebelle. Aux Origines du Communisme Cubain*, Paris: L'Harmattan.

Ota, C, DiCarlo, C. F. Burts, D.C., Laird, R. and Gioe, C. (2006). 'Training and Learning Needs of Adult Learners', *Journal of Extension*, December 2006, Vol. 44, No. 6, pp. 121-132.

Owen, H. (2008). *Open Space Technology: A User's Guide* (3rd ed.). Berrett-Koehler.

Palmer, G. (1987). *Unbridled Power: An Interpretation of New Zealand's Constitution and Government*. Oxford: Oxford University Press.

Parker, J. (2008). 'The Trades Union Congress and civil alliance building: Towards social movement unionism?' *Employee Relations*, 30(5), pp. 562-583.

(2011). 'Reaching out for strength within? "Social movement unionism" in a small country setting', *Industrial Relations Journal*, 42(4), pp. 392-403.

Parker, J., Nemani, M. and Arrowsmith, J. (2012). '(Un)muzzling the Watch Dogs: Collective Regulation and Working Women in New Zealand and Fiji'. Paper presented to the International Labour and Employment Relations Association (ILERA) Conference, Philadelphia, 2-5 July. Retrieved on 5 February 2017 from: http://ilera2012.wharton.upenn.edu/RefereedPapers/ParkerJane%20MaritinoNemani%20Jim%20Arrowsmith.pdf

Parker, J., Arrowsmith, J., Prowse, P. and Fells, R. (2016). 'The Living Wage: Concepts, Contexts and Future Concerns'. *Labour and Industry*, 26(1), pp. 1-7.

Parliament. House of Commons (2014) *Underachievement in Education by White Working Class Children*. London: The Stationery Office.

Peetz, D., Webb, C and Jones, M. (2003). *Activism Amongst Workplace Union Delegates, Industrial Relations*, Vol. 58, No. 2, Spring, pp. 354-358.

Piven, F.F. and Cloward, R.A. (1992). 'Normalizing Collective Protest', in Morris, A. and Mueller, C. (eds.) *Frontiers of Social Movement Theory*, New Haven: Yale University Press.

Poniatowska, E. (1992). *Tinisima*, trans. K. Silver. Albuquerque: University of New Mexico.

Portwood-Stacer, L. (2013). *Lifestyle politics and radical activism*. New York: Bloomsbury.

Prowse, P. and Fells, R. (2015). 'The UK Living Wage Regional Campaigns – An Analysis.' Paper presented at the Association of Industrial Relations Academics of Australia and New Zealand (AIRAANZ) Conference, University of Auckland, 3-5 February.

- (2016a). 'The Living Wage: Policy and Practice', *Industrial Relations Journal*, 47(2), pp. 144-162.

- (2016b). 'The Living Wage in the UK: An analysis of the GMB campaign in local government'. *Labour and Industry*, 26(1), pp. 58-73.

Quality Assurance Agency (2009). *Subject Benchmark Statement: Youth and Community Work*. Gloucester: QAA

Rancière, J. (1992). *The Ignorant Schoolmaster: Five Lessons in Intellectual Emancipation*, Stanford: Stanford University Press.

- (2004). 'Introducing disagreement', *Angelaki: Journal of the Theoretical Humanities*, 9(3), pp. 3-9.

Rasmussen, E., Foster, B., and Murrie, J. (2012). 'The Decline in Collectivism and Employer Attitudes and Behaviours: Facilitating a High-Skill, Knowledge Economy?' Paper presented at the ILERA Conference, Philadelphia, 2-5 July.

Reay, D., Crozier, G. and Clayton, J. (2009). '"Fitting in" or "standing out": working-class students in UK higher education', *British Educational Research Journal*, 36 (1) pp. 107-124.

Reynolds, D. and Kern, J. (2002). 'Labor and the Living Wage Movement', *Working USA*, Winter, 5(3), pp. 17-45.

Robertson, D. and Schuller, T. (1982). *Stewards, Members and Trade Union Training*. Glasgow: University of Glasgow Press.

Romero, A., Arce, S., and Cammarota, J. (2009). 'A barrio pedagogy: Identity, intellectualism, activism, and academic achievement through the evolution of critically compassionate intellectualism', *Race Ethnicity and Education*, 12(2), pp. 217-233.

Rosenberg, B. (2016). *CTU Monthly Economic Bulletin*, No. 181, August. Retrieved on 3 February 2017 from: http://www.union.org.nz/wp-content/

About Workable Books

Workable Books is a new publishing imprint dedicated to trade union related publications. Formed in 2017 by the General Federation of Trade Unions and New Internationalist, Workable Books believes that the stories, ideas, creativity and organizing and educational experiences of trade unionists need to be more widely shared throughout the world.

Our publishing objectives are not confined to any one particular subject area. We welcome suggestions for publications in any subject area which speak to the world of trade unionism: it could be photographs, paintings, memoirs, histories, ideas, plays, poetry, training manuals. You name it, if it relates to trade unionism we are interested.

Please send an outline of any proposals for publication to: workable@newint.org

NUPE *see* National Union of Public
Employees
NUT (National Union of Teachers)
education programme 139-40,
185-201

O'Grady, Frances 85
one-to-one meetings 153-4
oppression 18, 46-7, 72, 104, 141, 143,
211, 218, 219, 220, 224, 225
organizing
importance of education to 11, 12, 150
informal education for 167-8
strategic 129-32
Owen, Harrison 212
Oxfam International 134
Oxford and Working-Class Education
52, 59

Paid Educational Leave (PEL) 57;
see also day release
Paine, Thomas 18
Panama 256
Paraguay 256
Parker, Carl 139, 169
Parker, Jane 78, 80
Parks, Rosa 183-4
participant comments *see* feedback
passive learning 17, 39, 41, 44, 74, 121,
169, 170, 203, 217, 219, 232
Paterson, Owen 87
Pearson, Philip 87
peasant farmers, training for 257-8
Pedagogy of the Oppressed see Freire,
Paolo
PEL *see* Paid Educational Leave
Peña Vilaboa, José 245
Peoples Political Economy (PPE) 115,
116-18
Pérez, José Miguel 245
Peru 254, 256
philanthropy 68-9
Philosophy, Politics and Economics
(PPE) 8, 79, 115
pin the tail on the donkey 182
planning, educational 139, 162-8

Plebs' League 53, 101
POEU *see* Post Office Engineering
Union
political education 78-9, 100-14, 132-3
politics teaching 10; *see also* trade
union education
popular education 13, 14, 236
development 64-76
genesis of, in Cuba 236, 238-52
key concepts 16, 38-51
in Latin America 253-4
techniques 10-11
in universities 118-21, 141, 216-27
youth festivals 140, 202-15
see also critical pedagogy
Portela, Guillermo 250
Post Office Engineering Union
(POEU) 57
power structures, re-enforcement
of 42
PPE *see* Peoples Political Economy *and*
Philosophy, Politics and Economics
praxis 43, 116, 126, 216, 220, 222, 223,
227, 239
precarious employment 124, 131,
223, 255; *see also* gig economy *and*
zero-hours contracts
privatization 60, 107, 109, 135, 167, 186
psychology teaching 141, 216-27
Public and Commercial Services
Union 192
public services cuts 20, 64
public support for union activism 193

questioning 139, 156-9, 203

racism 34, 87, 88, 89, 97, 154, 183, 225
Rae, Nadine 138, 142
rallies and marches 154
Rancière, Jacques 48, 209
refugee crises 96
renewal, need for 140, 185-8
report-backs, managing 177-8
reports on education 25-6, 52, 59, 71, 208
representation
as education 7

uploads/2016/11/CTU-Monthly-Economic-Bulletin-181-August-2016.pdf

Ross, R. (2005). *Britain at Work. Voices from the Workplace 1945-1995* [Online]. Available at: http://www.unionhistory.info/britainatwork/narrativedisplay. php?type=tuandworkereducation

Rustin, M. (2016). 'The neoliberal university and its alternatives', *Soundings*, 63, pp. 147-177.

Ryall, S. and Blumenfeld, S. (2014). *The state of New Zealand Union membership in 2014*. Retrieved on 2 February 2017 from: http://www.victoria.ac.nz/ som/clew/files/The-state-of-New-Zealand-Union-membership-in-2014-FINALwithtables.pdf

- (2015). *Unions and Union Membership in New Zealand – report on 2015 Survey*. Retrieved on 17 February 2017 from: http://www.victoria.ac.nz/ som/clew/publications/New-Zealand-Union-membership-Survey-report-2015FINAL100217.pdf

Sahlberg, P. (2011). 'Finnish Lessons: What Can the World Learn from Educational Change in Finland?' New York: Teachers' College Press.

Salman, S. (2014). 'Why did Connor Sparrowhawk die in a specialist NHS unit?' *The Guardian*, 19 March (http://www.theguardian.com/society/2014/ mar/19/connor-sparrowhawk-death-nhs-care-unit-slade-house-learning-disabilities).

Schuller, T. (2004). *The Benefits of Learning*. London: Routledge.

Schuller, T. and Robertson, D. (1984). 'The Impact of Trade Union Education: a Framework for Evaluation', *Labour Studies Journal*, Spring, pp. 121-132.

Scipes, K. (1992). 'Understanding the New Labor Movements in the Third World: The Emergence of Social Movement Unionism', *Critical Sociology*, 19(2), pp. 81-101.

Seal, M. (2014). 'Philosophies of Youth Work: Post-modern Chameleons or Cherry Picking Charlatans', in Seal, M. and Frost, S. (2014)

- (2015). 'How We Teach' (internal document), Birmingham: Newman University.

Seal, M and Frost, S. (2014). *Philosophy and Youth and Community Work*. Lyme Regis: Russell House.

Seal, M and Harris, P. (2016). *Responding to Youth Violence through Youth Work*. Bristol: Policy Press.

Shaw, M. and Crowther, J. (2017). *Community Engagement: A Critical Guide for Practitioners*. [Online] http://www.populareducation.co.za/sites/default/files/ community_engagement_-_a_critical_guide.pdf (Accessed 20 June 2017]

Shedd, C. P. et al. (1955). *History of the World Alliance of Young Men's Christian Associations*, London: SPCK.

Shor, I. (1980). *Critical Teaching and Everyday Life*. Chicago: University of Chicago Press.

- (1992). *Empowering Education: Critical Education for Social Change* (2nd edition). Chicago: University of Chicago Press.

Simms, M., Holgate, J. and Heery, E. (2012). *Union Voices: Tactics and Tensions in UK Organising*. Ithaca: Cornell University Press.

Simon, B. (1987) 'Lessons in Elitism', *Marxism Today*, September, pp. 12-17.

(ed.) (1990). *The Search for Enlightenment: The Working Class And Adult Education In The Twentieth Century.* London: Lawrence and Wishart.

Smith, C, and S. McAdam (2017). 'In the middle and on the margins in perpetual motion: exploring the role of concepts in democratising knowledge production', *Radical Community Work Journal* (forthcoming).

Smith, M.K. (1994). Local Education, Buckingham: Open University Press.

Spence, J. (2006). 'Working with girls and young women: a broken history', *Drawing on the past: essays in the history of community and youth work.* Leicester: National Youth Agency, pp. 243-261.

Statistics NZ (2016). *Union membership and employment agreements – June 2016 quarter.* Retrieved on 7 February 2017 from: http://www.stats.govt.nz/browse_for_stats/income-and-work/employment_and_unemployment/improving-labour-market-statistics/union-memship-emplymt-agmt.aspx#union

Statistics NZ. (2014). *Flexibility and security in employment: Findings from the 2012 Survey of Working Life.* March. Wellington: Statistics NZ. Retrieved on 7 February 2017 from: http://www.stats.govt.nz/browse_for_stats/income-and-work/employment_and_unemployment/flexibility-security-employment.aspx

Stevenson, H. (2011). 'Coalition Education Policy: Thatcherism's Long Shadow', *FORUM*, 53(2), pp. 179-194.

Stevenson, H. and Mercer, J. (2015). 'Education Reform in England and the Emergence of Social Movement Unionism: The National Union of Teachers in England' in Bascia N. (ed), *Teacher Unions in Public Education: Politics, History and the Future.* London: Palgrave Macmillan

Street, W. (2011). 'A global union's direct action promotes organising in the US', *International Union Rights*, Vol 18, Issue 3, 2011.

Tattersall, A. (2005). 'There is Power in Coalition: A Framework for Assessing How and When Union-Community Coalitions are Effective and Enhance Union Power', *Labour and Industry*, 16(3), pp. 97-112.

- (2010). *Power and Coalition. Strategies for Strong Unions and Social Change.* Crows Nest, NSW: Allen and Unwin.

Taylor-Gooby, P. and Stoker, G. (2011). 'The Coalition Programme: A New Vision for Britain or Politics as Usual?' *The Political Quarterly*, Vol. 82, No 1, January-March 2011, pp. 4-15.

Taylor, P. (2013). *Performance Management and the New Workplace Tyranny: A Report for the Scottish Trades Union Congress*, Glasgow: University of Strathclyde.

TGWU Record (September 1950)

Thomas, H. (1971). *Cuba or the Pursuit of Freedom.* London: Eyre and Spottiswoode.

Thomson E.P. (1963). *The Making of the English Working Class.* London: Gollancz.

Titmuss, R. (1963). *Essays on the Welfare State* (2nd ed.). London : Unwin University Books.

Tolpuddle Martyrs Museum website (2017). 'Story of the Toldpuddle Martyrs' http://www.tolpuddlemartyrs.org.uk/story (Accessed 31 May 2017).

Topham (1970). 'Hull Portworkers' Day-Release Course', *The Industrial Tutor 1* (2), March, pp. 20-28.

Toynbee, P. and Walker, D. (2008). *Unjust Rewards: Exposing Greed and Inequality in Britain Today*, London: Granta.

Treen, M. (2015). 'How Unite took on the fast food companies over zero hours contracts and won!' 18 May. Retrieved on 18 March 2017 from: http://www.unite.org.nz/how_unite_took_on_the_fast_food_companies_over_zero_hour_contracts_and_won

TUC (1968). *Training Shop Stewards*, London: TUC.

TUC (2008). *A Green and Fair Future: For a Just Transition to a Low Carbon Economy*. Retrieved on 5 February 2017 from: https://www.tuc.org.uk/sites/default/files/documents/greenfuture.pdf

- (2010). *Trade Unions at Work: What They Are and What They Do*. May, London: TUC. Retrieved on 8 February 2017 from: https://www.tuc.org.uk/sites/default/files/unionsatwork.pdf

- (2013). *General Council and TUC Structure*. 5 April. Retrieved on 4 February 2017 from: https://www.tuc.org.uk/about-tuc/about_makingpolicy.cfm

- (2015). *TUC Directory 2015*. Retrieved on 4 February 2017 from: https://www.tuc.org.uk/sites/default/files/TUC_Directory_2015_Digital_Version.pdf

- (2016). *TUC Campaign Plan 2016-2017: Building Back Stronger*. August. Retrieved on 5 January from: https://www.tuc.org.uk/sites/default/files/TUC_Campaign_Plan_2016-17_Digital.pdf

- (2017a). *Britain's Unions*. Retrieved on 4 February 2017 from: https://www.tuc.org.uk/britains-unions-

- (2017b). Unionlearn at https://www.unionlearn.org.uk/tuc-education (Accessed 31 May 2017).

Turner, L. (2003). 'Reviving the labor movement: a comparative perspective', in D. B. Cornfield, H. J. McCammon (eds.), *Labor revitalization: Global perspectives and new initiatives*, pp. 23-58. Research in the Sociology of Work, 11. Emerald Group Publishing Limited.

UN (not dated). *Paris Agreement – Status of Ratification*. Retrieved on 7 February 2017 from: http://unfccc.int/paris_agreement/items/9444.php

UN High Commissioner for Refugees (2017). *Figures at a glance*. Retrieved on 8 February 2017 from: http://www.unhcr.org/figures-at-a-glance.html

Unite the Union (2011). *Unite Political Strategy*. London: Unite.

University Of Oxford (1908) *Oxford and Working-Class Education*. Oxford: University Of Oxford.

Vachon, T. and Brecher, J. (2016). 'Are union members more or less likely to be environmentalists?' *Labor Studies Journal*, 41(2), pp. 185-203.

Viz (2016). *Hell Below Zero*, issue 258 [Online]. Available at: http://viz.co.uk/

Vulliamy, D (1985). 'The Politics of Trade Union Education', draft paper, in Jowitt, J. A. and Taylor, R. K. S. (eds.), *The Politics of Adult Education*. Bradford:

Bradford Centre.

Waddington, J., Kahmann, M. and Hoffman, J. (2003). *United We Stand? A Comparison of the Trade Union Merger Process in Britain and Germany.* London: Anglo-German Foundation.

Welton, M. (1993). 'Canadian Workers' Education' in Edwards, R., *Adult Learners, Education and Training.* London: Routledge.

Whitney, R (2001). *State and Revolution in Cuba: Mass Mobilization and Political Change, 1920-1940.* Chapel Hill and London: University of North Carolina Press.

Wilkinson, R and Pickett, K. (2009). *The Spirit Level: Why Equality is Better for Everyone.* London: Allen Lane.

William. D. (2011). 'What is assessment for learning?' *Studies in Educational Evaluation 37,* pp. 3-14.

Wills, J. (2001). 'Community Unionism and Trade Union Renewal in the UK: Moving Beyond the Fragments at Least?' *Transactions of the Institute of British Geographers,* 26(4), pp. 465-483.

Wills, J. and Simms, M. (2004). 'Building reciprocal community unionism in the UK', *Capital and Class, 82,* pp. 59-84.

Wright Mills, C. (1959). *The Sociological Imagination.* Oxford: Oxford University Press.

Zachariah, M. (1986). *Revolution through Reform.* New York: Praeger.

Reading and resources

Items marked with an asterisk may be considered particularly helpful. We welcome suggestions for further additions. Please send these to doug@gftu.org.uk

*Atkins, John, 1981. *Neither Crumbs nor Condescension*, Workers' Education Association.

*Altenbaugh, Richard J., 1990. *Education for Struggle: The American Labor Colleges of the 1920s and 1930s (Labor & Social Change)*, Temple University Press.

Calveley, Moira (author), Steve Shelley (editor) 2007. *Trade Union Education. Learning with Trade Unions: A Contemporary Agenda in Employment Relations (Contemporary Employment Relations)*, Ashgate.

Corfield, Tony, 1969. *Epoch in Workers' Education*, Workers' Education Association.

Clegg, Hugh Armstrong, 1959. *Trade union education with special reference to the pilot areas: A report for the Workers' Educational Association.*

Craik, W.W. 1964. *Central Labour College*, Lawrence and Wishart.

Ball, Malcolm John, 2000. *Trade union education: a qualitative study of its contribution to participation and progression in adult learning*, Leeds Metropolitan University.

*Delp, Linda, et al, 2002. *Teaching for Change, Popular Education and the Labor Movement*, UCLA Centre for Labor Research and Education, Los Angeles, USA.

Doubleday, Christine, 1996. *Development of self-sufficiency in trade union education in Belarus: Project report*, Centre for Continuing Education, Hull.

Federation of Community Work Training Groups, and Association of Metropolitan Authorities, 1990. *Learning for Action, Community work and Participative Training*, AMA.

Fieldhouse, Roger, 1991. 'Conformity and Contradiction in English Responsible Body Adult Education, 1925-1950' in S. Westward and J. E Thomas, 1991, *The Politics of Adult Education*, NIACE.

*Fischer, Maria Clara, 1997. *Radical trade union education in practice? A study of CUT's Education Programme on Collective Bargaining.*

Fisher, John, 2005. *Bread on the water, A history of TGWU education 1922-2000*, Lawrence and Wishart.

Griggs, C., 1983. *The TUC and the Struggle for Education 1868-1925*, Falmer.

Hirson, Baruch (author), Lodge Tom (foreword), 2017. *Yours for the Union: Class and Community Struggles in South Africa*, Zed Books.

Holford, John, 1994. *Union education in Britain: A TUC Activity*, Department of Adult Education, University of Nottingham.

Irish Congress for Trade Unions, 1995. *Learning for a changing world: report of review group on trade union education and training.*

Lewis, 1993. *Leaders and Teachers: Adult Education and the Challenge of Labour in South Wales, 1906-1940*, University of Wales, Cardiff.

*Kelly, Thomas, 1962. *A History of Adult Education in Great Britain from the Middle Ages to the Twentieth Century.*

Kirton, Gill and Healy, Geraldine, 2002. *Talking union, learning union: a case study of women only trade union education* (Working paper series), University of Hertfordshire, Business School.

Lietard, P and Sorel B, 1984. *The Role of Trade Unions in Adult Education in France.*

Mace, J., and Yarnit, M., 1987. *Time Off to Learn,* Methuen, 1987.

MacLean, John, 2014. *Essential Writings and Speeches,* editor, Jonson, Will, Create Space Independent Publishing Platform.

Man, Kit Christopher, 2009. *Workers' Education in Hong Kong: Educational Duties of the Hong Kong Federation of Trade Unions: Past, Present and Future,* VDM Verlag.

Millar, J.P.M., 1979. *The Labour College Movement,* NCLC Publishing Society Limited, London.

Milton, Nan, 1973. *John MacLean,* London: Pluto Press.

Newman, Michael, 1993. *The Third Contract,* Sydney: Stewart Victor Publishing.

Nyman, Torre, 1991. *A guide to the teaching of collective bargaining: An Instructional Aid for Worker Students (Trade Union Functions and Services),* International Labour Office.

Ollis, Tracey, 2012. *A Critical Pedagogy of Embodied Education: Learning to Become an Activist (Postcolonial Studies in Education).*

*Schuller, Tom, 1981. *Is Knowledge Power?: Problems and Practice in Trade Union Education,* Aberdeen People's Press.

Schuller, Tom and Robertson, D., 1980. *The Impact of Trade Union Education on Steward/Member Relations,* Social Science Research Council.

Sherry, Dave, 2014. *John MacLean,* Bookmarks.

*Simon, Brian, 1965. *Education and the Labour Movement,* 1870-1920, Lawrence and Wishart.

*Simon, Brian (ed.), 1990. *The Search for Enlightenment: The Working Class and Adult Education in the Twentieth Century,* Lawrence & Wishart.

Thompson, Jane L, 1980. *Adult Education for a Change,* Hutchinson.

Tripathy, Sangam, 1994, *Organisation Through Education: a Report on Trade Union Education & Research Activities,* Hind Mazdoor Sabha.

Twitchin, John and Matthews Tony, 1976, *Trade Union Studies: A Course for Active Trade Unionists,* BBC.

Unknown author, 1990. *Training for full-time officers of trade unions,* Further Education Unit.

Unite the Union, 2013. *Unite Education, Theory and Practice, Beyond Functionalism, Unite National Workplace Reps and Health and Safety Certificate Courses: A discussion Document,* with a Foreword by Jim Mowatt.

Waugh, Colin, 2009, *'Plebs': The Lost Legacy of Independent Working-Class Education,* Post-16 Educator.

Yazykova, V.S., 1983. *The role of Soviet trade unions in the lifelong education of workers,* European Centre for Leisure and Education.

Index